AMERICA IN PERSPECTIVE

The United States through Foreign Eyes

AMERICA IN PERSPECTIVE

The United States through Foreign Eyes

❖❖❖❖❖❖❖❖❖❖❖❖

Edited,

with an Introduction and Notes

by

HENRY STEELE COMMAGER

RANDOM HOUSE

NEW YORK

First Printing

Acknowledgment is here made for our indebtedness to the following publishers, authors and agents for their courtesy in granting permission to reprint sections of books issued and copyrighted by them:

The Norwegian-American Historical Society for "Social Life and Customs of the Frontier" from *America in the Forties. The Letters of Ole Munch Raeder*, translated and edited by Gunnar J. Malmin.

DODD, MEAD & COMPANY, INC., for "The American Is an Electric Anglo-Saxon" from *Land of the Dollar* by George Warrington Steevens.

JOHN LANE THE BODLEY HEAD LIMITED for "Is America a Young or a Dying Nation?" from *Heretics* by G. K. Chesterton.

E. P. DUTTON & CO., INC., and JOHN MURRAY for "America Combines the Best Traits of Old-World Nations" from *The Inner Life of the United States* by Count Vay de Vaya.

A. P. WATT & SON and JAMES NISBET & CO., LTD., for "The American at Home and in His Club" from *From Connaught to Chicago* by George Birmingham. A. P. WATT & SON for "The Homeliness and the Friendliness of Americans" from *Pilgrim's Way* by John Buchan, by permission of Lady Tweedsmuir. For "The American Believes in Tomorrow" from *America at War* by Victor Vinde.

MRS. HUGO MUNSTERBERG for "A Philosopher Explains the American Passion for Money" from *The Americans* by Hugo Munsterberg.

HARPER & BROTHERS for "The Sentimentality, Kindness and Innocence of the Americans" from *Hail Columbia* by W. L. George. Copyright, 1921, by Harper & Brothers.

39677

OXFORD UNIVERSITY PRESS for "Americans Are Boys" from *I Americans* by Salvador de Madariaga.

NO YONG-PARK for "A Chinese View of the American Character" from *An Oriental View of American Civilization* by No Yong-Park.

MRS. RAOUL DE ROUSSY DE SALES for "Love in America" by Raoul de Roussy de Sales.

GEORGE ALLEN AND UNWIN LTD., for "The Mechanization and Standardization of American Life" from *Mysteries of the Soul* by Richard Müller-Freienfels.

ALFRED A. KNOPF, INC., for "A Cambridge Professor Celebrates the American Public School" from *The American Character* by Denis W. Brogan. Copyright, 1944, by Denis W. Brogan.

RINEHART & COMPANY, INC., for "Capitalism Nurtures America in Spiritual Lassitude" from *Little Golden America* by Ilya Ilf and Eugene Petrov. Copyright, 1937, by Rinehart & Company, Inc.

CONTENTS

Contents

INTRODUCTION

I

"WHAT kind of a people do they think we are?" cried Winston
Churchill at a famous moment in world history, and it was
a crucial question: it was in part because Hitler failed to appreciate the kind of people the British really were that the Nazi
bid for world power ended in catastrophe. His failure was
fundamental and pervasive. He failed to appreciate what kind
of people the Russians were. He failed—like his arrogant prede-
cessors in 1917—to appreciate what kind of people the Americans were. He failed to realize, as throughout history tyrants
have failed to realize, that a people's character is, in the last
analysis, the most important thing about them—more important
by far than statistics of armies and navies, of production or of
shipping or of finance. For material things cannot in themselves
achieve any thing. They count only where there is a will to use
them, and whether they count for weal or for woe depends
upon the way that they are used. What is, in the end, of decisive
importance are the intangible factors that we call character: the
things that are done and the things that are not done, the attitude toward the individual human being, the sense of responsibility toward society, the relations of the military and the civil-
ian, the position of women and of children, the role of the
school and of the church and of the courts, the concepts of
justice and of fair play, the ideals that are held up to children
and the pattern of conduct that is fixed for them, the moral
standards that are accepted and the moral values that are
cherished.

That each nation has its own character is taken for granted, and it is neither chauvinistic nor provincial to observe that the United States is no exception. Yet it is not a little remarkable that this should be so, and that it should have been so from the very beginning of the national experiment. For a national character is a product of inheritance, environment, and historical experience. The American inheritance was a heterogeneous one; the American environment—a continent containing within itself almost every extreme of climate, soil, and resources—was immensely complex; the American historical experience was brief and, for many of its beneficiaries, vicarious. Yet the first of our interpreters—Crèvecoeur—remarked how swift and how effective was the process of Americanization, and a hundred later commentators were to return to that theme, in indignation, in enthusiasm, and in wonder.

That by some alchemy, out of the blending of inheritance, environment, and experience, there came a distinctive American character, cannot be doubted. But precisely what were the lineaments of that character was not clear. Americans themselves were not skillful in drawing them. They took them, rather, for granted, as each individual takes his own character or his own physiognomy for granted. It is suggestive that although our literature is rich in description it is poor in interpretation: Cooper's *Gleanings in Europe* were more profound than his *Home as Found,* Hawthorne's *English Notebooks* more penetrating than his *American Notebooks,* and Emerson's *English Traits* more perspicacious than anything that he wrote on his own countrymen.

Happily we can turn for interpretation to hundreds of visitors who made it their business to observe, describe, analyze, and judge. No other people, it is safe to say, was ever so besieged by interpreters; none had its portrait painted, its habits described, its character analyzed, its soul probed so incessantly. The practice started before Independence and has continued unabated to the present day: the summer of 1947 saw the appearance of three new English books on America.

What is the explanation of this apparently insatiable curiosity about America? Is it that America was the most interesting of all countries, or the most attractive, or the most hospitable? Matthew Arnold, to be sure, thought not: his criticism of America was precisely that it was not *interesting*—the italics are his —yet even he found it necessary to write a book about it. But interesting, as William James remarked, is not a substantive term: nothing is really interesting in itself, only in relation to some thing or some body. Surely the thirty-five million immigrants who crossed the Atlantic to find homes in the New World found America interesting. And just as surely to the thousands of visitors who wrote books about it, it was interesting—as a curiosity or an entertainment, as an asylum or a refuge, as a catalytic agent or an experimental laboratory, as an object lesson in political depravity or an example of moral virtue, or, more frequently, as a combination of all these things.

The interest in America which animated the best of them— and their number is large—was profound. For they saw, from the beginning, that America held the key to the future: some, like the Italian Loria, thought that she held the key to the past as well, and that the newest of nations would reveal the history of the oldest. "I confess," wrote the incomparable Tocqueville, "that in America I saw more than America; I sought the image of democracy itself, with its inclinations, its character, its prejudices, and its passions, in order to learn what we have to fear or to hope from its progress." And he added that "the question here discussed is interesting not only to the United States but to the whole world; it concerns not a nation, but all mankind."

It was no idle prophecy. All mankind was, perforce, interested in the American experiment. Here was the largest, the best equipped, of all laboratories, and one whose findings were compulsory, as it were. What would be the consequences of political democracy, of social equality, of universal free education, of the intermixture of peoples and races, of new standards of material well-being? Could a federal system so extensive and so artificial endure? Could a democracy avoid degenerating into a tyranny of the majority? Could the arts and the sciences flourish in a society that was committed to the doctrine of equality? Could morality prosper without an established Church? The answers to these, and to scores of questions no less momentous, were to be found, it was thought, in America. And it was to these great and enduring questions that the most thoughtful and responsible foreign observers addressed themselves.

Nor were they, for the most part, disappointed. If the answers were not always clear, some of the confusion was in the minds of the observers, nor is it given to mortals to find ultimate answers to the most profound questions. Many of those who came over found what they were looking for, or merely confirmed what they already knew, for, as André Maurois has observed, "A people is a mirror in which each traveler contemplates his own image." Yet others—and they are chiefly those represented in this collection—were edified. What they saw, and reported, was relevant to the future, and because that future is with us, is relevant to our own day.

II

Our interest in these commentators is not so much in what they had to tell their own people as in what they have to tell us: in this matter we are justifiably parochial. Some of the interpretations were directed, in fact, to us: Grund, Gurowski, and Munsterberg, for example, wrote for their American audience, and Bryce and Brogan, it is safe to say, have been more widely read in America than in Britain. Most of our interpreters, however, looked for what was of interest to their own people. It might be supposed that they could tell us little that was relevant to our problems, little that we did not already know. Yet such a supposition, however logical, runs contrary to experience: biographies are usually more revealing than autobiographies and portraits than photographs. What they can, and do, tell us are mostly the obvious things, for it is in what a people take for granted that their character can be read—in the unformulated assumptions, the spontaneous reactions, the inevitable responses, the articles of faith. Americans, like any other people, are often in the position of the dullard who discovered with delight that all his life he had been writing prose.

We take for granted our pervasive social equality and do not appreciate the nature of class distinctions until we go abroad— until we go even to democratic England and discover the importance of the public-school accent. We take for granted the exalted status of women and the almost universal pampering of children, until we discover how these things alarm or horrify our visitors. We take for granted universal public education— until we familiarize ourselves with the statistics of secondary-school and university education abroad. We take for granted a political unity which enables us to travel from New York to California without customs barriers or change of money—until we travel over comparable distances in Europe. We take for granted, alas, a double standard of private and public morality, personal integrity and political venality—until we learn how that double standard shakes faith in democracy abroad. It is because foreign observers can see America without the assumptions and presuppositions that becloud the American vision, because they can, in fact, see America in perspective, that they are helpful.

What then do they tell us, these commentators who look at America from the perspective of the Old World? There are, altogether, several thousand of them, spread over a century and a half, representing every country, every point of view. At best the view which they seem to present to us is kaleidoscopic, at worst chaotic. Can we draw any conclusions from such disparate interpretations, can we find any unity in such diverse points of view? Can we, in any event, find common denominators in a selection of almost two score representative interpreters, a selection necessarily meager and inevitably arbitrary?

Surprisingly enough a real unity emerges from these heterogeneous selections, and it is not one imposed by any antecedent editorial discrimination but implicit in the material itself. We know that in all outward matters America has changed pro-

foundly in the century and a half since Independence, and that
these changes have been continuous and complex; we are sometimes inclined to suppose that there have been comparable
changes in the national character. That is not the conclusion to
be drawn from the findings of these foreign observers. They
report diversity, to be sure, but they conclude, too, in the words
of one of them, that "over confused diversity there broods a
higher unity." To the visitors of the seventeen-seventies and the
nineteen-forties, to Britons, Frenchmen, Germans, and Swedes,
America *meant* much the same thing.

What then was the permanent rather than the transient in the
American character as seen by these observers? What was the
abiding meaning of America in history? What were the recurring themes, the persistent traits? America was the land of
the future, and held the key to the future. "Westward the
course of empire takes its way . . . Time's noblest offspring is
the last," Bishop Berkeley had written, and the prophecy was
re-echoed decade after decade. "Americans are the western pilgrims," said Crèvecoeur, "who are carrying along with them
that great mass of arts, sciences, vigor, and industry, which began long since in the east; they will finish the great circle," and
one hundred and sixty years later, Victor Vinde concluded that
the American "knows there will be a tomorrow. He believes in
tomorrow." Throughout their history Americans have insisted
that the best was yet to be, and they have rarely been disappointed. America was the land of opportunity. Here the poor of
the Old World were given a second chance, here men achieved
a new stature, were endowed with a new dignity. "God made
America for the poor," said Dicey; "there is no other country
on earth which in so short a time has accomplished so much,"
asserted Mackay; and the enthusiastic Brissot remarked with delight "how the blessings of liberty can elevate the industry of
man, how they dignify his nature and dispose him to universal
fraternity." America was, above all, the land of equality. This
was the great theme which Tocqueville elaborated with con-
summate mastery, and the theme to which his ablest successors,

Mackay and Bryce and Munsterberg and Brogan, recurred. That equality was political; it was, until the twentieth century, economic; it was, above all, social and psychological. Much of that equality stemmed from the frontier, and America was a land molded by the frontier. "He who would see America in its proper light must visit our extended line of frontiers," wrote Crèvecoeur a century before Turner, and Ole Munch Raeder observed the leveling influence of the American west on judges, courts, and law. America was the land of experimentation. Everything here was new, as Francis Lieber discerned, everything had to be measured by new yardsticks. "In America," said the Pulszkys, "the spirit of progress is bold, and often encroaching . . . new ideas easily get a chance of being practically tried; the public at large does not shrink from testing at once different solutions of a problem." Equality, too, as Tocqueville pointed out, encouraged experimentation, for equality rejected the sovereign authority of the past, or of the great, and permitted every man to be his own authority—even on matters of language. Bryce more elaborately than any other commentator analyzed the American contribution to political experiments, and in the twentieth century Brogan returned to the theme. America was the land of industry, of energy, of vitality. "Excitability," wrote Gurowski, "is omnipotent in the American character," and George W. Steevens discovered that the American was an electric Anglo-Saxon. Only G. K. Chesterton struck an inharmonious—or merely a paradoxical—note. The explanations varied: climate, the frontier, the principle of equality, the intermixture of races—but whatever the particular explanation, the generalization was accepted by almost all observers from Crèvecoeur to Vinde. It was the combination of industry with natural wealth which accounted in large part for the material well-being of the American, and America was pre-eminently the land of plenty. "You are not much pressed to eat and drink," wrote Cobbett, "but such an abundance is spread before you . . . that you instantly lose all restraint." Perhaps no theme recurs more frequently, but it afforded few opportunities for philosophical interpretation and is not stressed here. It was the lush abundance of America that accounted, in part, for the generosity of its people, and America was the land of hospitality. The earliest visitors met it in the farms and in the villages; later visitors had to contend with it in mansions and banquet halls. Cobbett found it in rural Pennsylvania and Raeder in frontier Wisconsin and Harriet Martineau in Boston; Bourget thought it so extravagant as to be a national vice, but Birmingham thought that it contrasted happily with the prudence of the Old World and George Steevens delighted in it wherever he found it. The materialism which such physical well-being and such hospitality reflected could be interpreted as a virtue or as a vice, but whatever the interpretation, most observers were agreed that America was the land of materialism. "It would be well if they loved the real less and the ideal more," thought Dickens, but perhaps fame had brought him more hospitality than he could endure. Tocqueville explained American materialism as a consequence of equality, and Gurowski as a consequence of industrialism and commercialism; the first looked upon it as something to be overcome, the second as something to be proud of. "Money making," wrote the Polish critic, "continually extends the area of culture. It conquers the rugged face of nature, transforms the wilderness into a habitable and cultivated soil. In proportion as prosperity increases and expands, general civilization increases and expands." And Munsterberg too thought the American interest in money on the whole creditable. Notwithstanding the pervasive materialism of Americans, America was, most observers agreed, the land of exalted morals. This was a tribute all the more striking in the light of the general attribute of lawlessness. Tocqueville had analyzed the phenomenon, especially in its relation to the family, and he had found it, as usual, a manifestation of the principle of equality. Grund and Schaff found the explanation rather in religion which "presided over their councils"; Bryce traced it to more diverse factors. All agreed that sex morals were purer in America, female virtue safer, family relations more wholesome, than in Old-World nations. All agreed, too, on the elevated position which woman held in this country. America was the land of chivalry. "The age of chivalry is not gone," wrote Munsterberg; "until America it never came," and in one form or another a hundred commentators echoed this observation. Only the workingman, James Burn, thought American women spoiled, if not downright immoral, and only the novelist W. L. George suggested that women relieved from domestic duties and large families were to be pitied rather than envied. That there was a chasm between private and public morality was, however, argued with increasing insistence as the decades passed. Crèvecoeur thought that "we are the most perfect society now existing in the world," but Dickens, who was revolted by the licentiousness of the press, did not agree, nor for that matter did the judicious Bryce who more tellingly than any other exposed the venality of American politics. Political immorality was, indeed, the most pervasive of American vices, and few observers were able to extenuate it as they extenuated the American passion for money or American restlessness or American manners. Yet there was a paradox here, too, which the more astute interpreters did not fail to note. It was on his institutions, and particularly his political institutions, that the American fixed his patriotism. American patriotism was as new as American democracy, and dependent on it. It was not attached primarily to the soil, to a particular locality; it was not symbolized by a king or a nobility; it was inspired by abstractions—and this in the most practical of people—by the Constitution, equality, democracy, liberty. For these institutions Americans confessed a reverence otherwise alien to their character, nor were they deeply troubled by the gap between the ideal and the real, for in their minds the ideal assumed reality. For America was the land of perfectionism. The American knew that nothing was impossible, in his brave new world, and history confirmed his intuition. Progress was not, to him, a mere philosophical ideal but a commonplace of experience, and he could not understand why foreigners should see vulgar realities where he saw visions. He was outraged at any failure, at any imperfection even, could

not tolerate a depression or a military defeat, could not acquiesce
in any inadequacy of culture or, as Roussy de Sales pointed out,
even of marital felicity.

It all added up to a flattering picture, and this is, perhaps, one
of the more gratifying surprises of our investigation. For familiar as we are with the animadversions of a Trollope or a
Dickens, or a score of lesser commentators, we have supposed
that the foreign verdict on America was unfavorable. "The
feelings of the American people," as Mackay observed, "have
been wantonly and unnecessarily wounded by successive travelers who . . . have generally viewed them on the ludicrous
side," and every American schoolboy knows Lowell's famous
essay on a certain condescension in foreigners. The wanton attacks, the envy, the misunderstanding, the patronage, are all to
be found readily enough—Burn and Arnold and Madariaga are
examples here—but jaundiced criticism came from the second-
rate commentators rather than from the magisterial ones. The
most judicious, the most learned, the most perspicacious, the
most profound interpreters of America returned a verdict that
ranged from sympathy to enthusiasm.

That there were faults was acknowledged by even the most
friendly of our visitors, and the faults, like the virtues, seemed
to persist from generation to generation. What were the major
criticisms of the American experiment? The passion for equality, it was charged, made for mediocrity, for a general leveling
down of distinction and of talent. The concern for material
well-being produced a materialistic civilization, one in which
the arts flourished only by indulgence, as it were. The passion
for work, or for mere activity, left little time for the amenities
of life, and Americans were rude. An easygoing tolerance played
into the hands of the vulgar and the corrupt, permitted the invasion of privacy, the exaltation of the mediocre, the violation
of law and order. An excessive nervous vitality made for in-
stability and rootlessness, gave an air of impermanence to almost
everything that Americans undertook. The excessively high
value put upon woman led to a matriarchal society, and the con-

viction which animated all parents that their children must have
a better and easier life than they themselves had enjoyed produced successive generations of pampered brats. Most serious of
all, perhaps, was the charge of Tocqueville, reiterated by many
later interpreters, that democracy invited the tyranny of the
majority and that in the end popular rule might be metamor-
phosed into mob rule. Curiously enough not until almost the
twentieth century—Bryce is perhaps the earliest example—did
foreigners note the danger to democracy that came from the
wealthy minority rather than from the underprivileged majority.

Yet the dour prophecy of the tyranny of the majority was
confounded, and a hundred years after Tocqueville Americans
still observed the proprieties of the Constitution and cherished
their system of checks and balances. The observation can, without fatuousness, be enlarged to a generalization. America has, on
the whole, confounded her critics where they were pessimistic
rather than where they were optimistic.

III

These selections must speak for themselves, yet it is necessary
to say a word about them, if only in explanation. It should be
kept in mind that they are interpretations, not merely journalistic reports, that they are designed to discover the meaning of
America, not merely its appearance or habits or customs, certainly not its eccentricities and curiosities. As Henry Tucker-
man wrote almost a century ago, it is possible to find in foreign
views of America "every degree of sympathy and antipathy, of
refinement and vulgarity, of philosophical insight and shallow
impertinence, from coarse malice to dull good nature, and from
genial sense to repulsive bigotry." The vulgarity, the impertinence, the malice, the bigotry and, I trust, the dullness have been
excluded from this anthology, for it is not the sensational that I
have sought but the philosophical.

The task of selection presented serious difficulties. It is not
only that the number of volumes runs into the thousands, and

the number worth looking at into the hundreds, but that there are elementary difficulties in holding to any principle of selection. These are designed to be foreign views of America, yet what, after all, makes a view foreign? What gives the perspective so essential to interpretation? Is Crèvecoeur a foreign observer? He lived here for almost twenty years, and when he wrote it was as an "American Farmer." Are Schaff and Grund and Lieber and Gurowski foreigners? All of them settled down in the United States, regarded themselves, in the end, as Americans. And if Schaff is to be admitted to this anthology, why not Carl Schurz or Jacob Riis or Mary Antin or Edward Bok or any one of a dozen others who were born abroad and became Americanized? If Munsterberg is to be exploited, why not Santayana, whose career in many ways paralleled that of his Harvard colleague? In all these decisions I have had to follow my own judgment, and I do not suppose that others would invariably concur in that judgment. The selection from Schaff, for example, is taken from a series of addresses delivered in German to Germans, and this not long after Schaff had come to the United States. So, too, with Lieber: the "Letters" were written not long after Lieber arrived in this country and reflect the impact of the new world on a mind still open to fresh impressions. Grund and Gurowski, it seems to me, remained essentially alien in their point of view—and even in their style, while Munsterberg was deliberately interpreting America from the perspective of Old-World scholarship and philosophy.

All but one, or possibly two, of these commentators knew America at first hand. This requirement would seem to be obvious, yet it is by no means certain that it is sound. Hundreds of volumes of balderdash prove that physical acquaintance with America is no guaranty of understanding or judgment. Yet these pages could not be opened indiscriminately to all interpretations of America, to histories or criticisms or diplomatic documents. There had to be some principle of exclusion, and the logical thing was to exclude those who had not troubled to investigate America themselves. Yet I have not observed in this matter, however, a foolish consistency. The letters of Macaulay are included because they are interesting, important, and notorious, and because they represent a point of view that should not be ignored. The elaborate interpretation by Müller-Freienfels—who, for all I know, may have visited the United States—could not be omitted because it was a deliberate and on the whole successful attempt to view America in philosophical perspective.

Some famous names are absent, some notorious volumes have been ignored. Mrs. Trollope is not here, nor her more famous son; Ole Raeder has been preferred to the more familiar Fredrika Bremer, Müller-Freienfels to the ubiquitous Count Keyserling, and the delightful authors of *Little Golden America* to the belligerent Ilya Ehrenburg. These choices are of course personal; they do not involve any principle but represent merely my own preferences. Something of a principle was involved, however, in the selection of spokesmen for various countries and successive decades. I have tried to cover adequately a hundred and fifty years, and to find at least one interpreter for each decade, and I have been largely but not wholly successful in this. I have tried, further, to give adequate representation to as many countries as possible, and a statistical summary of that representation may not be irrelevant. Of the thirty-five selections eleven are English, four Scottish and two Irish, five are from France and four from Germany, two from Hungary, and one each from Norway, Sweden, Poland, Switzerland, Spain, China, and Russia. This is not, to be sure, proportional representation, but in this matter I was not a free agent. Any student can speedily satisfy himself that the best of interpretations, as well as the most voluminous, are the British, and that in the matter of interpreting America the French and the Germans are the only rivals of the Britons.

A word, finally, about the choice of material from the particular commentators. Here, again, I have been concerned with conclusions rather than merely with observations, and in a great many instances that principle left little room for choice. Where there was room for choice—as with Tocqueville, for example, or Bryce or Munsterberg or Brogan—I have been influenced by the desire to get illumination on diverse subjects. Thus I have selected from Tocqueville not the famous—and I think unhappy —chapter on the Tyranny of the Majority, but the lively and perspicacious comments on language and literature and on the military. Thus from Brogan I have taken not the highly controversial chapter on how the American people fight a war, but the unusually sympathetic essay on the American public schools —a subject not elsewhere represented.

It is interesting to find that these essays confirm our conventional judgment on our foreign interpreters. We have long believed that Tocqueville was the most profound, Bryce the most learned, of all the interpreters of America, and assuredly these selections justify that belief. The fame of Crèvecoeur is established—and deservedly. Arnold is as supercilious, Munsterberg as thorough, Chesterton as paradoxical, Birmingham as entertaining, Brogan as brilliant, as we have remembered them to be. Yet there are some agreeable discoveries. Alexander Mackay emerges as one of the best of all commentators. Francis Grund, clearly, should be better known; the saturnine Gurowski redeems himself from the faults of his Diary; the Pulszkys give us one of the most judicious of all comparative analyses of our civilization; Bourget has more solidity than we had suspected; G. W. Steevens and W. L. George reveal an interpretative talent of a high order. Nor is there any perceptible diminution either in the quantity or the quality of the interpretation in the twentieth century. The flood of commentary flows on unchecked, and Munsterberg, Müller-Freienfels, W. L. George and Denis Brogan compare not unfavorably with the giants of the nineteenth century. The question which Crèvecoeur asked at the very beginning of our national existence, and which after him a hundred philosophers have echoed, continues to command the interest of the world: What is the American, this new man?

HENRY STEELE COMMAGER
Rye, New York
June, 1947

AMERICA IN PERSPECTIVE
The United States through Foreign Eyes

WHAT IS AN AMERICAN?

MICHEL-GUILLAUME DE CRÈVECOEUR

NO interpretation of the American character in its formative period is more justly famous than this, the third "Letter
from an American Farmer" written sometime in the late
seventeen-seventies. The author of these letters, Michel
Guillaume de Crèvecoeur, had a long and romantic career
in two continents. Born in 1735—the date is somewhat
doubtful—near Caen, Normandy, Crèvecoeur served under
Montcalm in the Seven Years' War, explored the Great
Lakes and Ohio River country at a time when it was still
controlled by Indian tribes, and traveled widely in the
Middle and Southern Colonies. In 1765 he became a naturalized American and settled down to farming in Orange
County, New York, where he remained until his return to
France in 1780. It was during these years that he wrote the
Letters from an American Farmer and the delightful
Sketches of Eighteenth-Century America, not published until 1825 and only recently translated into English. Although
not an active Loyalist, Crèvecoeur had little sympathy with
the movement for independence and none at all for the
lawlessness which characterized the fighting in the frontier
country west of the Hudson. When he returned to America,
in 1783, it was to find his house in ashes, his wife dead, his
children scattered. Appointed French consul in New York,
he lingered on in America until 1790, then returned to
France where he lived until his death in 1813.

Crèvecoeur, who lived half of his mature life in America,
can scarcely be classified as a foreigner, and indeed, as his
letters and sketches reveal, he knew his adopted country
better than most native-born Americans did—knew it, understood it, and loved it.

❖❖❖❖❖❖❖

I wish I could be acquainted with the feelings and thoughts which must agitate the heart and present themselves to the mind of an enlightened Englishman, when he first lands on this continent. He must greatly rejoice, that he lived at a time to see this fair country discovered and settled; he must necessarily feel a share of national pride, when he views the chain of settlements which embellishes these extended shores. When he says to himself, this is the work of my countrymen, who, when convulsed by factions, afflicted by a variety of miseries and wants, restless and impatient, took refuge here. They brought along with them their national genius, to which they principally owe what liberty they enjoy, and what substance they possess. Here he sees the industry of his native country, displayed in a new manner, and traces in their works the embrios of all the arts, sciences, and ingenuity which flourish in Europe. Here he beholds fair cities, substantial villages, extensive fields, an immense country filled with decent houses, good roads, orchards, meadows, and bridges, where an hundred years ago all was wild, woody, and uncultivated!

What a train of pleasing ideas this fair spectacle must suggest! it is a prospect which must inspire a good citizen with the most heartfelt pleasure. The difficulty consists in the manner of viewing so extensive a scene. He is arrived on a new continent; a modern society offers itself to his contemplation, different from what he had hitherto seen. It is not composed, as in Europe, of great lords who possess every thing, and of a herd of people who have nothing. Here are no aristocratical families, no courts, no kings, no bishops, no ecclesiastical dominion, no invisible power giving to a few a very visible one; no great manufacturers employing thousands, no great refinements of luxury. The rich and the poor are not so far removed from each other as they are in Europe.

Some few towns excepted, we are all tillers of the earth, from Nova Scotia to West Florida. We are a people of cultivators, scattered over an immense territory, communicating with each other by means of good roads and navigable rivers, united by the silken bands of mild government, all respecting the laws without dreading their power, because they are equitable. We are all animated with the spirit of industry, which is unfettered, and unrestrained, because each person works for himself. If he travels through our rural districts, he views not the hostile castle, and the haughty mansion, contrasted with the clay-built hut and miserable cabbin, where cattle and men help to keep each other warm, and dwell in meanness, smoke, and indigence. A pleasing uniformity of decent competence appears throughout our habitations. The meanest of our log-houses is a dry and comfortable habitation. Lawyer or merchant are the fairest titles our towns afford; that of a farmer is the only appellation of the rural inhabitants of our country. It must take some time ere he can reconcile himself to our dictionary, which is but short in words of dignity, and names of honour. There, on a Sunday, he sees a congregation of respectable farmers and their wives, all clad in neat homespun, well mounted, or riding in their own humble waggons. There is not among them an esquire, saving the unlettered magistrate. There he sees a parson as simple as his flock, a farmer who does not riot on the labour of others. We have no princes, for whom we toil, starve, and bleed: we are the most perfect society now existing in the world. Here man is free as he ought to be; nor is this pleasing equality so transitory as many others are. Many ages will not see the shores of our great lakes replenished with inland nations, nor the unknown bounds of North America entirely peopled. Who can tell how far it extends? Who can tell the millions of men whom it will feed and contain? for no European foot has as yet travelled half the extent of this mighty continent!

The next wish of this traveller will be to know whence came all these people? they are a mixture of English, Scotch, Irish, French, Dutch, Germans, and Swedes. From this promiscuous breed, that race now called Americans have arisen.

The eastern provinces must indeed be excepted, as being the unmixed descendants of Englishmen. I have heard many wish they had been more intermixed also: for my part, I am no wisher; and think it much better as it has happened. They exhibit a most conspicuous figure in this great and variegated picture; they too enter for a great share in the pleasing perspective displayed in these thirteen provinces. I know it is fashionable to reflect on them; but I respect them for what they have done; for the accuracy and wisdom with which they have settled their territory; for the decency of their manners; for their early love of letters; their ancient college, the first in this hemisphere; for their industry, which to me, who am but a farmer, is the criterion of every thing. There never was a people, situated as they are, who, with so ungrateful a soil, have done more in so short a time. Do you think that the monarchical ingredients which are more prevalent in other governments, have purged them from all foul stains? Their histories assert the contrary.

In this great American asylum, the poor of Europe have by some means met together, and in consequence of various causes; to what purpose should they ask one another, what countrymen they are? Alas, two thirds of them had no country. Can a wretch who wanders about, who works and starves, whose life is a continual scene of sore affliction or pinching penury; can that man call England or any other kingdom his country? A country that had no bread for him, whose fields procured him no harvest, who met with nothing but the frowns of the rich, the severity of the laws, with jails and punishments; who owned not a single foot of the extensive surface of this planet? No! urged by a variety of motives, here they came. Every thing has tended to regenerate them; new laws, a new mode of living, a new social system; here they are become men: in Europe they were as so many useless plants, wanting vegetative mould, and refreshing showers; they withered, and were mowed down by want, hunger, and war: but now, by the power of transplantation, like all other plants, they have taken root and flourished! Formerly they were not numbered in any civil list of their country, except in those of the poor; here they rank as citizens. By what invisible power has this surprizing metamorphosis been performed? By that of the laws and that of their industry. The laws, the indulgent laws, protect them as they arrive, stamping on them the symbol of adoption; they receive ample rewards for their labours; these accumulated rewards procure them lands; those lands confer on them the title of freemen; and to that title every benefit is affixed which men can possibly require. This is the great operation daily performed by our laws. From whence proceed these laws? From our government. Whence that government? It is derived from the original genius and strong desire of the people, ratified and confirmed by government. This is the great chain which links us all, this is the picture which every province exhibits, Nova Scotia excepted. There the crown has done all; either there were no people who had genius, or it was not much attended to: the consequence is, that the province is very thinly inhabited indeed; the power of the crown, in conjunction with the musketos, has prevented men from settling there. Yet some part of it flourished once, and it contained a mild harmless set of people. But for the fault of a few leaders the whole were banished. The greatest political error the crown ever committed in America, was to cut off men from a country which wanted nothing but men!

What attachment can a poor European emigrant have for a country where he had nothing? The knowledge of the language, the love of a few kindred as poor as himself, were the only cords that tied him: his country is now that which gives him land, bread, protection, and consequence: *Ubi panis ibi patria*, is the motto of all emigrants. What then is the American, this new man? He is either an European, or the descendant of an European; hence that strange mixture of blood, which you will find in no other country. I could point out to you a man, whose grandfather was an Englishman, whose wife was Dutch, whose son married a French woman, and whose present four sons have now four wives of different nations. *He* is an American, who, leaving behind him all his ancient prejudices and manners, receives new ones from the new mode of life he has embraced, the new government he obeys, and the new rank he holds. He becomes an American by being received in the broad lap of our great *Alma Mater*.

Here individuals of all nations are melted into a new race of men, whose labours and posterity will one day cause great change in the world. Americans are the western pilgrims, who are carrying along with them that great mass of arts, sciences, vigour, and industry, which began long since in the east; they will finish the great circle. The Americans were once scattered all over Europe; here they are incorporated into one of the finest systems of population which has ever appeared, and which will hereafter become distinct by the power of the different climates they inhabit. The American ought, therefore, to love this country much better than that wherein either he or his forefathers were born. Here the rewards of his industry follow with equal steps the progress of his labour; his labour is founded on the basis of nature, *self-interest*; can it want a stronger allurement? Wives and children, who before in vain demanded of him a morsel of bread, now, fat and frolicsome, gladly help their father to clear those fields whence exuberant crops are to arise to feed and to clothe them all; without any part being claimed, either by a despotic prince, a rich abbot, or a mighty lord. Here religion demands but little of him; a small voluntary salary to the minister, and gratitude to God; can he refuse these? The American is a new man, who acts upon new principles; he must therefore entertain new ideas, and form new opinions. From involuntary idleness, servile dependence, penury, and useless labour, he has passed to toils of a very different nature, rewarded by ample subsistence.—This is an American. . . .

I wish I were able to trace all my ideas; if my ignorance prevents me from describing them properly, I hope I shall be able to delineate a few of the outlines, which are all I propose.

Those who live near the sea, feed more on fish than on flesh, and often encounter that boisterous element. This renders them more bold and enterprising; this leads them to neglect the confined occupations of the land. They see and converse with a variety of people; their intercourse with mankind becomes extensive. The sea inspires them with a love of traffic, a desire of transporting produce from one place to another; leads them to a variety of resources, which supply the place of labour. Those who inhabit the middle settlements, by far the most numerous, must be very different; the simple cultivation of the earth purifies them; but the indulgences of the government, the soft remonstrances of religion, the rank of independent free-holders, must necessarily inspire them with sentiments, very little known in Europe among people of the same class. What do I say? Europe has no such class of man; the early knowledge they acquire, the early bargains they make, give them a great degree of sagacity. As freemen, they will be litigious; pride and obstinacy are often the cause of law suits; the nature of our laws and governments may be another. As citizens, it is easy to imagine, that they will carefully read the newspapers, enter into every political disquisition, freely blame or censure governors and others. As farmers, they will be careful and anxious to get as much as they can, because what they get is their own. As northern men, they will love the chearful cup. As Christians, religion curbs them not in their opinions; the general indulgence leaves every one to think for himself in spiritual matters; the laws inspect our actions; our thoughts are left to God. Industry, good living, selfishness, litigiousness, country politics, the pride of freemen, religious indifference, are their characteristics. If you recede still farther from the sea, you will come into more modern settlements; they exhibit the same strong lineaments, in a ruder appearance. Religion seems to have still less influence, and their manners are less improved.

Now we arrive near the great woods, near the last inhabited districts; there men seem to be placed still farther
beyond the reach of government, which in some measure
leaves them to themselves. How can it pervade every corner?
as they were driven there by misfortunes, necessity of beginnings, desire of acquiring large tracts of land, idleness,
frequent want of economy, ancient debts; the reunion of
such people does not afford a very pleasing spectacle. When
discord, want of unity and friendship—when either drunken-
ness or idleness prevail in such remote districts—contention,
inactivity, and wretchedness must ensue. There are not the
same remedies to these evils as in a long established community. The few magistrates they have, are in general little
better than the rest; they are often in a perfect state of war;
that of man against man, sometimes decided by blows, sometimes by means of the law; that of man against every wild
inhabitant of these venerable woods, of which they are come
to dispossess them. There men appear to be no better than
carnivorous animals of a superior rank, living on the flesh of
wild animals when they can catch them; and when they are
not able, they subsist on the grain.

He who would wish to see America in its proper light, and
have a true idea of its feeble beginnings and barbarous rudiments, must visit our extended line of frontiers where the last
settlers dwell, and where he may see the first labours of settlement, the mode of clearing the earth, in all their different
appearances; where men are wholly left dependent on their
native tempers, and on the spur of uncertain industry, which
often fails, when not sanctified by the efficacy of a few moral
rules. There, remote from the power of example, and check
of shame, many families exhibit the most hideous parts of
our society. They are a kind of forlorn hope, preceding by
ten or twelve years the most respectable army of veterans
which come after them. In that space, prosperity will polish
some, vice and the law will drive off the rest, who uniting
again with others like themselves will recede still farther;

making room for more industrious people, who will finish their improvements, convert the log-house into a convenient habitation, and rejoicing that the first heavy labours are finished, will change in a few years that hitherto barbarous country into a fine, fertile, well regulated district.

Such is our progress, such is the march of the Europeans toward the interior parts of this continent. In all societies there are off-casts; this impure part serves as our precursors or pioneers; my father himself was one of that class; but he came upon honest principles, and was therefore one of the few who held fast; by good conduct and temperance, he transmitted to me his fair inheritance, when not above one in fourteen of his contemporaries had the same good fortune.

Forty years ago, this smiling country was thus inhabited; it is now purged, a general decency of manners prevails throughout; and such has been the fate of our best countries.

Exclusive of those general characteristics, each province has its own, founded on the government, climate, mode of husbandry, customs, and peculiarity of circumstances. Europeans submit insensibly to these great powers, and become in the course of a few generations, not only Americans in general, but either Pennsylvanians, Virginians, or provincials under some other name. Whoever traverses the continent, must easily observe those strong differences, which will grow more evident in time. The inhabitants of Canada, Massachusetts, the middle provinces, the southern ones will be as different as their climates; their only points of unity will be those of religion and language.

As I have endeavoured to shew you how Europeans become Americans; it may not be disagreeable to shew you likewise how the various Christian sects introduced, wear out, and how religious indifference becomes prevalent. When any considerable number of a particular sect happen to dwell contiguous to each other, they immediately erect a temple, and there worship the Divinity agreeably to their own peculiar ideas. Nobody disturbs them. If any new sect springs up in Europe, it may happen that many of its professors will come and settle in America. As they bring their zeal with them, they are at liberty to make proselytes if they can, and to build a meeting and to follow the dictates of their consciences; for neither the government nor any other power interferes. If they are peaceable subjects, and are industrious, what is it to their neighbours how and in what manner they think fit to address their prayers to the Supreme Being? But if the sectaries are not settled close together, if they are mixed with other denominations, their zeal will cool for want of fuel, and will be extinguished in a little time. Then the Americans become as to religion, what they are as to country, allied to all. In them the name of Englishman, Frenchman, and European is lost, and in like manner, the strict modes of Christianity as practised in Europe are lost also. . . .

Thus have I faintly and imperfectly endeavoured to trace our society from the sea to our woods! Yet you must not imagine that every person who moves back, acts upon the same principles, or falls into the same degeneracy. Many families carry with them all their decency of conduct, purity of morals, and respect of religion; but these are scarce, the power of example is sometimes irresistible. Even among these back-settlers, their depravity is greater or less, according to what nation or province they belong. Were I to adduce proofs of this, I might be accused of partiality. If there happens to be some rich intervals, some fertile bottoms, in those remote districts, the people will there prefer tilling the land to hunting, and will attach themselves to it; but even on these fertile spots you may plainly perceive the inhabitants to acquire a great degree of rusticity and selfishness.

It is in consequence of this straggling situation, and the astonishing power it has on manners, that the back-settlers of both the Carolinas, Virginia, and many other parts, have been long a set of lawless people; it has been even dangerous to travel among them. Government can do nothing in so

extensive a country; better it should wink at these irregulari-
ties, than that it should use means inconsistent with its usual
mildness. Time will efface those stains: in proportion as the
great body of population approaches them they will reform,
and become polished and subordinate. Whatever has been
said of the four New England provinces, no such degeneracy
of manners has ever tarnished their annals; their back-settlers
have been kept within the bounds of decency, and government, by means of wise laws, and by the influence of religion.
What a detestable idea such people must have given to
natives of the Europeans! They trade with them, the worst
of people are permitted to do that which none but persons
of the best characters should be employed in. They get
drunk with them, and often defraud the Indians. Their
avarice, removed from the eyes of their superiors, knows no
bounds; and aided by a little superiority of knowledge, these
traders deceive them, and even sometimes shed blood. Hence
those shocking violations, those sudden devastations which
have so often stained our frontiers, when hundreds of innocent people have been sacrificed for the crimes of a few. It
was in consequence of such behaviour, that the Indians took
the hatchet against the Virginians in 1774. Thus are our first
steps trod, thus are our first trees felled, in general, by the
most vicious of our people; and thus the path is opened for
the arrival of a second and better class, the true American
freeholders; the most respectable set of people in this part of
the world: respectable for their industry, their happy independence, the great share of freedom they possess, the good
regulation of their families, and for extending the trade and
dominion of our mother country.

Europe contains hardly any other distinctions but lords
and tenants; this fair country alone is settled by freeholders,
the possessors of the soil they cultivate, members of the government they obey, and the framers of their own laws, by
means of their representatives. This is a thought which you
have taught me to cherish; our distance from Europe, far

from diminishing, rather adds to our usefulness and consequence as men and subjects. Had our forefathers remained there, they would only have crouded it, and perhaps prolonged those convulsions which had shook it so long. Every industrious European who transports himself here, may be compared to a sprout growing at the foot of a great tree; it enjoys and draws but a little portion of sap; wrench it from the parent roots, transplant it, and it will become a tree bearing fruit also. Colonists are therefore entitled to the consideration due to the most useful subjects; a hundred families barely existing in some parts of Scotland, will here in six years, cause an annual exportation of 10,000 bushels of wheat: 100 bushels being but a common quantity for an industrious family to sell, if they cultivate good land. It is here, then, that the idle may be employed, the useless become useful, and the poor become rich: but by riches I do not mean gold and silver; we have but little of those metals; I mean a better sort of wealth, cleared lands, cattle, good houses, good clothes, and an increase of people to enjoy them.

There is no wonder that this country has so many charms, and presents to Europeans so many temptations to remain in it. A traveller in Europe becomes a stranger as soon as he quits his own kingdom; but it is otherwise here. We know, properly speaking, no strangers; this is every person's country; the variety of our soils, situations, climates, governments, and produce, hath something which must please every body. No sooner does an European arrive, no matter of what condition, than his eyes are opened upon the fair prospects; he hears his language spoke, he retraces many of his own country manners, he perpetually hears the names of families and towns with which he is acquainted; he sees happiness and prosperity in all places disseminated; he meets with hospitality, kindness, and plenty every where: he beholds hardly any poor, he seldom hears of punishments and executions; and he wonders at the elegance of our towns, those miracles of industry and freedom. He cannot admire enough our rural districts, our convenient roads, good taverns, and our many accommodations; he involuntarily loves a country where every thing is so lovely. When in England, he was a mere Englishman; here he stands on a larger portion of the globe, not less than its fourth part, and may see the productions of the north, in iron and naval stores; the provisions of Ireland, the grain of Egypt, the indigo, the rice of China. He does not find, as in Europe, a crouded society, where every place is over-stocked; he does not feel that perpetual collision of parties, that difficulty of beginning, that contention which oversets so many.

There is room for every body in America: has he any particular talent, or industry? he exerts it in order to procure a livelihood, and it succeeds. Is he a merchant? the avenues of trade are infinite; is he eminent in any respect? he will be employed and respected. Does he love a country life? pleasant farms present themselves; he may purchase what he wants, and thereby become an American farmer. Is he a labourer, sober and industrious; he need not go many miles, nor receive many informations before he will be hired, well fed at the table of his employer, and paid four or five times more than he can get in Europe. Does he want uncultivated lands? thousands of acres present themselves, which he may purchase cheap. Whatever be his talents or inclinations, if they are moderate, he may satisfy them. I do not mean, that every one who comes will grow rich in a little time; no, but he may procure an easy, decent maintenance, by his industry. Instead of starving, he will be fed; instead of being idle, he will have employment; and these are riches enough for such men as come over here. The rich stay in Europe; it is only the middling and poor that emigrate. Would you wish to travel in independent idleness, from north to south, you will find easy access, and the most chearful reception at every house; society without ostentation, good cheer without pride, and every decent diversion which the country affords, with little expense. It is no wonder that the European who has lived here a few years, is desirous to remain; Europe with all its pomp, is not to be compared to this continent, for men of middle stations or labourers.

An European, when he first arrives, seems limited in his intentions, as well as in his views; but he very suddenly alters his scale; two hundred miles formerly appeared a very great distance; it is now but a trifle; he no sooner breathes our air than he forms schemes, and embarks in designs he never would have thought of in his own country. There the plenitude of society confines many useful ideas, and often extinguishes the most laudable schemes which here ripen into maturity. Thus Europeans become Americans.

But how is this accomplished in that croud of low, indigent people, who flock here every year from all parts of Europe? I will tell you; they no sooner arrive than they immediately feel the good effects of that plenty of provisions we possess: they fare on our best food, and are kindly entertained; their talents, character, and peculiar industry are immediately enquired into; they find countrymen every where disseminated, let them come from whatever part of Europe.

Let me select one as an epitome of the rest; he is hired, he goes to work, and works moderately; instead of being employed by a haughty person, he finds himself with his equal, placed at the substantial table of the farmer, or else at an inferior one as good; his wages are high, his bed is not like that bed of sorrow on which he used to lie: if he behaves with propriety, and is faithful, he is caressed, and becomes, as it were, a member of the family. He begins to feel the effects of a sort of resurrection; hitherto he had not lived, but simply vegetated; he now feels himself a man, because he is treated as such; the laws of his own country had overlooked him in his insignificancy; the laws of this cover him with their mantle. Judge what an alteration there must arise in the mind and thoughts of this man; he begins to forget his former servitude and dependence; his heart involuntarily swells and glows; this first swell inspires him with those new thoughts which constitute an American. What love can he entertain for a country where his existence was a burden to him! if he is a generous good man, the love of his new adoptive parent, will sink deep into his heart. He looks around, and sees many a prosperous person, who but a few years before was as poor as himself. This encourages him much; he begins to form some little scheme, the first, alas, he ever formed in his life. If he is wise, he thus spends two or three years, in which time he acquires knowledge, the use of tools, the modes of working the lands, felling trees, &c. This prepares the foundation of a good name, the most useful acquisition he can make. He is encouraged; he has gained friends; he is advised and directed; he feels bold; he purchases some land; he gives all the money he has brought over, as well as what he has earned, and trusts to the God of harvests for the discharge of the rest. His good name procures him credit; he is now possessed of the deed, conveying to him and his posterity the fee simple, and absolute property of two hundred acres of land, situated on such a river. What an epocha in this man's life! He is become a freeholder, from perhaps a German boor—he is now an American, a Pennsylvanian. He is naturalized; his name is enrolled with those of the other citizens of the province. Instead of being a vagrant, he has a place of residence; he is called the inhabitant of such a county, or of such a district, and for the first time in his life counts for something; for hitherto he had been a cypher. I only repeat what I have heard many say, and no wonder their hearts should glow, and be agitated with a multitude of feelings, not easy to describe. From nothing to start into being; from a servant to the rank of master; from being the slave of some despotic prince, to become a free man, invested with lands, to which every municipal blessing is annexed! What a change indeed! It is in consequence of that change, that he becomes an American.

This great metamorphosis has a double effect; it extinguishes all his European prejudices; he forgets that mechanism of subordination, that servility of disposition which poverty had taught him; and sometimes he is apt to forget it too much, often passing from one extreme to the other. If he is a good man, he forms schemes of future prosperity; he proposes to educate his children better than he has been educated himself; he thinks of future modes of conduct, feels an ardour to labour he never felt before. Pride steps in, and leads him to every thing that the laws do not forbid: he respects them; with a heart-felt gratitude he looks toward that government from whose wisdom all his new felicity is derived, and under whose wings and protection he now lives. These reflexions constitute him the good man and the good subject.

Ye poor Europeans, ye, who sweat and work for the great —ye, who are obliged to give so many sheaves to the church, so many to your lords, so many to your government, and have hardly any left for yourselves—ye, who are held in less estimation than favourite hunters or useless lap-dogs—ye, who only breathe the air of nature, because it cannot be withheld from you; it is here that ye can conceive the possibility of those feelings I have been describing; it is here the laws of naturalization invite every one to partake of our great labours and felicity, to till unrented, untaxed lands!

Many, corrupted beyond the power of amendment, have brought with them all their vices, and, disregarding the advantages held out to them, have gone on in their former career of iniquity, until they have been overtaken and punished by our laws. It is not every emigrant who succeeds; no, it is only the sober, the honest, and industrious: happy those, to whom this transition has served as a powerful spur to labour, to prosperity, and to the good establishment of children, born in the days of their poverty: and who had no other portion to expect, but the rags of their parents, had it not been for their happy emigration. Others again, have been led astray by this enchanting scene; their new pride, instead of leading them to the fields, has kept them in idleness; the idea of possessing lands is all that satisfies them—though surrounded with fertility, they have mouldered away their time in inactivity, misinformed husbandry, and ineffectual endeavours. . . .

After a foreigner from any part of Europe is arrived, and become a citizen; let him devoutly listen to the voice of our great parent, which says to him, "Welcome to my shores, distressed European; bless the hour in which thou didst see my verdant fields, my fair navigable rivers, and my green mountains!—If thou wilt work, I have bread for thee; if thou wilt be honest, sober and industrious, I have greater rewards to confer on thee—ease and independence. I will give thee fields to feed and clothe thee; a comfortable fire-side to sit by, and tell thy children by what means thou hast prospered; and a decent bed to repose on. I shall endow thee, beside, with the immunities of a freeman. If thou wilt carefully educate thy children, teach them gratitude to God, and reverence to that government, that philanthropic government, which has collected here so many men and made them happy, I will also provide for thy progeny: and to every good man this ought to be the most holy, the most powerful, the most earnest wish he can possibly form, as well as the most consolatory prospect when he dies. Go thou, and work and till; thou shalt prosper, provided thou be just, grateful and industrious." 1793

Crèvecoeur, *Letters from an American Farmer.*

2

WHY THE AMERICANS ARE
A HAPPY PEOPLE

JACQUES PIERRE BRISSOT DE WARVILLE

LESS penetrating than Crèvecoeur, but even more enthusiastic, was Brissot de Warville. Born at Ouraville, near
Chartres, young Ouraville—or Warville as he later called it
—early attached himself to the revolutionary cause in
France, and in the mid-eighties was thrown into the Bastille
for his attacks on the old regime. Liberated through the efforts of the Duc d' Orleans, Brissot visited America, in 1788,
gathering material for his *Travels in the United States* which
was published in London four years later. The outbreak
of the Revolution sent him hurrying back to France, eager
to establish in his native land those institutions of liberty and
equality which had aroused his admiration in the New
World. A leader of the Gironde, he soon fell out of favor
with the extremists, however, and in 1793 he was proscribed
and sent to the guillotine.

Like his successor, Tocqueville, Brissot was interested in
America not so much for its own sake as for the lessons it
might hold for France. His *Travels*—from whose preface
this extract is taken—is nevertheless valuable for its description of American economy at the time of the establishment
of the new Constitutional government.

❖❖❖❖❖❖❖

O FRENCHMEN who wish for this valuable instruction,
study the Americans of the present day. Open this
book; you will here see to what degree of prosperity the
blessings of freedom can elevate the industry of man; how
they dignify his nature, and dispose him to universal fra-

ternity; you will here learn by what means liberty is preserved; that the great secret of its duration is in good morals. It is a truth that the observation of the present state of America demonstrates at every step. Thus you will see, in these Travels, the prodigious effects of liberty on morals, on industry, and on the amelioration of men. You will see those stern Presbyterians, who, on the first settlement of their country, infected with the gloomy superstitions of Europe, could erect gibbets for those who thought differently from themselves. You will see them admitting all sects to equal charity and brotherhood, rejecting those superstitions which, to adore the Supreme Being, make martyrs of part of the human race. Thus you will see all the Americans, in whose minds the jealousy of the mother country had disseminated the most absurd prejudices against foreign nations, abjure those prejudices, reject every idea of war, and open the way to an universal confederation of the human race. You will see independent America contemplating no other limits but those of the universe, no other restraint but the laws made by her representatives. You will see them attempting all sorts of speculations; opening the fertile bosom of the soul, lately covered by forests; tracing unknown seas; establishing new communications, new markets; naturalizing, in their country, those precious manufactures which England had reserved to herself; and by this accumulation of the means of industry, they change the balance that was formerly against America, and turn it to their advantage. You will see them faithful to their engagements, while their enemies are proclaiming their bankruptcy. You will see them invigorating their minds, and cultivating their virtues; reforming their government, employing only the language of reason to convince the refractory; multiplying everywhere moral institutions and patriotic establishments; and, above all, never separating the idea of public from private virtues. Such is the consoling picture, which these Travels will offer to the friend of Liberty. . . .

Can a people without government be happy? Yes, if you can suppose a whole people with good morals; and this is not a chimera. Will you see an example? Observe the Quakers of America. Though numerous, though dispersed over the surface of Pennsylvania, they have passed more than a century, without municipal government, without police, without coercive measures, to administer the State, or to govern the hospitals. And why? See the picture of their manners; you will there find the explanation of the phenomenon.

Coercive measures and liberty never go together; a free people hates the former; but if these measures are not employed how will you execute the law? By the force of reason and good morals—take away these, and you must borrow the arm of violence, or fall into anarchy. If, then, a people wishes to banish the dishonorable means of coercion, they must exercise their reason, which will show them the necessity of a constant respect for the law.

The exercise of this faculty produces among the Americans a great number of men designated by the name of principled men. This appellation indicates the character of a class of men so little known among us that they have not acquired a name. There will be one formed, I have no doubt; but, in the meantime, I see none but vibrating, vacillating beings, who do good by enthusiasm, and never by reflection. There can be no durable revolution, but where reflection marks the operation, and matures the ideas. It is amongst those men of principle that you find the true heroes of humanity, the Howards, Fothergills, Penns, Franklins, Washingtons, Sidneys and Ludlows. . . .

In a word, my countrymen, would you be always free, always independent in your elections, and in your opinions? Would you confine the executive power within narrow limits, and diminish the number of your laws? . . . Morals supply perfectly the necessity of laws; laws supply but imperfectly, and in a miserable manner, the place of morals.

Would you augment your population, that chief wealth of nations? Would you augment the ease of individuals, industry, agriculture, and everything that contributes to general prosperity?—Have morals!

Such is the double effect of morals in the United States, whose form of government still frightens pusillanimous and superstitious men. The portraits offered to view, in these Travels, will justify that republicanism which knaves calumniate with design, which ignorant men do not understand, but which they will learn to know and respect. How can we better judge of a government than by its effects? Reasoning may deceive; experience is always right. If liberty produces good morals, and diffuses information, why do freemen continue to carp at that kind of government, which, being founded on the greatest degree of liberty, secures the greatest degree of prosperity? . . .   Paris, April 21, 1791

Brissot de Warville, *New Travels in the United States of America.*

3

THE MATERIAL WELL-BEING
OF THE AMERICANS

WILLIAM COBBETT

WILLIAM COBBETT, like Crèvecoeur, belongs almost as much to American history and literature as to the history and literature of his native country. Born in Surrey, England, in 1762, Cobbett first came to the United States in 1792, eking out a living by teaching English to French refugees in Philadelphia. Caught up in the bitter conflict between Federalists and Jeffersonians, he discovered a talent for vituperative journalism that made him invaluable to the Federalists. Under the pseudonym "Porcupine" he savagely attacked Jefferson and the Francophiles in a series of pamphlets and in *Porcupine's Gazette*. So malevolent were his criticisms that even Federalist President John Adams considered deporting him, and his libels on the famous Dr. Benjamin Rush cost him five thousand dollars. In 1800 Cobbett returned to England, where he supervised a twelve-volume edition of his writings and lent his pen to the support of William Pitt. Antagonized by the Peace of Amiens, however, he broke with Pitt, and devoted himself once more to his favorite journalism—vitriolic attack. Twice he incurred fines of one thousand pounds for his attacks upon the government, and in 1809 he was jailed for two years for the same offense. In 1817 he fled once more to America, to escape persecution and staggering debts. His views, meantime, had undergone something of a revolution: he was now a confirmed democrat and an admirer of American institutions. His chief interest, however, was not in politics but in agriculture, and his *Year's Residence in America* (1818) was devoted largely to a description of American husbandry. After his return to England, Cobbett entered Parliament, but his last years were relatively quiet and innocuous. He died in 1835, leaving a reputation as the Junius of his generation.

◇◇◇◇◇◇

ALL these are, generally speaking, the same as those of the people of England. The French call this people *Les Anglo-Americains*: and, indeed, what are they else? Of the manners and customs somewhat peculiar to America I have said so much, here and there, in former chapters, that I can hardly say anything new here upon these matters. But, as *society* is naturally a great thing with a gentleman, who thinks of coming hither with his wife and children, I will endeavor to describe the society that he will find here. To give general descriptions is not so satisfactory as it is to deal a little in particular instances; to tell of what one has seen and experienced. This is what I shall do; and, in this chapter I wish to be regarded as addressing myself to a most worthy and public-spirited gentleman of moderate fortune, in Lancashire, who, with a large family, now balances whether he shall come, to stay.

Now, then, my dear Sir, this people contains very few persons very much raised in men's estimation, above the general mass; for, though there are some men of immense *fortunes*, their wealth does very little indeed in the way of purchasing even the outward signs of respect; and, as to *adulation*, it is not to be purchased with love or money. Men, be they what they may, are generally called by their *two names*, without any thing prefixed or added. I am one of the greatest men in this country at present; for people in general call me "*Cobbett*," though the Quakers provokingly persevere in putting the *William* before it, and my old friends in Pennsylvania, use even the word *Billy*, which, in the very sound of the letters, is an antidote to every thing like thirst for distinction.

Fielding, in one of his romances, observes, that there are but few cases, in which a husband can be justified in availing himself of the right which the law gives him to bestow manual chastisement upon his wife, and that one of these, he thinks, is when any pretensions to superiority of blood make their appearance in her language and conduct. They have a better cure for this malady here; namely, silent, but ineffable contempt.

It is supposed, in England, that this equality of estimation must beget a general coarseness and rudeness of behavior. Never was there a greater mistake. No man likes to be treated with disrespect; and, when he finds that he can obtain respect only by treating others with respect, he will use that only means. When he finds that neither haughtiness nor wealth will bring him a civil word, he becomes civil himself; and, I repeat it again and again, this is a country of *universal civility*.

The causes of hypocrisy are the fear of loss and the hope of gain. Men crawl to those, whom, in their hearts, they despise, because they fear the effects of their ill-will and hope to gain by their good-will. The circumstances of all ranks are so easy here that there is no cause for hypocrisy; and the thing is not of so fascinating a nature, that men should love it for its own sake.

The boasting of wealth, and the endeavoring to disguise poverty, these two acts, so painful to contemplate, are almost total strangers in this country; for, no man can gain adulation or respect by his wealth, and no man dreads the effects of poverty, because no man sees any dreadful effects arising from poverty.

That anxious eagerness to get on, which is seldom unaccompanied with some degree of envy of more successful neighbors, and which has its foundation first in a dread of future want, and next in a desire to obtain distinction by means of wealth; this anxious eagerness, so unamiable in itself, and so unpleasant an inmate of the breast, so great a sourer of the temper, is a stranger to America, where accidents and losses, which would drive an Englishman half mad, produce but very little agitation.

From the absence of so many causes of uneasiness, of envy, of jealousy, of rivalship, and of mutual dislike, society, that is to say, the intercourse between man and man, and family and family, becomes easy and pleasant; while the universal plenty is the cause of universal hospitality. I know, and have ever known, but little of the people in the cities and towns in America; but the difference between them and the people in the country can only be such as is found in all other countries. As to the manner of living in the country, I was, the other day, at a gentleman's house, and I asked the lady for her bill of fare for the year. I saw fourteen fat hogs weighing about twenty score a piece, which were to come into the house the next Monday; for here they slaughter them all in one day. This led me to ask, "Why, in God's name, what do you eat in a year?" The bill of fare was this, for this present year: about this same quantity of hog-meat: four beeves: and forty-six fat sheep! Besides the suckling pigs (of which we had then one on the table), besides lambs, and besides the produce of seventy hen fowls, not to mention good parcels of geese, ducks and turkeys, but not to forget a garden of three-quarters of an acre and the butter of ten cows, not one ounce of which is ever sold! What do you think of that? Why, you will say, this must be some great overgrown farmer, that has swallowed up half the country; or some nabob sort of merchant. Not at all. He has only one hundred and fifty four acres of land (all he consumes is of the produce of this land), and he lives in the same house that his English-born grandfather lived in.

When the hogs are killed, the house is full of work. The sides are salted down as pork. The hams are smoked. The lean meats are made into sausages, of which, in this family, they make about two hundred weight. These latter, with broiled fish, eggs, dried beef, dried mutton, slices of ham, tongue, bread, butter, cheese, short cakes, buckwheat cakes, sweet meats of various sorts, and many other things, make up the breakfast fare of the year, and a dish of beef steaks is frequently added.

When one sees this sort of living, with the houses full of good beds, ready for the guests as well as the family to sleep in, we cannot help perceiving, that this is that "English hospitality," of which we have read so much; but which Boroughmongers, taxes and pawns have long since driven out of England. . . .

Their forefathers brought the English hospitality with them; for, when they left the country, the infernal Borough-monger Funding system had not begun. The Stuarts were religious and prerogative tyrants; but they were not, like their successors, the Boroughmongers, taxing, plundering tyrants. Their quarrels with their subjects were about mere words; with the Boroughmongers it is a question of purses and strong-boxes, of goods and chattels, lands and tenements. Confiscation is their word; and you must submit, be hanged, or flee. They take away men's property at their pleasure, without any appeal to any tribunal. They appoint Commis-sioners to seize what they choose. There is, in fact, no law of property left. The Bishop-begotten and hell-born system of funding has stripped England of every vestige of what was her ancient character. Her hospitality along with her freedom have crossed the Atlantic; and here they are to shame our ruffian tyrants, if they were sensible of shame, and to give shelter to those who may be disposed to deal them distant blows.

It is not with a little bit of dry toast, so neatly put in a rack; a bit of butter so round and small; a little milk pot so pretty and so empty; an egg for you, the host and hostess not liking eggs. It is not with looks that seem to say, "don't eat too much, for the taxgatherer is coming." It is not thus that you are received in America. You are not much asked, not much pressed, to eat and drink; but, such an abundance is spread before you, and so hearty and so cordial is your reception, that you instantly lose all restraint, and are tempted to feast whether you be hungry or not. And, though the manner and style are widely different in different houses, the abundance everywhere prevails. This is the strength of the government: a happy people: and no government ought to have any other strength.

But, you may say, perhaps, that plenty, however great, is not all that is wanted. Very true: for the mind is of more account than the carcass. But, here is mind too. These repasts, amongst people of any figure, come forth under the superintendence of industrious and accomplished housewives, or their daughters, who all read a great deal, and in whom that gentle treatment from parents and husbands, which arises from an absence of racking anxiety, has created an habitual, and even an hereditary good humor. These ladies can converse with you upon almost any subject, and the ease and gracefulness of their behavior are surpassed by those of none of even our best-tempered English women. They fade at an earlier age than in England; but, till then, they are as beautiful as the women in Cornwall, which contains, to my thinking, the prettiest women in our country. However, young or old, blooming or fading, well or ill, rich or poor, they still preserve their good humor.

There are very few really ignorant men in America of native growth. Every farmer is more or less of a reader. There is no brogue, no provincial dialect. No class like that which the French call peasantry, and which degrading appellation the miscreant spawn of the Funds have, of late years, applied to the whole mass of the most useful of the people in England, those who do the work and fight the battles. And, as to the men, who would naturally form your acquaintances, they, I know from experience, are as kind, frank, and sensible men as are, on the general run, to be found in England, even with the power of selection. They are all well-informed; modest without shyness; always free to communicate what they know, and never ashamed to acknowledge that they have yet to learn. You never hear them boast of their possessions, and you never hear them complaining of their wants. They have all been readers from their youth up; and there are few subjects upon which they cannot converse with you, whether of a political or scientific nature. At any rate, they always hear with patience. I do not know that I ever heard a native American interrupt another man while he was speaking. Their sedateness and coolness, the deliberate manner in which they say and do every thing, and the slowness and reserve with which they express their assent; these are very wrongly estimated, when they are taken for marks of a want of feeling. It must be a tale of woe indeed, that will bring a tear from an American's eye; but any trumped-up story will send his hand to his pocket, as the ambassadors from the beggars of France, Italy and Germany can fully testify.

However, you will not, for a long while, know what to do for want of the quick responses of the English tongue, and the decided tone of the English expression. The loud voice: the hard squeeze of the hand: the instant assent or dissent: the clamorous joy: the bitter wailing: the ardent friendship: the deadly enmity: the love that makes people kill themselves: the hatred that makes them kill others. All these belong to the characters of Englishmen, in whose minds and hearts every feeling exists in the extreme. To decide the question, which character is, upon the whole, best, the American or the English, we must appeal to some third party. But it is no matter: we cannot change our natures. For my part, who can, in nothing think or act by halves, I must belie my very nature, if I said that I did not like the character of my own countrymen best. We all like our own parents and children better than other people's parents and children, not because they are better, but because they are ours: because they belong to us and we to them, and because

we must resemble each other. There are some Americans that
I like full as well as I do any man in England; but, if, nation
against nation, I put the question home to my heart, it instantly decides in favor of my countrymen. . . .

There is one thing in the Americans, which though its
proper place was further back, I have reserved, or rather
kept back to the last moment. It has presented itself several
times; but I have turned from the thought, as men do from
thinking of any mortal disease that is at work in their frame.
It is not covetousness; it is not niggardliness; it is not insincerity; it is not enviousness; it is not cowardice, above all
things: it is drinking. Aye, and that too, amongst but too
many men who, one would think, would loath it. You can
go into hardly any man's house, without being asked to drink
wine, or spirits, even in the morning. They are quick at
meals, are little eaters, seem to care little about what they
eat, and never talk about it. This, which arises out of the
universal abundance of good and even fine eatables, is very
amiable. You are here disgusted with none of those eaters by
reputation that are found especial amongst the Parsons, in
England: fellows that unbutton at it. Nor do the Americans
sit and tope much after dinner, and talk on till they get into
nonsense and smut, which last is a sure mark of a silly and,
pretty generally, even of a base mind. But, they tipple: and
the infernal spirits they tipple, too! The scenes that I witnessed at Harrisburgh, I shall never forget. I almost wished
(God forgive me!) that there were Boroughmongers here
to tax these drinkers: they would soon reduce them to a
moderate dose. Any nation that feels itself uneasy with its
fulness of good things has only to resort to an application of
Boroughmongers. These are by no means nice feeders or of
contracted throat: they will suck down anything from the
poor man's pot of beer to the rich man's lands and tenements.

The Americans preserve their gravity and quietness and
good-humor even in their drink; and so much the worse. It

were far better for them to be as noisy and quarrelsome as the English drunkards; for then the odiousness of the vice would be more visible, and the vice itself might become less frequent. Few vices want an apology, and drinking has not only its apologies but its praises: for, besides the appellation of generous wine, and the numerous songs, some in very elegant and witty language, from the pens of debauched men of talents, drinking is said to be necessary, in certain cases at least, to raise the spirits, and to keep out cold. Never was anything more false. Whatever intoxicates must enfeeble in the end, and whatever enfeebles must chill. It is very well known, in the Northern countries, that, if the cold be such as to produce danger of frost biting, you must take care not to drink strong liquors.

To see this beastly vice in young men is shocking. At one of the taverns at Harrisburgh there were several as fine young men as I ever saw. Well-dressed, well-educated, polite, and everything but sober. What a squalid, drooping, sickly set they looked in the morning!

Even little boys at, or under twelve years of age, go into stores, and tip off their drams! I never struck a child, in anger, in my life, that I recollect; but, if I were so unfortunate as to have a son to do this, he having had an example to the contrary in me, I would, if all other means of reclaiming him failed, whip him like a dog, or, which would be better, make him an outcast from my family.

However, I must not be understood as meaning, that this tippling is universal amongst gentlemen; and, God be thanked, the women of any figure in life do by no means give in to the practice; but abhor it as much as well-bred women in England, who, in general, no more think of drinking strong liquors, than they do of drinking poison.

I shall be told that men in the harvest field must have something to drink. To be sure, where perspiration almost instantly carries off the drink, the latter does not remain so long to burn the liver, or whatever else it does burn. But, I much question the utility even here; and I think, that in the long run, a water drinker would beat a spirit drinker at anything, provided both had plenty of good food. And, besides, beer, which does not burn, at any rate, is within everyone's reach in America, if he will but take the trouble to brew it.

A man, at Botley, whom I was very severely reproaching for getting drunk and lying in the road, whose name was James Isaacs, and who was, by the by, one of the hardest workers I ever knew, said, in answer, Why, no, Sir, Noah and Lot were two very good men, you know, and yet they loved a drop of drink. Yes, you drunken fool, replied I, but you do not read that Isaac ever got drunk and rolled about the road. I could not help thinking, however, that the Bible Societies, with the wise Emperor Alexander and the Holy Alliance at their head, might as well (to say nothing about the cant of the thing) leave the Bible to work its own way. I had seen Isaacs dead drunk, lying stretched out, by my front gate, against the public highway; and if he had followed the example of Noah, he would not have endeavored to excuse himself in the modest manner that he did, but would have affixed an everlasting curse on me and my children to all generations.

The soldiers, in the regiment that I belonged to, many of whom served in the American war, had a saying, that the Quakers used the word "tired" in place of the word "drunk." Whether any of them do ever get tired themselves, I know not; but, at any rate, they most resolutely set their faces against the common use of spirits. They forbid their members to retail them; and, in case of disobedience, they disown them.

However, there is no remedy but the introduction of beer, and I am very happy to know, that beer is, every day, becoming more and more fashionable. At Bristol in Pennsylvania, I was pleased to see excellent beer in clean and nice pewter pots. Beer does not kill. It does not eat out the vitals and take the color from the cheek. It will make men tired, indeed, by midnight; but it does not make them half dead in the morning.

Cobbett, *A Year's Residence in America.*

4

"TEN YEARS IN AMERICA
ARE LIKE A CENTURY
ELSEWHERE"

FRANCIS LIEBER

ALTHOUGH born and educated in Germany, Francis Lieber belongs to American history and scholarship; indeed were it not that his *Letters to a Gentleman in Germany* were written shortly after his arrival in America, he could not properly be admitted to this volume. Born in Berlin, in 1800, Lieber fought as a mere boy at Waterloo and Namur. Even in youth he was inclined toward radicalism, and in 1819 he was arrested as a dangerous character and forbidden to study at any university except Jena. Here he received the degree of doctor of philosophy in 1820 and then—with the relaxation of the restriction on his movements—studied further at Halle, Dresden, and Berlin. His enthusiasm for liberty led him to enlist in the Greek War for Independence, but, disillusioned, he made his way to Rome, where for a short time he lived with the great historian Niebuhr. On his return to Germany he found himself once more involved with the government, and in 1826 fled to London. The next year found young Lieber in Boston, busily cultivating the friendship of such men as Justice Story, Edward Everett, and George Ticknor. With the assistance of Judge Story and other friends he launched the Encyclopaedia Americana. It was during these early years in the United States that Lieber wrote his *Letters to a Gentleman in Germany*—letters recording enthusiastically the prosperity and freedom of the New World.

Lieber's later career is familiar to every student of Ameri-

can political thought. For twenty years he was Professor of
history and political economy at the University of South
Carolina; in 1857 he was appointed to the chair of political
science at Columbia College; and later taught in the Columbia University law school. He drew up the famous Code for
the Government of Armies, which became General Order
No. 100, and formed the basis of military law in the
United States and elsewhere; he wrote voluminously on
political theory, philosophy, penology, and international law;
and as friend and adviser to statesmen he exercised a far-
reaching influence on American politics.

◇◇◇◇◇◇◇

WHAT distances and cheapness! The steamboat which I
found here for Chicago, I think I have already mentioned; in fine, distances are not considered in this country
as in Europe; if they were, we should not have crept much
beyond the Alleghany mountains by this time. And what is
the reason that a thousand miles in the United States are not
as much as a thousand miles in Europe? There are several
reasons for it, in my opinion. First, the early settlers had to
think of many thousand miles off, whenever they thought
of their beloved home. Thus, a far different unit by which
to estimate other distances was laid down in their minds. It
is clear that a person settling a hundred miles from them
could not appear far away to those who had their original
home some thousand miles off; and, although a generation
born on this continent soon grew up, their relations to Europe
still continued to be of such a character that all considered
themselves intimately connected with her; and even to this
day, we feel that, as to everything in science and civilization,
we are closely connected with Europe; and a lady in New
York thinks no more of going to Havre or Liverpool than a
lady in London of going to Paris.

This feeling, together with the vast unsettled continent
before them, induced people to push on and settle at great

distances, especially as the life of the early colonists was such as to develop a daring spirit of enterprise, which gradually has settled down into a fixed trait of American character. General Moreau, when residing in this country—so said a French gentleman, an acquaintance of mine—believed that no soldier would be equal to an American, if well and thoroughly disciplined (to be sure, the present militia would require some "rubbings"), because, said he, "An American doubts of nothing." It was true what Moreau observed, that an American doubts of nothing; sometimes owing to enterprising boldness, sometimes to want of knowledge or to self-confidence, always, in a measure, to the fact that want of success in an enterprise is not followed in the United States by obloquy or ridicule, even though the undertaking may have been injudicious. This, though often calculated to mislead, is, on the whole, an excellent thing; and, even supposing a man to have miscalculated his strength in one attempt, he may take better care the next time.

This spirit of enterprise and adventure pushed new settlers far into all directions; a consequence of which is that we now dwell in a vast country, inhabited by people of the same language, and living under the same laws—another reason why distances appear shorter to us. The comparatively small number of mountain chains is a third cause of the same singular fact. As we require objects by which to judge distances—thus, for instance, objects, seen over a wide expanse of water, appear nearer to us, than when the view lies across an equally extensive tract of land—so a distance by land, if we have to pass through many different languages and governments, and over mountains, appears to us greater than if no such intervening objects existed. In the Atlantic states, people are, besides, so familiar with voyages to Canton, the Pacific, Buenos Aires, etc., that I have seen in Europe more bustle in a family, a member of which was going to a university, perhaps some sixty miles off, than I have here when the son or brother was embarking for China or the Manilas. The steamboats—which greatly facilitate traveling, the population being scattered over so vast a country—and the migratory disposition of the American in general, originally caused by the above given reasons, contribute, in turn, their full part to the production of the same effect. The next nation after the Americans in this respect are the English, whose possessions in all quarters of the globe would make them consider distances as still less than the Americans, were their own country not itself so very confined. Every mile has there its full value.

Not distances alone are measured here by a standard different from that of other countries; time, too, receives a different value, but it is measured by a smaller standard than in Europe. An American wants to perform within a year what others do within a much longer period. Ten years in America are like a century in Spain. The United States really change in some respects more within ten years than a country like Spain has within a hundred. England moves, in all practical affairs, quicker than the continent: The United States move quicker still, in some respects, than England. There are many reasons for this more rapid movement which I will not oblige you to read; let me only observe that it influences all relations of life. According to recent statements, a female servant in London remains, on average, four hundred and sixty-two days in the same situation. I have no doubt that, if similar accounts could be obtained from Germany, we would find that they remain much longer there in the same place, and the corresponding period in New York would average much less. Sometimes individuals long for a stationary country, where things remain in their place for some time, and where one does not feel all the time as if tied to the wing of a windmill. This desire is very natural: whether they would be pleased by a change for a long time or not is quite a different question. For the rest, the choice is not with the nations. There are, at present, two classes of nations, which, in all your inquiries, you must strictly distinguish from each other; namely, moving nations and stationary nations. The former would be utterly ruined, were they to counteract their own impetus. I speak here chiefly of industry, and diffusion and application of knowledge. This movement has become with them one of the "historical tasks" which they have to perform. They must have steamboats, though a sailing boat may grace the landscape a thousand times more: they must have railroads, though traveling on them be a dull thing.

Lieber, *Letters to a Gentleman in Germany*.

5

THE PERVASIVE INFLUENCE
OF DEMOCRACY

ALEXIS DE TOCQUEVILLE

IT is over one hundred years since young Alexis de Tocqueville—just turned thirty—brought out the first two volumes of his *Democracy in America*, yet that work remains the classic analysis of the influence of democracy on the society, economy, and government of the United States. Born in Paris, in 1800, and trained to the law, Tocqueville was sent to the United States in 1831 by his government to investigate the penitentiary system of this country. But he was interested in much more than the prison and penal system; he was interested in the new phenomenon of a society dominated by democratic principles, and fascinated by the manner in which those principles permeated every institution in American life. "I confess," he wrote, "that in America I saw more than America; I sought the image of democracy itself, with its inclinations, its character, its prejudices, and its passions, in order to learn what we have to fear or hope from its progress." Convinced that democracy was bound to spread, Tocqueville was concerned, above all, to understand its implications for the Old World and, above all, for France. He was the first philosophical historian to write of the American experiment in democracy, the first political scientist to make democracy the primary object of realistic investigation. No other analyst, American or foreign, has traced so skillfully or so thoroughly the subtle and complex ramifications of the democratic principle in our society, nor has any other, except Bryce, commented so shrewdly on the strength and the weakness of American democracy.

Tocqueville's book, the first two volumes of which ap-

peared in 1835, the next two in 1840, was at once hailed as
a classic, and Tocqueville himself was elected to the French
Academy. He continued for some years in public life, became a member and vice-president of the assembly, and, for
a few months, minister of foreign affairs, but with the
triumph of Louis Napoleon he withdrew in disgust from
politics and returned to scholarship. The most notable work
of his latter years is his *Ancient Regime and the Revolution.*
He died at Cannes, at the comparatively young age of fifty-
eight.

It is exceptionally difficult to make a selection from
Tocqueville, for almost every page cries out for reproduction. We have chosen here some of his observations on the
influence of democracy on language, literature, and history,
and portions of his chapters on armies and war among democratic nations. The translation is that by the Englishman,
Henry Reeve.

◇◇◇◇◇◇◇

INFLUENCES OF DEMOCRACY UPON LANGUAGE
AND LITERATURE

ALTHOUGH America is perhaps in our days the civilized
country in which literature is least attended to, a large
number of persons are nevertheless to be found there who
take an interest in the productions of the mind, and who
make them, if not the study of their lives, at least the charm
of their leisure hours. But England supplies these readers
with the larger portion of the books which they require.
Almost all important English books are republished in the
United States. The literary genius of Great Britain still darts
its rays into the recesses of the forests of the New World.
There is hardly a pioneer's hut which does not contain a few
odd volumes of Shakespeare. I remember that I read the
feudal play of *Henry V* for the first time in a log-house.

Not only do the Americans constantly draw upon the

treasures of English literature, but it may be said with truth that they find the literature of England growing on their own soil. The larger part of that small number of men in the United States who are engaged in the composition of literary works are English in substance, and still more so in form. Thus they transport into the midst of democracy the ideas and literary fashions which are current among the aristocratic nation they have taken for their model. They paint with colours borrowed from foreign manners; and as they hardly ever represent the country they were born in as it really is, they are seldom popular there. The citizens of the United States are themselves so convinced that it is not for them that books are published, that before they can make up their minds upon the merit of one of their authors they generally wait till his fame has been ratified in England, just as in pictures the author of an original is held to be entitled to judge of the merit of a copy. The inhabitants of the United States have then at present, properly speaking, no literature. The only authors whom I acknowledge as American are the journalists. They, indeed, are not great writers, but they speak the language of their countrymen, and make themselves heard by them. Other authors are aliens; they are to the Americans what the imitators of the Greeks and Romans were to us at the revival of learning—an object of curiosity, not of general sympathy. They amuse the mind, but they do not act upon the manners of the people.

I have already said that this state of things is very far from originating in democracy alone, and that the causes of it must be sought for in several peculiar circumstances independent of the democratic principle. If the Americans, retaining the same laws and social condition, had had a different origin, and had been transported into another country, I do not question that they would have had a literature. Even as they now are, I am convinced that they will ultimately have one; but its character will be different from that which marks the American literary productions of our time, and that character will be peculiarly its own. Nor is it impossible to trace this character beforehand. . . .

Let us transport ourselves into the midst of a democracy, not unprepared by ancient traditions and present culture to partake in the pleasures of the mind. Ranks are there intermingled and confounded; knowledge and power are both infinitely subdivided, and, if I may use the expression, scattered on every side. Here, then, is a motley multitude, whose intellectual wants are to be supplied. These new votaries of the pleasures of the mind have not all received the same education: they do not possess the same degree of culture as their fathers, nor any resemblance to them—nay, they perpetually differ from themselves, for they live in a state of incessant change of place, feelings, and fortunes. The mind of each member of the community is therefore unattached to that of his fellow-citizens by tradition or by common habits; and they never have had the power, the inclination, nor the time to concert together. It is, however, from the bosom of this heterogeneous and agitated mass that authors spring; and from the same source their profits and their fame are distributed. I can understand without difficulty that, under these circumstances, I must expect to meet in the literature of such a people with but few of those strict conventional rules which are admitted by readers and by writers in aristocratic ages. If it should happen that the men of some one period were agreed upon any such rules, that would prove nothing for the following period; for among democratic nations each new generation is a new people. Among such nations, then, literature will not easily be subjected to strict rules, and it is impossible that any such rules should ever be permanent.

In democracies it is by no means the case that all the men who cultivate literature have received a literary education; and most of those who have some tinge of *belles-lettres* are either engaged in politics, or in a profession which only allows them to taste occasionally and by stealth the pleasures of the mind. These pleasures, therefore, do not constitute the principal charm of their lives; but they are considered as a transient and necessary recreation amid the serious labours of life. Such men can never acquire a sufficiently intimate knowledge of the art of literature to appreciate its more delicate beauties; and the minor shades of expression must escape them. As the time they can devote to letters is very short, they seek to make the best use of the whole of it. They prefer books which may be easily procured, quickly read, and which require no learned research to be understood. They ask for beauties, self-proffered and easily enjoyed; above all, they must have what is unexpected and new. Accustomed to the struggle, the crosses, and the monotony of practical life, they require rapid emotions, startling passages —truths or errors brilliant enough to rouse them up, and to plunge them at once, as if by violence, into the midst of a subject.

Why should I say more? or who does not understand what is about to follow, before I have expressed it? Taken as a whole, literature in democratic ages can never present, as it does in the periods of aristocracy, an aspect of order, regularity, science, and art; its form will, on the contrary, ordinarily be slighted, sometimes despised. Style will frequently be fantastic, incorrect, overburdened, and loose—almost always vehement and bold. Authors will aim at rapidity of execution, more than at perfection of detail. Small productions will be more common than bulky books; there will be more wit than erudition, more imagination than profundity; and literary performances will bear marks of an untutored and rude vigour of thought—frequently of great variety and singular fecundity. The object of authors will be to astonish rather than to please, and to stir the passions more than to charm the taste. Here and there, indeed, writers will doubtless occur who will choose a different track, and who will, if they are gifted with superior abilities, succeed in finding readers, in spite of their defects or their better qualities; but these exceptions will be rare, and even the authors who shall so depart from the received practice in the main subject of their works, will always relapse into it in some lesser details. . . .

Democracy not only infuses a taste for letters among the trading classes, but introduces a trading spirit into literature. In aristocracies, readers are fastidious and few in number; in democracies, they are far more numerous and far less difficult to please. The consequence is, that among aristocratic nations no one can hope to succeed without immense exertions, and that these exertions may bestow a great deal of fame, but never can earn much money; while among democratic nations, a writer may flatter himself that he will obtain at a cheap rate a meagre reputation and a large fortune. For this purpose he need not be admired; it is enough that he is liked. The ever-increasing crowd of readers, and their continual craving for something new, insure the sale of books which nobody much esteems.

In democratic periods the public frequently treat authors as kings do their courtiers; they enrich, and they despise them. What more is needed by the venal souls which are born in courts, or which are worthy to live there? Democratic literature is always infested with a tribe of writers who look upon letters as a mere trade: and for some few great authors who adorn it you may reckon thousands of idea-mongers. . . .

A very superficial survey of the literary remains of the ancients will suffice to convince us that if those writers were sometimes deficient in variety, or fertility in their subjects, or in boldness, vivacity, or power of generalization in their thoughts, they always displayed exquisite care and skill in their details. Nothing in their works seems to be done hastily or at random: every line is written for the eye of the connoisseur, and is shaped after some conception of ideal beauty. No literature places those fine qualities, in which the writers of democracies are naturally deficient, in bolder relief than that of the ancients; no literature, therefore, ought to be more studied in democratic ages. This study is better suited than any other to combat the literary defects inherent in those ages: as for their more praiseworthy literary qualities, they will spring up of their own accord, without its being necessary to learn to acquire them.

It is important that this point should be clearly understood. A particular study may be useful to the literature of a people, without being appropriate to its social and political wants. If men were to persist in teaching nothing but the literature of the dead languages in a community where every one is habitually led to make vehement exertions to augment or to maintain his fortune, the result would be a very polished, but a very dangerous, race of citizens. For as their social and political condition would give them every day a sense of wants which their education would never teach them to supply, they would perturb the State, in the name of the Greeks and Romans, instead of enriching it by their productive industry.

It is evident that in democratic communities the interest of individuals, as well as the security of the commonwealth, demands that the education of the greater number should be scientific, commercial, and industrial, rather than literary. Greek and Latin should not be taught in all schools; but it is important that those who by their natural disposition or their fortune are destined to cultivate letters or prepared to relish them, should find schools where a complete knowledge of ancient literature may be acquired, and where the true scholar may be formed. A few excellent universities would do more toward the attainment of this object than a vast number of bad grammar-schools, where superfluous matters, badly learned, stand in the way of sound instruction in necessary studies. . . .

If the reader has rightly understood what I have already said on the subject of literature in general, he will have no difficulty in comprehending that species of influence which a democratic social condition and democratic institutions may exercise over language itself, which is the chief instrument of thought.

American authors may truly be said to live more in England than in their own country; since they constantly study the English writers, and take them every day for their models. But such is not the case with the bulk of the population, which is more immediately subjected to the peculiar causes acting upon the United States. It is not then to the written but to the spoken language that attention must be paid if we would detect the modifications which the idiom of an aristocratic people may undergo when it becomes the language of a democracy.

Englishmen of education, and more competent judges than I can be myself of the nicer shades of expression, have frequently assured me that the language of the educated classes in the United States is notably different from that of the educated classes in Great Britain. They complain not only that the Americans have brought into use a number of new words—the difference and the distance between the two countries might suffice to explain that much—but that these new words are more especially taken from the jargon of parties, the mechanical arts, or the language of trade. They assert, in addition to this, that old English words are often used by the Americans in new acceptations; and lastly, that the inhabitants of the United States frequently intermingle their phraseology in the strangest manner, and sometimes place words together which are always kept apart in the language of the mother-country. . . .

In aristocracies, language must naturally partake of that state of repose in which everything remains. Few new words are coined, because few new things are made; and even if new things were made, they would be designated by known words, whose meaning has been determined by tradition. If it happens that the human mind bestirs itself at length, or is roused by light breaking in from without, the novel expressions which are introduced are characterized by a degree of learning, intelligence, and philosophy which shows that they do not originate in a democracy. After the fall of Constantinople had turned the tide of science and literature toward the west, the French language was almost immediately invaded by a multitude of new words, which had all Greek or Latin roots. An erudite neologism then sprang up in France which was confined to the educated classes, and which produced no sensible effect, or at least a very gradual one, upon the people. All the nations of Europe successively exhibited the same change. Milton alone introduced more than six hundred words into the English language, almost all derived from the Latin, the Greek, or the Hebrew. The constant agitation which prevails in a democratic community tends unceasingly, on the contrary, to change the character of the language, as it does the aspect of affairs. In the midst of this general stir and competition of minds a great number of new ideas are formed, old ideas are lost, or reappear, or are subdivided into an infinite variety of minor shades. The consequence is, that many words must fall into desuetude, and others must be brought into use.

Democratic nations love change for its own sake; and this is seen in their language as much as in their politics. Even when they do not need to change words, they sometimes feel a wish to transform them. The genius of a democratic people is not only shown by the great number of words they bring into use, but also by the nature of the ideas these new words represent. Among such a people the majority lays down the law in language as well as in everything else; its prevailing spirit is as manifest in that as in other respects. But the majority is more engaged in business than in study—in political and commercial interests than in philosophical speculation or literary pursuits. Most of the words coined or adopted for its use will therefore bear the mark of these habits; they will mainly serve to express the wants of business, the passions of party, or the details of the public administration. In these departments the language will constantly spread, while on the other hand it will gradually lose ground in metaphysics and theology. . . .

In the absence of knowledge of the dead languages, democratic nations are apt to borrow words from living tongues; for their mutual intercourse becomes perpetual, and the inhabitants of different countries imitate each other the more readily as they grow more like each other every day.

But it is principally upon their own languages that democratic nations attempt to perpetrate innovations. From time to time they resume forgotten expressions in their vocabulary, which they restore to use; or they borrow from some particular class of the community a term peculiar to it, which they introduce with a figurative meaning into the language of daily life. Many expressions which originally belonged to the technical language of a profession or a party are thus drawn into general circulation.

The most common expedient employed by democratic nations to make an innovation in language consists in giving some unwonted meaning to an expression already in use. This method is very simple, prompt, and convenient; no learning is required to use it aright, and ignorance itself rather facilitates the practice; but that practice is most dangerous to the language. When a democratic people doubles the meaning of a word in this way, they sometimes render the signification which it retains as ambiguous as that which it acquires. An author begins by a slight deflection of a known expression from its primitive meaning, and he adapts it, thus modified, as well as he can to his subject. A second writer twists the sense of the expression in another way; a third takes possession of it for another purpose; and as there is no common appeal to the sentence of a permanent tribunal which may definitely settle the signification of the word, it remains in an ambiguous condition. The consequence is that writers hardly ever appear to dwell upon a single thought, but they always seem to point their aim at a knot of ideas, leaving the reader to judge which of them has been hit. This is a deplorable consequence of democracy. . . .

The principle of equality necessarily introduces several other changes into language. In aristocratic ages, when each nation tends to stand aloof from all others and likes to have distinct characteristics of its own, it often happens that several peoples which have a common origin become nevertheless estranged from each other, so that, without ceasing to understand the same language, they no longer all speak it in the same manner. In these ages each nation is divided into a certain number of classes, which see but little of each other, and do not intermingle. Each of these classes contracts, and invariably retains, habits of mind peculiar to itself, and adopts by choice certain words and certain terms, which afterward pass from generation to generation, like their estates. The same idiom then comprises a language of the poor and a language of the rich—a language of the citizen and a language of the nobility—a learned language and a vulgar one. The deeper the divisions, and the more impassable the barriers of society become, the more must this be the case. . . . When, on the contrary, men, being no longer restrained by ranks, meet on terms of constant intercourse—when castes are destroyed, and the classes of society are recruited and intermixed with each other, all the words of a language are mingled. Those which are unsuitable to the greater number perish; the remainder form a common store, whence every one chooses pretty nearly at random. Almost all the different dialects which divided the idioms of European nations are manifestly declining; there is no patois in the New World, and it is disappearing every day from the old countries.

The influence of this revolution in social conditions is as much felt in style as it is in phraseology. Not only does every one use the same words, but a habit springs up of using them without discrimination. The rules which style had set up are almost abolished: the line ceases to be drawn between expressions which seem by their very nature vulgar, and others which appear to be refined. Persons springing from different ranks of society carry the terms and expressions they are accustomed to use with them, into whatever circumstances they may pass; thus the origin of words is lost like the origin of individuals, and there is as much confusion in language as there is in society. . . .

I shall not quit this topic without touching on a feature of democratic languages which is perhaps more characteristic of them than any other. It has already been shown that democratic nations have a taste, and sometimes a passion, for general ideas, and that this arises from their peculiar merits and defects. This liking for general ideas is displayed in democratic languages by the continual use of generic terms or abstract expressions, and by the manner in which they are employed. This is the great merit and the great imperfection of these languages. Democratic nations are passionately addicted to generic terms or abstract expressions, because these modes of speech enlarge thought, and assist the operations of the mind by enabling it to include several objects in a small compass. . . .

These abstract terms which abound in democratic languages, and which are used on every occasion without attaching them to any particular fact, enlarge and obscure the thoughts they are intended to convey; they render the mode of speech more succinct, and the idea contained in it less clear. But with regard to language, democratic nations prefer obscurity to labour. I know not, indeed, whether this loose style has not some secret charm for those who speak and write among these nations. As the men who live there are frequently left to the efforts of their individual powers of mind, they are almost always a prey to doubt; and as their situation in life is for ever changing, they are never held fast to any of their opinions by the certain tenure of their fortunes. Men living in democratic countries are, then, apt to entertain unsettled ideas, and they require loose expressions to convey them. As they never know whether the idea they express to-day will be appropriate to the new position they may occupy to-morrow, they naturally acquire a liking for abstract terms. An abstract term is like a box with a false bottom: you may put in it what ideas you please, and take them out again without being observed. . . .

Historians who write in aristocratic ages are wont to refer all occurrences to the particular will or temper of certain individuals; and they are apt to attribute the most important revolutions to very slight accidents. They trace out the smallest causes with sagacity, and frequently leave the greatest unperceived. Historians who live in democratic ages exhibit precisely opposite characteristics. Most of them attribute hardly any influence to the individual over the destiny of the race, nor to citizens over the fate of a people; but, on the other hand, they assign great general causes to all petty incidents. These contrary tendencies explain each other.

When the historian of aristocratic ages surveys the theatre of the world, he at once perceives a very small number of prominent actors, who manage the whole piece. These great personages, who occupy the front of the stage, arrest the observation, and fix it on themselves; and while the historian is bent on penetrating the secret motives which make them speak and act, the rest escape his memory. The importance of the things which some men are seen to do, gives him an exaggerated estimate of the influence which one man may possess; and naturally leads him to think that, in order to explain the impulses of the multitude, it is necessary to refer them to the particular influence of some one individual.

When, on the contrary, all the citizens are independent of one another, and each of them is individually weak, no one is seen to exert a great, or still less a lasting power, over the community. At first sight, individuals appear to be absolutely devoid of any influence over it; and society would seem to advance alone by the free and voluntary concurrence of all the men who compose it. This naturally prompts the mind to search for that general reason which operates upon so many men's faculties at the same time, and turns them simultaneously in the same direction. . . .

M. de Lafayette says somewhere in his *Memoirs* that the exaggerated system of general causes affords surprising consolations to second-rate statesmen. I will add that its effects are not less consolatory to second-rate historians; it can always furnish a few mighty reasons to extricate them from the most difficult part of their work, and it indulges the indolence or incapacity of their minds, while it confers upon them the honours of deep thinking.

For myself, I am of opinion that at all times one great portion of the events of this world are attributable to general facts, and another to special influences. These two kinds of cause are always in operation: their proportion only varies. General facts serve to explain more things in democratic than in aristocratic ages, and fewer things are then assignable to special influences. At periods of aristocracy the reverse takes place: special influences are stronger, general causes weaker—unless, indeed, we consider as a general cause the fact itself of the inequality of conditions, which allows some individuals to baffle the natural tendencies of all the rest. The historians who seek to describe what occurs in democratic societies are right, therefore, in assigning much to general causes, and in devoting their chief attention to discover them; but they are wrong in wholly denying the special influence of individuals, because they cannot easily trace or follow it.

The historians who live in democratic ages are not only prone to assign a great cause to every incident, but they are also given to connect incidents together, so as to deduce a system from them. In aristocratic ages, as the attention of historians is constantly drawn to individuals, the connection of events escapes them; or rather, they do not believe in any such connection. To them the clue of history seems every instant crossed and broken by the step of man. In democratic ages, on the contrary, as the historian sees much more of actions than of actors, he may easily establish some kind of sequence and methodical order among the former. Ancient literature, which is so rich in fine historical compositions, does not contain a single great historical system, while the poorest of modern literatures abound with them. It would appear that the ancient historians did not make sufficient use of those general theories which our historical writers are ever ready to carry to excess.

Those who write in democratic ages have another more dangerous tendency. When the traces of individual action upon nations are lost, it often happens that the world goes on to move, though the moving agent is no longer discoverable. As it becomes extremely difficult to discern and to analyse the reasons which, acting separately on the volition of each member of the community, concur in the end to produce movement in the old mass, men are led to believe that this movement is involuntary, and that societies unconsciously obey some superior force ruling over them. But even when the general fact which governs the private volition of all individuals is supposed to be discovered upon the earth, the principle of human free will is not secure. A cause sufficiently extensive to affect millions of men at once, and sufficiently strong to bend them all together in the same direction, may well seem irresistible: having seen that mankind do yield to it, the mind is close upon the inference that mankind cannot resist it.

Historians who live in democratic ages, then, not only deny that the few have any power of acting upon the destiny of a people, but they deprive the people themselves of the power of modifying their own condition, and they subject them either to an inflexible Providence, or to some blind necessity. According to them, each nation is indissolubly bound by its position, its origin, its precedents, and its character, to a certain lot which no efforts can ever change. They involve generation in generation, and thus, going back from age to age, and from necessity to necessity, up to the origin of the world, they forge a close and enormous chain, which girds and binds the human race. To their minds it is not enough to show what events have occurred: they would fain show that events could not have occurred otherwise. They take a nation arrived at a certain stage of its history, and they affirm that it could not but follow the track which brought it thither. It is easier to make such an assertion than to show by what means the nation might have adopted a better course.

In reading the historians of aristocratic ages, and especially those of antiquity, it would seem that, to be master of his lot, and to govern his fellow-creatures, man requires only to be master of himself. In perusing the historical volumes which our age has produced, it would seem that man is utterly powerless over himself and over all around him. The historians of antiquity taught how to command: those of our time teach only how to obey; in their writings the author often appears great, but humanity is always diminutive. If this doctrine of necessity, which is so attractive to those who write history in democratic ages, passes from authors to their readers, till it infects the whole mass of the community and gets possession of the public mind, it will soon paralyse the activity of modern society, and reduce Christians to the level of the Turks. . . . Our contemporaries are but too prone to doubt of the human free will, because each of them feels himself confined on every side by his own weakness; but they are still willing to acknowledge the strength and independence of men united in society. Let not this principle be lost sight of; for the great object in our time is to raise the faculties of men, not to complete their prostration.

WARFARE AMONG DEMOCRATIC PEOPLES

THE same interests, the same fears, the same passions which deter democratic nations from revolutions, deter them also from war; the spirit of military glory and the spirit of revolution are weakened at the same time and by the same causes. The ever-increasing numbers of men of property—lovers of peace, the growth of personal wealth which war so rapidly consumes, the mildness of manners, the gentleness of heart, those tendencies to pity which are engendered by the equality of conditions, that coolness of understanding which renders men comparatively insensible to the violent and poetical excitement of arms—all these causes concur to quench the military spirit. I think it may be admitted as a general and constant rule that, among civilized nations, the warlike passions will become more rare and less intense in proportion as social conditions shall be more equal. War is nevertheless an occurrence to which all nations are subject, democratic nations as well as others. Whatever taste they may have for peace, they must hold themselves in readiness to repel aggression, or, in other words, they must have an army.

Fortune, which has conferred so many peculiar benefits upon the inhabitants of the United States, has placed them in the midst of a wilderness, where they have, so to speak, no neighbours: a few thousand soldiers are sufficient for their wants; but this is peculiar to America, not to democracy. The equality of conditions, and the manners as well as the institutions resulting from it, do not exempt a democratic people from the necessity of standing armies, and their armies always exercise a powerful influence over their fate. It is therefore of singular importance to inquire what are the natural propensities of the men of whom these armies are composed.

Among aristocratic nations, especially among those in which birth is the only source of rank, the same inequality exists in the army as in the nation; the officer is noble, the soldier is a serf; the one is naturally called upon to command, the other to obey. In aristocratic armies, the private soldier's ambition is therefore circumscribed within very narrow limits. Nor has the ambition of the officer an unlimited range. An aristocratic body not only forms a part of the scale of ranks in the nation, but it contains a scale of ranks within itself: the members of whom it is composed are placed one above another, in a particular and unvarying manner. Thus one man is born to the command of a regiment, another to that of a company; when once they have reached the utmost object of their hopes, they stop of their own accord, and remain contented with their lot. There is, besides, a strong cause, which, in aristocracies, weakens the officer's desire of promotion. Among aristocratic nations, an officer, independently of his rank in the army, also occupies an elevated rank in society; the former is almost always in his eyes only an appendage to the latter. A nobleman who embraces the profession of arms follows it less from motives of ambition than from a sense of the duties imposed on him by his birth. He enters the army in order to find an honourable employment for the idle years of his youth, and to be able to bring back to his home and his peers some honourable recollections of military life; but his principal object is not to obtain by that profession either property, distinction, or power, for he possesses these advantages in his own right, and enjoys them without leaving his home.

In democratic armies all the soldiers may become officers, which makes the desire of promotion general, and immeasurably extends the bounds of military ambition. The officer, on his part, sees nothing which naturally and necessarily stops him at one grade more than at another; and each grade has immense importance in his eyes, because his rank in society almost always depends on his rank in the army. Among democratic nations it often happens that an officer has no property but his pay, and no distinction but that of military honours: consequently as often as his duties change, his fortune changes, and he becomes, as it were, a new man. What was only an appendage to his position in aristocratic armies has thus become the main point, the basis of his whole condition.

Under the old French monarchy officers were always called by their titles of nobility; they are now always called by the title of their military rank. This little change in the forms of language suffices to show that a great revolution has taken place in the constitution of society and in that of the army. In democratic armies the desire of advancement is almost universal: it is ardent, tenacious, perpetual; it is strengthened by all other desires, and only extinguished with life itself. But it is easy to see that, of all armies in the world, those in which advancement must be slowest in time of peace are the armies of democratic countries. As the number of commissions is naturally limited, while the number of competitors is almost unlimited, and as the strict law of equality is over all alike, none can make rapid progress—many can make no progress at all. Thus the desire of advancement is greater, and the opportunities of advancement fewer, there than elsewhere. All the ambitious spirits of a democratic army are consequently ardently desirous of war, because war makes vacancies, and warrants the violation of that law of seniority which is the sole privilege natural to democracy.

We thus arrive at this singular consequence, that of all armies those most ardently desirous of war are democratic armies, and of all nations those most fond of peace are democratic nations: and, what makes these facts still more extraordinary, is that these contrary effects are produced at the same time by the principle of equality.

All the members of the community, being alike, constantly harbour the wish, and discover the possibility, of changing their condition and improving their welfare: this makes them fond of peace, which is favourable to industry, and allows every man to pursue his own little undertakings to their completion. On the other hand, this same equality makes soldiers dream of fields of battle, by increasing the value of military honours in the eyes of those who follow the profession of arms, and by rendering those honours accessible to all. In either case the inquietude of the heart is the same, the taste for enjoyment as insatiable, the ambition of success as great —the means of gratifying it are alone different.

These opposite tendencies of the nation and the army expose democratic communities to great dangers. When a military spirit forsakes a people, the profession of arms immediately ceases to be held in honour, and military men fall to the lowest rank of the public servants: they are little esteemed, and no longer understood. The reverse of what takes place in aristocratic ages then occurs; the men who enter the army are no longer those of the highest, but of the lowest rank. Military ambition is only indulged in when no other is possible. Hence arises a circle of cause and consequence from which it is difficult to escape: the best part of the nation shuns the military profession because that profession is not honoured, and the profession is not honoured because the best part of the nation has ceased to follow it. It is then no matter of surprise that democratic armies are often restless, ill-tempered, and dissatisfied with their lot, although their physical condition is commonly far better and their discipline less strict than in other countries. The soldier feels that he occupies an inferior position, and his wounded pride either stimulates his taste for hostilities which would render his services necessary, or gives him a turn for revolutions, during which he may hope to win by force of arms the political influence and personal importance now denied him. The composition of democratic armies makes this last-mentioned danger much to be feared. In democratic communities almost every man has some property to preserve; but democratic armies are generally led by men without property, most of whom have little to lose in civil broils. The bulk of the nation is naturally much more afraid of revolutions than in the ages of aristocracy, but the leaders of the army much less so.

Moreover, as among democratic nations . . . the wealthiest, the best educated, and the most able men seldom adopt the military profession, the army, taken collectively, eventually forms a small nation by itself, where the mind is less enlarged, and habits are more rude than in the nation at large. Now, this small uncivilized nation has arms in its possession, and alone knows how to use them: for, indeed, the pacific temper of the community increases the danger to which a democratic people is exposed from the military and turbulent spirit of the army. Nothing is so dangerous as an army amid an unwarlike nation; the excessive love of the whole community for quiet continually puts its constitution at the mercy of the soldiery.

It may, therefore, be asserted, generally speaking, that if democratic nations are naturally prone to peace from their interests and their propensities, they are constantly drawn to war and revolutions by their armies. Military revolutions, which are scarcely ever to be apprehended in aristocracies, are always to be dreaded among democratic nations. These perils must be reckoned among the most formidable which beset their future fate, and the attention of statesmen should be sedulously applied to find a remedy for the evil.

When a nation perceives that it is inwardly affected by the restless ambition of its army, the first thought which occurs is to give this inconvenient ambition an object by going to war. I speak no ill of war: war almost always enlarges the mind of a people, and raises their character. In some cases it is the only check to the excessive growth of certain propensities which naturally spring out of the equality of conditions, and it must be considered as a necessary corrective to certain inveterate diseases to which democratic communities are liable. War has great advantages, but we must not flatter ourselves that it can diminish the danger I have just pointed out. That peril is only suspended by it, to return more fiercely when the war is over; for armies are much more impatient of peace after having tasted military exploits. War could only be a remedy for a people which should always be athirst for military glory. I foresee that all the military rulers who may rise up in great democratic nations will find it easier to conquer with their armies than to make their armies live at peace after conquest. There are two things which a democratic people will always find very difficult—to begin a war, and to end it.

Again, if war has some peculiar advantages for democratic nations, on the other hand it exposes them to certain dangers which aristocracies have no cause to dread to an equal extent. I shall only point out two of these. Although war gratifies the army, it embarrasses and often exasperates that countless multitude of men whose minor passions every day require peace in order to be satisfied. Thus there is some risk of its causing, under another form, the disturbance it is intended to prevent. No protracted war can fail to endanger the freedom of a democratic country. Not, indeed, that after every victory it is to be apprehended that the victorious generals will possess themselves by force of the supreme power, after the manner of Sylla and Cæsar: the danger is of another kind. War does not always give over democratic communities to military government, but it must invariably and immeasurably increase the powers of civil government; it must almost compulsorily concentrate the direction of all men and the management of all things in the hands of the administration. If it lead not to despotism by sudden violence, it prepares men for it more gently by their habits. All those who seek to destroy the liberties of a democratic nation ought to know that war is the surest and the shortest means to accomplish it. This is the first axiom of the science.

One remedy, which appears to be obvious when the ambition of soldiers and officers becomes the subject of alarm, is to augment the number of commissions to be distributed by increasing the army. This affords temporary relief, but it plunges the country into deeper difficulties at some future period. To increase the army may produce a lasting effect in an aristocratic community, because military ambition is there confined to one class of men, and the ambition of each individual stops, as it were, at a certain limit; so that it may be possible to satisfy all who feel its influence. But nothing is gained by increasing the army among a democratic people, because the number of aspirants always rises in exactly the same ratio as the army itself. Those whose claims have been satisfied by the creation of new commissions are instantly succeeded by a fresh multitude beyond all power of satisfaction; and even those who were but now satisfied soon begin to crave more advancement; for the same excitement prevails in the ranks of the army as in the civil classes of democratic society, and what men want is not to reach a certain grade, but to have constant promotion. Though these wants may not be very vast, they are perpetually recurring. Thus a democratic nation, by augmenting its army, only allays for a time the ambition of the military profession, which soon becomes even more formidable, because the number of those who feel it is increased. I am of opinion that a restless and turbulent spirit is an evil inherent in the very constitution of democratic armies, and beyond hope of cure. The legislators of democracies must not expect to devise any military organization capable by its influence of calming and restraining the military profession: their efforts would exhaust their powers before the object is attained.

The remedy for the vices of the army is not to be found in the army itself, but in the country. Democratic nations are naturally afraid of disturbance and of despotism; the object is to turn these natural instincts into well-digested, deliberate, and lasting tastes. When men have at last learned to make a peaceful and profitable use of freedom, and have felt its blessing—when they have conceived a manly love of order, and have freely submitted themselves to discipline—these same men, if they follow the profession of arms, bring into it, unconsciously and almost against their will, these same habits and manners. The general spirit of the nation being infused into the spirit peculiar to the army, tempers the opinions and desires engendered by military life, or represses them by the mighty force of public opinion. Teach but the citizens to be educated, orderly, firm, and free, the soldiers will be disciplined and obedient. Any law which, in repressing the turbulent spirit of the army, should tend to diminish the spirit of freedom in the nation, and to overshadow the notion of law and right, would defeat its object: it would do much more to favour, than to defeat, the establishment of military tyranny.

After all, and in spite of all precautions, a large army amid a democratic people will always be a source of great danger; the most effectual means of diminishing that danger would be to reduce the army, but this is a remedy which all nations have it not in their power to use.

It is a part of the essence of a democratic army to be very numerous in proportion to the people to which it belongs, as I shall hereafter show. On the other hand, men living in democratic times seldom choose a military life. Democratic nations are therefore soon led to give up the system of voluntary recruiting for that of compulsory enlistment. The necessity of their social condition compels them to resort to the latter means, and it may easily be foreseen that they will all eventually adopt it. When military service is compulsory, the burden is indiscriminately and equally borne by the whole community. This is another necessary consequence of the social condition of these nations, and of their notions. The government may do almost whatever it pleases, provided it appeals to the whole community at once: it is the unequal distribution of the weight, not the weight itself, which commonly occasions resistance. But as military service is common to all the citizens, the evident consequence is that each of them remains but for a few years on active duty. Thus it is in the nature of things that the soldier in democracies only passes through the army, while among most aristocratic nations the military profession is one which the soldier adopts, or which is imposed upon him, for life.

This has important consequences. Among the soldiers of a democratic army, some acquire a taste for military life, but the majority being enlisted against their will, and ever ready to go back to their homes, do not consider themselves as seriously engaged in the military profession, and are always thinking of quitting it. Such men do not contract the wants, and only half partake in the passions, which that mode of life engenders. They adapt themselves to their military duties, but their minds are still attached to the interests and the duties which engaged them in civil life. They do not, therefore, imbibe the spirit of the army—or rather, they infuse the spirit of the community at large into the army, and retain it there. Among democratic nations the private soldiers remain most like civilians: upon them the habits of the nation have the firmest hold, and public opinion most influence. It is by the instrumentality of the private soldiers especially that it may be possible to infuse into a democratic army the love of freedom and the respect of rights, if these principles have once been successfully inculcated on the people at large. The reverse happens among aristocratic nations, where the soldiery have eventually nothing in common with their fellow-citizens, and where they live among them as strangers, and often as enemies. In aristocratic armies the officers are the conservative element, because the officers alone have retained a strict connection with civil society, and never forego their purpose of resuming their place in it sooner or later: in democratic armies the private soldiers stand in this position, and from the same cause. . . .

Any army is in danger of being conquered at the outset of a campaign, after a long peace; any army which has long been engaged in warfare has strong chances of victory: this truth is peculiarly applicable to democratic armies. In aristocracies the military profession, being a privileged career, is held in honour even in time of peace. Men of great talents, great attainments, and great ambition embrace it; the army is in all respects on a level with the nation, and frequently above it. We have seen, on the contrary, that among a democratic people the choicer minds of the nation are gradually drawn away from the military profession, to seek by other paths distinction, power, and especially wealth. After a long peace—and in democratic ages the periods of peace are long—the army is always inferior to the country itself. In this state it is called into active service; and until war has altered it, there is danger for the country as well as for the army.

I have shown that in democratic armies, and in time of peace, the rule of seniority is the supreme and inflexible law of advancement. This is not only a consequence, as I have before observed, of the constitution of these armies, but of the constitution of the people, and it will always occur. Again, as among these nations the officer derives his position in the country solely from his position in the army, and as he draws all the distinction and the competency he enjoys from the same source, he does not retire from his profession, or is not superannuated, till toward the extreme close of life. The consequence of these two causes is, that when a democratic people goes to war after a long interval of peace all the leading officers of the army are old men. I speak not only of the generals, but of the non-commissioned officers, who have most of them been stationary, or have only advanced step by step. It may be remarked with surprise, that in a democratic army after a long peace all the soldiers are mere boys, and all the superior officers in declining years; so that the former are wanting in experience, the latter in vigour. This is a strong element of defeat, for the first condition of successful generalship is youth: I should not have ventured to say so if the greatest captain of modern times had not made the observation. . . .

A long peace not only fills democratic armies with elderly officers, but it also gives to all the officers habits both of body and mind which render them unfit for actual service. The man who has long lived amid the calm and lukewarm atmosphere of democratic manners can at first ill adapt himself to the harder toils and sterner duties of warfare; and if he has not absolutely lost the taste for arms, at least he has assumed a mode of life which unfits him for conquest.

Among aristocratic nations, the ease of civil life exercises less influence on the manners of the army, because among those nations the aristocracy commands the army: and an aristocracy, however plunged in luxurious pleasures, has always many other passions besides that of its own well-being, and to satisfy those passions more thoroughly its well-being will be readily sacrificed.

I have shown that in democratic armies, in time of peace, promotion is extremely slow. The officers at first support this state of things with impatience, they grow excited, restless, exasperated, but in the end most of them make up their minds to it. Those who have the largest share of ambition and of resources quit the army; others, adapting their tastes and their desires to their scanty fortunes, ultimately look upon the military profession in a civil point of view. The quality they value most in it is the competency and security which attend it: their whole notion of the future rests upon the certainty of this little provision, and all they require is peaceably to enjoy it. Thus not only does a long peace fill an army with old men, but it frequently imparts the views of old men to those who are still in the prime of life.

I have also shown that among democratic nations in time of peace the military profession is held in little honour and indifferently followed. This want of public favour is a heavy discouragement to the army; it weighs down the minds of the troops, and when war breaks out at last, they cannot immediately resume their spring and vigour. No similar cause of moral weakness occurs in aristocratic armies: there the officers are never lowered either in their own eyes or in those of their countrymen, because, independently of their military greatness, they are personally great. But even if the influence of peace operated on the two kinds of armies in the same manner, the results would still be different. When the officers of an aristocratic army have lost their warlike spirit and the desire of raising themselves by service, they still retain a certain respect for the honour of their class, and an old habit of being foremost to set an example. But when the officers of a democratic army have no longer the love of war and the ambition of arms, nothing whatever remains to them.

I am therefore of opinion that, when a democratic people engages in a war after a long peace, it incurs much more risk of defeat than any other nation; but it ought not easily to be cast down by its reverses, for the chances of success for such an army are increased by the duration of the war. When a war has at length, by its long continuance, roused the whole community from their peaceful occupations and ruined their minor undertakings, the same passions which made them attach so much importance to the maintenance of peace will be turned to arms. War, after it has destroyed all modes of speculation, becomes itself the great and sole speculation, to which all the ardent and ambitious desires which equality engenders are exclusively directed. Hence it is that the self-same democratic nations which are so reluctant to engage in hostilities sometimes perform prodigious achievements when once they have taken the field. As the war attracts more and more of public attention, and is seen to create high reputations and great fortunes in a short space of time, the choicest spirits of the nation enter the military profession: all the enterprising, proud, and martial minds, no longer of the aristocracy solely, but of the whole country, are drawn in this direction. As the number of competitors for military honours is immense, and war drives every man to his proper level, great generals are always sure to spring up. A long war produces upon a democratic army the same effects that a revolution produces upon a people; it breaks through regulations, and allows extraordinary men to rise above the common level. Those officers whose bodies and minds have grown old in peace, are removed, or superannuated, or they die. In their stead a host of young men are pressing on, whose frames are already hardened, whose desires are extended and inflamed by active service. They are bent on advancement at all hazards, and perpetual advancement; they are followed by others with the same passions and desires, and after these are others yet unlimited by aught but the size of the army. The principle of equality opens the door of ambition to all, and death provides chances for ambition. Death is constantly thinning the ranks, making vacancies, closing and opening the career of arms.

There is, moreover, a secret connection between the military character and the character of democracies, which war brings to light. The men of democracies are naturally passionately eager to acquire what they covet, and to enjoy it on easy conditions. They for the most part worship chance, and are much less afraid of death than of difficulty. This is the spirit which they bring to commerce and manufactures; and this same spirit, carried with them to the field of battle, induces them willingly to expose their lives in order to secure in a moment the rewards of victory. No kind of greatness is more pleasing to the imagination of a democratic people than military greatness—a greatness of vivid and sudden lustre, obtained without toil, by nothing but the risk of life. Thus, while the interests and the tastes of the members of a democratic community divert them from war, their habits of mind fit them for carrying on war well; they soon make good soldiers, when they are roused from their business and their enjoyments. If peace is peculiarly hurtful to democratic armies, war secures to them advantages which no other armies ever possess: and these advantages, however little felt at first, cannot fail in the end to give them the victory. An aristocratic nation, which in a contest with a democratic people does not succeed in ruining the latter at the outset of the war, always runs a great risk of being conquered by it.

It is a very general opinion, especially in aristocratic countries, that the great social equality which prevails in democracies ultimately renders the private soldier independent of the officer, and thus destroys the bond of discipline. This is a mistake, for there are two kinds of discipline, which it is important not to confound. When the officer is noble and the soldier is a serf—one rich, the other poor—the former educated and strong, the latter ignorant and weak—the strictest bond of obedience may easily be established between the two men. The soldier is broken in to military discipline, as it were, before he enters the army; or rather, military discipline is nothing but an enhancement of social servitude. In aristocratic armies the soldier will soon become insensible to everything but the orders of his superior officers; he acts without reflection, triumphs without enthusiasm, and dies without complaint: in this state he is no longer a man, but he is still a most formidable animal trained for war.

A democratic people must despair of ever obtaining from soldiers that blind, minute, submissive, and invariable obedience which an aristocratic people may impose on them without difficulty. The state of society does not prepare them for it, and the nation might be in danger of losing its natural advantages if it sought artificially to acquire advantages of this particular kind. Among democratic communities, military discipline ought not to attempt to annihilate the free spring of the faculties; all that can be done by discipline is to direct it; the obedience thus inculcated is less exact, but it is more eager and more intelligent. It has its root in the will of him who obeys: it rests not only on his instinct, but on his reason; and consequently it will often spontaneously become more strict as danger requires it. The discipline of an aristocratic army is apt to be relaxed in war, because that discipline is founded upon habits, and war disturbs those habits. The discipline of a democratic army, on the contrary, is strengthened in sight of the enemy, because every soldier then clearly perceives that he must be silent and obedient in order to conquer.

The nations which have performed the greatest warlike achievements knew no other discipline than that which I speak of. Among the ancients none were admitted into the armies but freemen and citizens, who differed but little from one another, and were accustomed to treat each other as

equals. In this respect it may be said that the armies of antiquity were democratic, although they came out of the
bosom of aristocracy; the consequence was that in those armies a sort of fraternal familiarity prevailed between the officers and the men. Plutarch's lives of great commanders furnish convincing instances of the fact: the soldiers were in the
constant habit of freely addressing their general, and the general listened to and answered whatever the soldiers had to
say: they were kept in order by language and by example,
far more than by constraint or punishment; the general was
as much their companion as their chief. I know not whether
the soldiers of Greece and Rome ever carried the minutiæ of
military discipline to the same degree of perfection as the
Russians have done; but this did not prevent Alexander from
conquering Asia—and Rome, the world.

When the principle of equality is in growth, not only
among a single nation, but among several neighbouring nations at the same time, as is now the case in Europe, the inhabitants of these different countries, notwithstanding the
dissimilarity of language, of customs, and of laws, nevertheless resemble each other in their equal dread of war and their
common love of peace. It is in vain that ambition or anger
puts arms in the hands of princes; they are appeased in spite
of themselves by a species of general apathy, and goodwill,
which makes the sword drop from their grasp, and wars become more rare. As the spread of equality, taking place in
several countries at once, simultaneously impels their various
inhabitants to follow manufactures and commerce, not only
do their tastes grow alike, but their interests are so mixed and
entangled with one another that no nation can inflict evils
on other nations without those evils falling back upon itself;
and all nations ultimately regard war as a calamity, almost as
severe to the conqueror as to the conquered. Thus, on the
one hand, it is extremely difficult in democratic ages to draw
nations into hostilities; but, on the other hand, it is almost impossible that any two of them should go to war without em-

broiling the rest. The interests of all are so interlaced, their opinions and their wants so much alike, that none can remain quiet when the others stir. Wars, therefore, become more rare, but when they break out they spread over a larger field. Neighbouring democratic nations not only become alike in some respects, but they eventually grow to resemble each other in almost all. This similitude of nations has consequences of great importance in relation to war. . . .

A great aristocratic people cannot either conquer its neighbours, or be conquered by them, without great difficulty. It cannot conquer them, because all its forces can never be collected and held together for a considerable period: it cannot be conquered, because an enemy meets at every step small centres of resistance by which invasion is arrested. War against an aristocracy may be compared to war in a mountainous country; the defeated party has constant opportunities of rallying its forces to make a stand in a new position. Exactly the reverse occurs among democratic nations: they easily bring their whole disposable force into the field, and when the nation is wealthy and populous it soon becomes victorious; but if ever it is conquered, and its territory invaded, it has few resources at command; and if the enemy takes the capital, the nation is lost. This may very well be explained: as each member of the community is individually isolated and extremely powerless, no one of the whole body can either defend himself or present a rallying-point to others. Nothing is strong in a democratic country except the State; as the military strength of the State is destroyed by the destruction of the army, and its civil power paralysed by the capture of the chief city, all that remains is only a multitude without strength or government, unable to resist the organized power by which it is assailed. I am aware that this danger may be lessened by the creation of provincial liberties, and consequently of provincial powers, but this remedy will always be insufficient. For after such a catastrophe not only is the population unable to carry on hostilities, but it may be apprehended that they will not be inclined to attempt it.

In accordance with the law of nations adopted in civilized countries, the object of wars is not to seize the property of private individuals, but simply to get possession of political power. The destruction of private property is only occasionally resorted to for the purpose of attaining the latter object. When an aristocratic country is invaded after the defeat of its army, the nobles, although they are at the same time the wealthiest members of the community, will continue to defend themselves individually rather than submit; for if the conqueror remained master of the country, he would deprive them of their political power, to which they cling even more closely than to their property. They therefore prefer fighting to subjection, which is to them the greatest of all misfortunes; and they readily carry the people along with them because the people has long been used to follow and obey them, and besides has but little to risk in the war. Among a nation in which equality of conditions prevails, each citizen, on the contrary, has but a slender share of political power, and often has no share at all; on the other hand, all are independent, and all have something to lose; so that they are much less afraid of being conquered, and much more afraid of war, than an aristocratic people. It will always be extremely difficult to decide a democratic population to take up arms, when hostilities have reached its own territory. Hence the necessity of giving to such a people the rights and the political character which may impart to every citizen some of those interests that cause the nobles to act for the public welfare in aristocratic countries.

It should never be forgotten by the princes and other leaders of democratic nations that nothing but the passion and the habit of freedom can maintain an advantageous contest with the passion and the habit of physical well-being. I can conceive nothing better prepared for subjection, in case of defeat, than a democratic people without free institutions. . . .

I shall add but a few words on civil wars, for fear of exhausting the patience of the reader. Most of the remarks which I have made respecting foreign wars are applicable *a fortiori* to civil wars. Men living in democracies are not naturally prone to the military character; they sometimes assume it, when they have been dragged by compulsion to the field; but to rise in a body and voluntarily to expose themselves to the horrors of war, and especially of civil war, is a course which the men of democracies are not apt to adopt. None but the most adventurous members of the community consent to run into such risks; the bulk of the population remains motionless. But even if the population were inclined to act, considerable obstacles would stand in their way; for they can resort to no old and well-established influence which they are willing to obey—no well-known leaders to rally the discontented, as well as to discipline and to lead them —no political powers subordinate to the supreme power of the nation, which afford an effectual support to the resistance directed against the government. In democratic countries the moral power of the majority is immense, and the physical resources which it has at its command are out of all proportion to the physical resources which may be combined against it. Therefore the party which occupies the seat of the majority, which speaks in its name and wields its power, triumphs instantaneously and irresistibly over all private resistance; it does not even give such opposition time to exist, but nips it in the bud. Those who in such nations seek to effect a revolution by force of arms have no other resource than suddenly to seize upon the whole engine of government as it stands, which can better be done by a single blow than by a war; for as soon as there is a regular war, the party which represents the State is always certain to conquer. The only case in which a civil war could arise is, if the army should divide itself into two factions, the one raising the standard of rebellion, the other remaining true to its allegiance. An army constitutes a small community, very closely united together, endowed with great powers of vitality, and able to supply its own wants for some time. Such a war might be bloody, but it could not be long; for either the rebellious army would gain over the government by the sole display of its resources, or by its first victory, and then the war would be over; or the struggle would take place, and then that portion of the army which should not be supported by the organized powers of the State would speedily either disband itself or be destroyed. It may, therefore, be admitted as a general truth, that in ages of equality civil wars will become much less frequent and less protracted.

Tocqueville, *Democracy in America.*

6

ECCENTRICITY AND ORIGINALITY IN THE AMERICAN CHARACTER

HARRIET MARTINEAU

OF early English travelers in America, only Dickens and Mrs. Trollope created a greater sensation than Harriet Martineau. This remarkable woman, who had been born in Norwich, England, at the beginning of the century, had early embarked upon a career of authorship and had made something of a sensation by her *Illustrations of Political Economy* which translated the economic doctrines of Adam Smith and Ricardo into popular stories. This remarkable volume catapulted the obscure young lady into fame, and she hastened to capitalize upon it. In 1834 she embarked on a two-year tour of the United States, the results of which appeared in her *Society in America* (1836) and *A Retrospect of Western Travel* (1838), from which this excerpt is taken. A devout Unitarian, author of many tracts on Unitarianism, and sister to the famous James Martineau, she was received with open arms by the Unitarians of New England, and from them as well as from her own experiences she derived a somewhat extreme view of the institution of slavery which she promptly transcribed into her volumes. Sponsored by Judge Story, she had an opportunity to meet the great and the near great in America, and she gave her impressions of these, and of American society, in a lively style well larded with moralizing. "Nothing," wrote *Blackwood's Magazine* sourly, "can rectify a reformer's vision, and no conviction of inadequacy prevent any of the class from lecturing all mankind." Miss Martineau's later writings include novels, histories, studies of philosophy, education, and domestic economy. She died in 1876.

Every state of society has, happily, its originals; men and women who, in more or fewer respects, think, speak, and act, naturally and unconsciously, in a different way from the generality of men. There are several causes from which this generality may arise, particularly in a young community less gregarious than those of the civilized countries of the world.

The commonest of these causes in a society like that of the United States is, perhaps, the absence of influences to which almost all other persons are subject. The common pressure being absent in some one direction, the being grows out in that direction, and the mind and character exhibit more or less deformity to the eyes of all but the individual most concerned. The back States afford a full harvest of originals of this class; while in England, where it is scarcely possible to live out of society, such are rarely to be found.

Social and professional eccentricity comes next. When local and professional influences are inadequately balanced by general ones, a singularity of character is produced, which is not so agreeable as it is striking and amusing. Of this class of characters few examples are to be seen at home; but, instead of them, something much worse, which is equally rare in America. In England we have confessors to tastes and pursuits, and martyrs to passions and vices, which arise out of a highly artificial state of society. In England we have a smaller proportion of grave, innocent, professional buffoons; but in America there are few or no fashionable ingrained profligates, few or no misers.

In its possession of a third higher class, it is reasonable and delightful to hope that there is no superiority in the society of any one civilized country over that of any other. Of men and women who have intellectual power to modify the general influences to which, like others, they are subject, every nation has its share. In every country there have been beings who have put forth more or less of the godlike power involved in their humanity, whereby they can stem the current of circumstance, deliberately form the purpose of their life, and prosecute it, happen what may. The number is not large anywhere, but the species is nowhere unknown.

A yet smaller class of yet nobler originals remains; those who, with the independent power of the last mentioned, are stimulated by strong pressure of circumstance to put forth their whole force, and form and achieve purposes in which not only their own life, but the destiny of others, is included. Such, being the prophets and redeemers of their age and country, rise up when and where they are wanted. The deed being ripe for the doing, the doer appears. The field being white for harvest, the reaper shows himself at the gate, whether the song of fellow-reapers cheers his heart, or lions are growling in his solitary path.

Many English persons have made up their minds that there is very little originality in America, except in regions where such men as David Crockett grow up. In the wilds of Tennessee and Kentucky twenty years ago, and now in Arkansas and Missouri, where bear-hunting and the buffalo chase are still in full career, it is acknowledged that a man's natural bent may be seen to advantage, and his original force must be fully tested. But it is asked, with regard to America, whether there is not much less than the average amount of originality of character to be found in the places where men operate upon one another. It is certain that there is an intense curiosity in Americans about English oddities; and a prevailing belief among themselves that England is far richer in humorists than the United States. It is also true that the fickleness and impressibleness of the Americans (particularly of the New Englanders) about systems of science, philosophy, and morals, exceed anything ever seen or heard of in the sober old country; but all this can prove only that the nation and its large divisions are not original in character, and not that individuals of that character are wanting.

It should be remembered that one great use of a metropolis, if not the greatest, is to test everything for the benefit of the whole of the rest of the country. The country may, according to circumstances, be more or less ready to avail itself of the benefit; but the benefit exists and waits for acceptance. Now the Americans have no metropolis. Their cities are all provincial towns. It may be, in their circumstances, politically good that they should have the smallest possible amount of centralization; but the want of this centralization is injurious to their scientific and philosophical progress and dignity, and, therefore, to their national originality. A conjurer's trip through the English counties is very like the progress of a lecturer or newly imported philosopher through the American cities. The wonder, the excitement, the unbounded credulity are much alike in the two cases; but in the English village there may be an old man under the elm smiling good-naturedly after the show without following after it; or a sage young man who could tell how the puppets are moved as well as if he saw the wires. And so it is in American cities. The crowd is large, but everybody is not in it; the believers are many, but there are some who foresee how soon the belief will take a new turn. . . .

The Americans appear to me an eminently imaginative people. The unprejudiced traveler can hardly spend a week among them without being struck by this every day. At a distance it is seen clearly enough that they do not put their imaginative power to use in literature and the arts; and it does certainly appear perverse enough to observers from the Old World that they should be imitative in fictions (whether of the pen, the pencil, stone, or marble), and imaginative in their science and philosophy, applying their sober good sense to details, but being sparing of it in regard to principles. This arbitrary direction of their imaginative powers, or, rather,

its restriction to particular departments, is, I believe and
trust, only temporary. As their numbers increase and their
society becomes more delicately organized; when, consequently, the pursuit of literature, philosophy, and art shall
become as definitely the business of some men as politics and
commerce now are of others, I cannot doubt that the re-
straints of imitation will be burst through, and that a plenitude of power will be shed into these departments as striking
as that which has made the organization of American commerce (notwithstanding some defects) the admiration of the
world, and vindicated the originality of American politics in
theory and practice. . . .

However this may be, it is certain that there are individuals existing everywhere, in the very heart of Boston itself,
as original as Sam Weller and David Crockett, or any other
self-complacent mortal who finds scope for his humors amid
the kindly intricacies of London or the canebrakes of Tennessee. . . .

There must be very many local and professional oddities
in a country like America, where individuals fill a larger
space in society, and are less pressed upon by influences,
other than local and professional, than in Old World communities. A judge in the West is often a remarkable person-
age to European eyes. I know one who unites all the odd
characteristics of the order so as to be worth a close study.
Before I left home, a friend desired me to bring her something, she did not care what, that should be exclusively American, something which could not be procurable anywhere
else. When I saw this judge I longed to pack him up, and
direct him, per next packet from New York, to my friend,
for he was the first article I met with that could not by any
possibility have been picked up anywhere out of the United
States. He was about six feet high, lank as a flail, and seeming
to be held together only by the long-tailed drab greatcoat
into which he was put. He had a quid in his cheek whenever
I saw him, and squirted tobacco-juice into the fireplace or

elsewhere at intervals of about twenty seconds. His face was long and solemn, his voice monotonous, and his manner dogmatical to a most amusing degree. He was a dogged republican, with an uncompromising hatred of the blacks, and with an indifferent sort of pity for all foreigners. This last feeling probably induced him to instruct me on various matters. He fixed his eyes on the fire, and talked on for my edification, but without taking express notice of the presence of any one, so that his lecture had the droll appearance of being a formal soliloquy. In the same speech he declared that no man was made by God to run wild through a forest who was not able to comprehend Christianity at sight; missions to the heathen being therefore sanctioned from heaven itself; and that men with a dark skin cannot, in three years, learn the name of a rope or the point of the compass, and that they are therefore meant to be slaves. It seemed to me that he was bound to suspend the operation of the law against all colored persons on the ground of their incapacity, their lack of understanding of the common affairs of life. But the ground of their punishment in this life seemed to be that they might be as wise as they pleased about the affairs of the next. He proceeded with his enunciations, however, without vouchsafing an explanation of these mysteries. It must be an awkward thing to be either a heathen or a Negro under his jurisdiction, if he acts upon his own doctrines. . . .

Martineau, *Retrospect of Western Travel*.

7

THE AMERICAN IDIOM AND AMERICAN PRUDERY

FREDERICK MARRYAT

WHEN Captain Marryat visited the United States in 1837 he was already famous as the author of *Captain Faithful*, *Peter Simple*, *Midshipman Easy*, and other sea stories that have held their popularity to this day. Born in London in 1792, Marryat had fought in many naval battles during the last years of the Napoleonic wars, rising to the rank of Captain in the Royal Navy. In 1830, however, he resigned his commission in order to devote all of his time to literature. Widely traveled on the Continent, he was eager to compare New World civilization with the Old and, as his mother was a native of Boston, he was predisposed to see the best side of America. Yet his ingrained suspicion of democracy and of leveling made it difficult for him to understand or appreciate what he found in America, and his famous *Diary*, from which this selection is taken, was on the whole supercilious and superficial—but invariably amusing.

THE Americans boldly assert that they speak better English than we do, and I was rather surprised not to find a statistical table to that effect in Mr. Carey's publication. What I believe the Americans would imply by the above assertion is that you may travel through all the United States and find less difficulty in understanding, or in being understood, than in some of the counties of England, such as Cornwall, Devonshire, Lancashire, and Suffolk. So far they are correct; but it is remarkable how very debased the language has become in a short period in America. There are few provincial dialects in England much less intelligible than the following. A Yankee girl, who wished to hire herself out, was asked if she had any followers, or sweethearts? After a little hesitation, she replied, "Well, now, can't exactly say; I bees a sorter courted, and a sorter not; reckon more a sorter yes than a sorter no." In many points the Americans have to a certain degree obtained that equality which they profess; and, as respects their language, it certainly is the case. If their lower classes are more intelligible than ours, it is equally true that the higher classes do not speak the language so purely or so classically as it is spoken among the well-educated English. The peculiar dialect of the English counties is kept up because we are a settled country; the people who are born in a country live in, and die in, it, transmitting their sites of labor or of amusement to their descendants, generation after generation, without change; consequently, the provincialisms of the language become equally hereditary. Now, in America, they have a dictionary containing many thousands of words which, with us, are either obsolete, or are provincialisms, or are words necessarily invented by the Americans. When the people of England emigrated to the States, they came from every county in England, and each county brought its provincialisms with it. These were admitted into the general stock; and were since all collected and bound up by one Mr. Webster. With the exceptions of a few words coined for local uses (such as snags and sawyers, on the Mississippi), I do not recollect a word which I have not traced to be either a provincialism of some English county, or else to be obsolete English. There are a few from the Dutch, such as stoup, for the porch of a door, etc. I was once talking with an American about Webster's dictionary, and he observed, "Well, now, sir, I understand it's the only one used in the Court of St. James, by the king, queen, and princesses, and that by royal order."

The upper classes of the Americans do not, however, speak or pronounce English according to our standard; they appear to have no exact rule to guide them, probably from a want of any intimate knowledge of Greek or Latin. You seldom hear a derivation from the Greek pronounced correctly, the accent being generally laid upon the wrong syllable. In fact, every one appears to be independent, and pronounces just as he pleases.

But it is not for me to decide the very momentous question, as to which nation speaks the best English. The Americans generally improve upon the inventions of others; probably they may have improved upon our language. . . .

I cannot conclude this chapter without adverting to one or two points peculiar to the Americans. They wish, in everything, to improve upon the old country, as they call us, and affect to be excessively refined in their language and ideas; but they forget that very often in the covering, and the covering only, consists the indecency, and that, to use the old aphorism—"Very nice people are people with very nasty ideas."

They object to everything nude in statuary. When I was at the house of Governor Everett at Boston, I observed a fine cast of the Apollo Belvedere, but, in compliance with general opinion, it was hung with drapery, although Governor Everett himself is a gentleman of refined mind and high classical attainments, and quite above such ridiculous sensitiveness. In language it is the same thing: there are certain words which are never used in America, but an awkward substitute is employed. I cannot particularize them after this preface, lest I should be accused of indelicacy myself. I may, however, state one little circumstance, which will prove the correctness of what I say.

When at Niagara Falls, I was escorting a young lady with whom I was on friendly terms. She had been standing on a piece of rock, the better to view the scene, when she slipped down, and was evidently hurt by the fall; she had in fact grazed her shin. As she limped a little in walking home, I said, "Did you hurt your leg much?" She turned from me, evidently much shocked, or much offended; and not being aware that I had committed any very heinous offense, I begged to know what was the reason of her displeasure. After some hesitation, she said that as she knew me well, she would tell me that the word leg was never mentioned before ladies. I apologized for my want of refinement, which was attributable to my having been accustomed only to English society, and added, that as such articles must occasionally be referred to, even in the most polite circles of America, perhaps she would inform me by what name I might mention them without shocking the company. Her reply was that the word limb was used; "Nay," continued she, "I am not so particular as some people are, for I know those who always say limb of a table, or limb of a piano-forte."

There the conversation dropped; but a few months afterwards I was obliged to acknowledge that the young lady was correct when she asserted that some people were more particular than even she was.

I was requested by a lady to escort her to a seminary for young ladies, and on being ushered into the reception room, conceive my astonishment at beholding a square piano-forte with four limbs. However, that the ladies who visited their daughters might feel in its full force the extreme delicacy of the mistress of the establishment, and her care to preserve in their utmost purity the ideas of the young ladies under her charge, she had dressed all these four limbs in modest little trousers, with frills at the bottom of them!

Marryat, *A Diary in America.*

RELIGION AND MORALITY PRESIDE OVER THEIR COUNCILS

FRANCIS GRUND

FEW commentators on America had a more cosmopolitan experience than Francis Grund. Born in Bohemia in 1805, he studied in Vienna, taught at a military academy in Rio de Janeiro, practiced journalism in Philadelphia, served as consul at Antwerp and Le Havre and as diplomatic agent to the South German States, and in 1863, the last year of his life, returned to Philadelphia to edit the *Age*. His interests were almost as varied as his activities. Besides elementary texts on algebra, geometry, chemistry, and philosophy, he wrote a campaign life of William Henry Harrison, a study of Aristocracy in America, a handbook for immigrants, and the two volume work on *The Americans in their Moral, Social, and Political Relations* (1837) from which this chapter is taken. An eminently philosophical observer, Grund, like Tocqueville, was interested in the effect of the notion of equality on morals, religion, politics, and the position of women.

THE religious habits of the Americans form not only the basis of their private and public morals, but have become so thoroughly interwoven with their whole course of legislation that it would be impossible to change them without affecting the very essence of their government. Not only are the manners and habits of a people, at all times, stronger than the positive law, but the latter itself is never readily obeyed without becoming reduced to a custom. It is to the manners and habits of a nation we must look for the continuance of their government. In France, where the people have for ages been accustomed to an absolute and despotic government, where every historical monument, every palace, every work of art, nay, the very furniture of their rooms, speak monarchy, we perceive constant anomalies in society, from the legislative halls down to the meanest public resort; simply because the people are accustomed to feel one way, and constrained to reason and act in another. They possess yet the forms of religion, which have ceased to convey to them a meaning; they have yet the splendor of a throne, without any of the feelings of loyalty; they have all the titles and pretensions of their ancient nobles, with the most unbounded love of equality. Yet, with all their political excitability, and their theoretical attachment to republicanism, they are constantly lulled asleep by monarchical principles without offering any other resistance than the sensation which the fact itself produces, when set off by the pen of an editor. An Englishman or an American would feel the encroachment on his liberty, because it would oblige him to change his habits, which he is less prepared to do, than to surrender a positive right. American liberty is further advanced in the minds of the people than even in the laws themselves. It has become an active principle which lives with, and animates the nation, and of which their political constitution is but a facsimile.

Whatever contributes to confirm a people in the habitual exercise of freedom is an additional guarantee of its continuance; and whatever has been instrumental in procuring that freedom, or is associated with it in their minds, must be preserved with religious care, lest liberty itself should suffer in their estimation. This is the case with the doctrines of Christianity in the United States. Religion has been the basis of the most important American settlements; religion kept their little community together; religion assisted them in their revolutionary struggle; it was religion to which they appealed in defending their rights, and it was religion, in fine, which taught them to prize their liberties. It is with the solemnities of religion that the Declaration of Independence is yet annually read to the people from the pulpit, or that Americans celebrate the anniversaries of the most important events in their history. It is to religion they have recourse whenever they wish to impress the popular feeling with anything relative to their country; and it is religion which assists them in all their national undertakings. The Americans look upon religion as a promoter of civil and political liberty; and have, therefore, transferred to it a large portion of the affection which they cherish for the institutions of their country. In other countries, where religion has become the instrument of oppression, it has been the policy of the liberal party to diminish its influence; but in America its promotion is essential to the constitution.

Religion presides over their councils, aids in the execution of the laws, and adds to the dignity of the judges. Whatever is calculated to diminish its influence and practice has a tendency to weaken the government, and is, consequently, opposed to the peace and welfare of the United States. It would have a direct tendency to lessen the respect for the law, to bring disorder into their public deliberations, and to retard the administration of justice.

The deference which the Americans pay to morality is scarcely inferior to their regard for religion, and is, in part, based upon the latter. The least solecism in the moral conduct of a man is attributed to his want of religion, and is visited upon him as such. It is not the offense itself, but the outrage on society, which is punished. They see in a breach of morals a direct violation of religion; and in this, an attempt to subvert the political institutions of the country. These sentiments are all-powerful in checking the appearance of vice, even if they are not always sufficient to preclude its existence.

With Argus-eyes does public opinion watch over the words and actions of individuals, and, whatever may be their private sins, enforces at least a tribute to morality in public.

My meaning cannot be misunderstood. It is but the open violation of the law, which comes before the forum of the judge; for our secret transgressions we shall have to account with our God. Public virtue must be guarded against the pernicious influence of example; vice must be obliged to conceal itself, in order not to tincture society in general. In this consists the true force and wholesome influence of public opinion. It becomes a mighty police-agent of morality and religion, which not only discovers crimes, but partly prevents their commission. The whole people of the United States are empanelled as a permanent jury to pronounce their verdict of "guilty" or "not guilty" on the conduct and actions of men, from the President down to the laborer; and there is no appeal from their decision. Public opinion may sometimes be unjust for a long time, especially in reference to politicians, but it hardly ever remains so, and there is no injury which it inflicts, which it is not in its power to remedy.

Another proof of the high premium at which morality is held in the United States consists in its influence on the elections of officers. In Europe, a man of genius is almost privileged. If he be a poet or an artist, allowances are made for the extravagance of his fancy, or the peculiarity of his appetites. If he be a statesman, his individual wanderings are forgotten for the general good he bestows on the nation; if he be a soldier, the wounds he may inflict upon virtue and unguarded innocence are pardoned for the sake of those he may have received in defending his country; and even the clergy have their offenses excused, in consideration of the morals which they promote by their spiritual functions. No such compensation takes place in the United States. Private virtue overtops the highest qualifications of the mind, and is indispensable to the progress even of the most acknowledged talents. This, in many instances, clips the wings of genius, by substi-

tuting a decent mediocrity in the place of brilliant but vicious talents; but the nation at large is nevertheless a gainer
in the practice.

It must be remembered that the Americans are already in
possession of most political advantages other nations are
striving to obtain; and that their principal care, therefore, is
rather to preserve what they have acquired than to enlarge
their possessions; and for this purpose virtue and honest simplicity are infinitely preferable to the ambitious designs of
towering talents. If morality, which is now the common law
of the country, were once to be dispensed with in favor of
certain individuals—if the exactions which are now made of
every member of the community were to relax with regard
to the peculiarly gifted, then the worst and most dangerous
aristocracy would be introduced, which would not only
shake the foundation of society, but eventually subvert the
government. Talent, in a republic, must be valued principally in proportion as it is calculated to promote public good;
every additional regard for it enriches only the possessor; and
the Americans are too prudent a people to enrich and elevate
individuals with the property and wealth of the nation.

The moment a candidate is presented for office, not only
his mental qualifications for the functions he is about to assume, but also his private character are made the subject of
criticism. Whatever he may have done, said, or listened to,
from the time he left school to the present moment is sure to
be brought before the public. The most trifling incidents
which are calculated to shed a light on his motives or habits
or thinking are made the subject of the most uncompromising
scrutiny; and facts and circumstances, already buried in ob-
livion, are once more brought before the judging eye of the
people. This, undoubtedly, gives rise to a vast deal of personal abuse and scurrility, and may even disturb the domestic
peace of families; but then the candidates for office are comparatively few, while the people, who are to be benefited or
injured by their election, are many; they are all presenting

themselves of their own accord, and the people compelled to be their judges; they have friends to defend and extol their virtues, and they must therefore expect to have enemies, who will endeavor to tarnish their fair reputation. We may have pity on a repentant culprit—we may be roused to indignation by the condemnation of an innocent person; but we would not, on that account, abolish the trial by jury, or shut our courts of justice, which are instituted not only for the punishment but also for the prevention of crime. The process of an American election resembles that of a Roman canonization; the candidate must be fairly snatched from the clutches of the devil's advocate, before he can be admitted to the unrestrained enjoyment of paradise. If, in this manner, some are prevented from becoming saints, who have a just title to that dignity, it may also serve to prevent a heathen worship of idols, which would divert the people from the true faith.

It is an erroneous maxim, to consider American institutions as they are calculated to affect individuals: they are made for the people, and intended to benefit the majority. The consideration of quality must necessarily, in many instances, yield to the reflection on quantity; and a small benefit extended to large numbers, be preferred to a signal advantage conferred on a favored few. The American government, possessing little coercive power, cannot introduce sudden changes either for the better or worse, and is, therefore, less able to correct an abuse, if it is once introduced and sanctioned by the majority, than any other government in the world. It is consequently of the greatest importance that public morality should be preserved at any price, and that the people themselves should compose the tribunal before which the offenders are to be tried. It is their noblest privilege to be themselves the guardians of their moral and religious rights, without which their political immunities would soon become crippled and destroyed. In this manner they will not always secure the greatest talents, but generally the moral integrity of their leaders; they will not easily sacrifice peace to national glory, but promote the tranquil happiness of millions; their career will not be one of brilliant triumph, but it will be less sullied with political crimes; they will not give birth to a Caesar or an Augustus, but be spared the mourning for Brutus.

Morality, in America, is not only required of a statesman, but is equally necessary in every occupation of life. The merchant who employs a clerk, the master-workman who employs a journeyman, the gentleman who hires a servant, will all make morality an indispensable condition of contract. In this they are as much guided by their own choice, as by the opinions of their neighbors, and the community in general. An inferior workman of "steady habits" is almost always preferred to one possessed of the highest business qualifications, but with a doubtful moral character. Thus, a married man will be sooner trusted than one who is single; because "he has given hostage to fortune," and possesses what Bacon calls "an impediment to mischief." A man of sober habits will be sooner employed than one addicted to intemperance; and a clumsy, but moral servant will more readily obtain a situation, than one who is expert and vicious. Religion will, in all, be considered as a pledge of morality; and a lax observance of religious duties, as a bad index to their private virtues. In short, morality and religion are as indispensable to the laboring classes in the United States as powerful and well-formed limbs and a correct use of the understanding. They will often atone for a variety of other imperfections; but without them every other qualification becomes useless, and only serves to aggravate the despair of success.

There is one particular sentiment pervading all classes of Americans, which, though something similar exists in England, is in no other country carried to the same extent, or productive of the same consequences. I mean the universal respect for women, and the protection offered them, to whatever order of society they may belong. Ladies are respected, or rather command respect, everywhere, especially in Eng-

land; but in no country are the penalties fixed by the law, or
the received customs of society, on a breach of decorum, so
severe as in the United States. The commission of such an
offense not only excludes a man from society, but influences
his business, his character, his reputation, his prospects in life,
and every reasonable chance of success. No rank or standing
proves sufficient to protect him against the denunciations of
the public; no repentance can atone for an offense once
known to the world. Of all the crimes against society, the
Americans seem to be bent upon visiting this with the most
unrelenting severity; of all that obtain forgiveness, this alone
seems to form an exception.

Neither is this protection, as I have said before, only offered to ladies, or to those whose education and family entitle
them to particular consideration, as is the case in Europe; it
extends to all classes without distinction, and is even more
favorable to the lower orders than to those who are supposed
to be above them.

If a man of fortune and reputation were to ruin an innocent girl, or be guilty of a breach of promise, were it but to
a waiting-woman, it would no less affect his standing in society, and expose him to the revenge of the public. Neither
ladies nor gentlemen would plead his cause; and his only
chance of escape from punishment would be to satisfy the
injured party.

Where a feeling of this kind is too general, and acts alike
on every member of society, it cannot be the result of a mere
polite etiquette, but must be based on a principle which is
deeply rooted in the mind, and forms part of the national
code of morals. Its advantages in promoting early marriages,
and preserving the sanctity of the marriage vow, are incalculable, and are the best comment on the rapid increase of
population and the domestic happiness, which is enjoyed
throughout the United States. . . .

I consider the domestic virtue of the Americans as the
principal source of all their other qualities. It acts as a pro-

moter of industry, as a stimulus to enterprise, and as the most powerful restrainer of public vice. It reduces life to its simplest elements, and makes happiness less dependent on precarious circumstances; it ensures the proper education of children, and acts, by the force of example, on the morals of the rising generation: in short, it does more for the preservation of peace and good order than all the laws enacted for that purpose; and is a better guarantee for the permanency of the American government than any written instrument, the constitution itself not excepted.

No government could be established on the same principle as that of the United States, with a different code of morals. The American Constitution is remarkable for its simplicity; but it can only suffice a people habitually correct in their actions, and would be utterly inadequate to the wants of a different nation. Change the domestic habits of the Americans, their religious devotion, and their high respect for morality, and it will not be necessary to change a single letter of the Constitution in order to vary the whole form of their government. The circumstances being altered, the same causes would no longer produce the same effects; and it is more than probable that the disparity which would then exist between the laws and the habits of those whom they are destined to govern, would not only make a different government desirable, but absolutely necessary, to preserve the nation from ruin.

The moral and domestic habits of the Americans must necessarily exercise an important influence on the acquisition and accumulation of property. A single man encounters often more difficulties in making his way through the world, than one whose early marriage has increased his stimulus to exertion. The man who has a family is double pledged to virtue, and has, in every additional member, a monitor to industry and frugality. In a country like America, where so much depends on individual enterprise, the effect of it, when anyway ably directed, can never long remain doubtful; especially when it is seconded and approved of by the community in general. Accordingly, there are but few single men largely engaged in commerce, or any other kind of enterprise, and less who, in the state, are capable of accumulating fortunes. The most enterprising merchants and shipowners, the first manufacturers, and the proprietors of the largest estates in the country are married men; and, what is still more remarkable, have acquired their property, not before, but after, their marriage.

This example of prosperity, in the marriage-state, and the consequently greater facilities of credit of married men act as a premium on matrimony; and enable men to provide for their wives and children, who, without them, might have been unable to provide for themselves. But when the foundation of a fortune is once laid, its increase and accumulation follow as a matter of course, unless some unexpected calamity should blast the hope of success. The moment a man is known to have acquired a little property by his own industry, he receives credit for ingenuity and perseverance, and is trusted on account of these virtues. His means become, in this manner, much more enlarged than his estate: and it depends chiefly on the resources of his own mind, what advantages he will draw from his position.

But if the acquisition and accumulation of property in the United States are made comparatively easy, and credit given to those who succeed in it, a proportionally larger discredit must attach itself to those who are unfortunate and poor; and this is really carried to a melancholy extent, although, from the unexampled prosperity of the country, there are few to whom it will apply. A man in America is not despised for being poor in the outset—three-fourths of all that are rich have begun in the same way—but every year which passes, without adding to his prosperity, is a reproach to his understanding or industry; and if he should become old without having acquired some property, or showing reasons which prevented his success, if he should not enjoy a reputation as a scholar or a professional man, then I am afraid he will be doubly punished; by his own helpless situation, and the want of sympathy in others. But in this case, it is not the want of property, which deprives him of the consideration of his fellow-beings: it is the want of talent, ingenuity, perseverance, or enterprise, which might have insured his success. Hence an American will seldom complain of losses, want of business, or prosperity in general. The sympathy he might create in his friends would rather injure than benefit him; and would, at best, but destroy his credit with the rest. In the United States, if a man has made a bad bargain, he is sure to keep the secret to himself, lest his business talent should be doubted; if he has been unfortunate in a speculation, he will find a remedy in another, without lamenting the loss; and should he even be ruined, he will put on a good face, arrange himself with his creditors, and start anew, cautioned by his former experience.

This habit, of depending chiefly on themselves, produces in the Americans a spirit of independence, scarcely to be found in any other nation. It stifles complaints of all sorts; makes them support heavy times and calamities with patience; and inspires them with hope and energy when oppressed with loss and misfortunes. During a residence of many years in the United States, I have had frequent intercourse with all classes of society, but do not remember having heard a single individual complain of misfortunes; and I have never known a native American to ask for charity. No country in the world has such a small number of persons supported at the public expense; and of that small number one half are foreign paupers. An American, embarrassed in his pecuniary circumstances, can hardly be prevailed upon to ask or accept the assistance of his own relations; and will, in many instances, scorn to have recourse to his own parents. Even an unsuccessful politician will leave the field without a groan, not to appear overcome by his antagonist; and, whatever be his secret anguish, show a bright countenance to the public. Happiness and prosperity are so popular in the United States that no one dares to show himself an exception to the rule; and avoiding carefully the semblance of misfortune, they generally succeed in reality, and become that which they have always been striving to appear.

Grund, *The Americans in their Moral, Social and Political Relations.*

9

IT WOULD BE WELL IF THEY LOVED THE REAL LESS AND THE IDEAL MORE

CHARLES DICKENS

PERHAPS the most famous of all visitors to America was Charles Dickens. He was just thirty when, in 1842, he made the first of two visits to this country, but he was already famous as the author of the *Pickwick Papers*, *Nicholas Nickleby*, and *The Old Curiosity Shop*, and he was received everywhere with open arms. Yet wearied with over-much attention, irritated by the minor discomforts of travel and hotel life, and outraged by what he thought the transparent hypocrisy of slavery in a nation that professed devotion to liberty, he conceived a poor opinion of American society and institutions. This opinion found expression first in the *American Notes*—of which this selection is the concluding chapter—and more memorably in *Martin Chuzzlewit*. Most Americans felt that these books were not only gross caricatures on American society, but bad manners and bad taste, and Dickens himself came to regret them. Yet much that he had to say was true, and certainly his strictures on the press of that day were deserved.

THERE are many passages in this book, where I have been at some pains to resist the temptation of troubling my readers with my own deductions and conclusions: preferring that they should judge for themselves, from such premises as I have laid before them. My only object in the outset, was, to carry them with me faithfully wheresoever I went: and that task I have discharged.

But I may be pardoned, if on such a theme as the general character of the American people, and the general character of their social system, as presented to a stranger's eyes, I desire to express my own opinions in a few words, before I bring these volumes to a close.

They are, by nature, frank, brave, cordial, hospitable, and affectionate. Cultivation and refinement seem but to enhance their warmth of heart and ardent enthusiasm; and it is the possession of these latter qualities in a most remarkable degree, which renders an educated American one of the most endearing and most generous of friends. I never was so won upon, as by this class; never yielded up my full confidence and esteem so readily and pleasurably, as to them; never can make again, in half-a-year, so many friends for whom I seem to entertain the regard of half a life.

These qualities are natural, I implicitly believe, to the whole people. That they are, however, sadly sapped and blighted in their growth among the mass; and that there are influences at work which endanger them still more, and give but little present promise of their healthy restoration; is a truth that ought to be told.

It is an essential part of every national character to pique itself mightily upon its faults, and to deduce tokens of its virtue or its wisdom from their very exaggeration. One great blemish in the popular mind of America, and the prolific parent of an innumerable brood of evils, is Universal Distrust. Yet the American citizen plumes himself upon this spirit, even when he is sufficiently dispassionate to perceive the ruin it works; and will often adduce it, in spite of his own reason, as an instance of the great sagacity and acuteness of the people, and their superior shrewdness and independence.

"You carry," says the stranger, "this jealousy and distrust into every transaction of public life. By repelling worthy men from your legislative assemblies, it has bred up a class of candidates for the suffrage, who, in their every act, disgrace your Institutions and your people's choice. It has rendered you so fickle, and so given to change, that your inconstancy has passed into a proverb; for you no sooner set up an idol firmly, than you are sure to pull it down and dash it into fragments: and this, because directly you reward a benefactor, or a public servant, you distrust him, merely because he *is* rewarded; and immediately apply yourselves to find out, either that you have been too bountiful in your acknowledgments, or he remiss in his deserts. Any man who attains a high place among you, from the President downwards, may date his downfall from that moment; for any printed lie that any notorious villain pens, although it militate directly against the character and conduct of a life, appeals at once to your distrust, and is believed. You will strain at a gnat in the way of trustfulness and confidence, however fairly won and well deserved; but you will swallow a whole caravan of camels, if they be laden with unworthy doubts and mean suspicions. Is this well, think you, or likely to elevate the character of the governors or the governed, among you?"

The answer is invariably the same: "There's freedom of opinion here, you know. Every man thinks for himself, and we are not to be easily overreached. That's how our people come to be suspicious."

Another prominent feature is the love of "smart" dealing: which gilds over many a swindle and gross breach of trust; many a defalcation, public and private; and enables many a knave to hold his head up with the best, who well deserves a halter: though it has not been without its retributive operation, for this smartness has done more in a few years to impair the public credit, and to cripple the public resources, than dull honesty, however rash, could have effected in a century. The merits of a broken speculation, or a bankruptcy, or of a successful scoundrel, are not gauged by its or his observance of the golden rule, "Do as you would be done by," but are considered with reference to their smartness. I recollect, on both occasions of our passing that ill-fated Cairo on the Mississippi, remarking on the bad effects such gross deceits must have when they exploded, in generating a want of confidence abroad, and discouraging foreign investment: but I was given to understand that this was a very smart scheme by which a deal of money had been made: and that its smartest feature was, that they forgot these things abroad, in a very short time, and speculated again, as freely as ever. The following dialogue I have held a hundred times: "Is it not a very disgraceful circumstance that such a man as So and So should be acquiring a large property by the most infamous and odious means, and notwithstanding all the crimes of which he has been guilty, should be tolerated and abetted by your Citizens? He is a public nuisance, is he not?" "Yes, sir." "A convicted liar?" "Yes, sir." "He has been kicked, and cuffed, and caned?" "Yes, sir." "And he is utterly dishonourable, debased, and profligate?" "Yes, sir." "In the name of wonder, then, what is his merit?" "Well, sir, he is a smart man."

In like manner, all kinds of deficient and impolitic usages are referred to the national love of trade; though, oddly enough, it would be a weighty charge against a foreigner that he regarded the Americans as a trading people. The love of trade is assigned as a reason for that comfortless custom, so very prevalent in country towns, of married persons living in hotels, having no fireside of their own, and seldom meeting from early morning until late at night, but at the hasty public meals. The love of trade is a reason why the literature of America is to remain for ever unprotected: "For we are a trading people, and don't care for poetry:" though we *do*, by the way, profess to be very proud of our poets: while healthful amusements, cheerful means of recreation, and wholesome fancies, must fade before the stern utilitarian joys of trade.

These three characteristics are strongly presented at every

turn, full in the stranger's view. But, the foul growth of America has a more tangled root than this; and it strikes its fibres, deep in its licentious Press.

Schools may be erected, East, West, North, and South; pupils be taught, and masters reared, by scores upon scores of thousands; colleges may thrive, churches may be crammed, temperance may be diffused, and advancing knowledge in all other forms walk through the land with giant strides: but while the newspaper press of America is in, or near, its present abject state, high moral improvement in that country is hopeless. Year by year, it must and will go back; year by year, the tone of public feeling must sink lower down; year by year, the Congress and the Senate must become of less account before all decent men; and year by year, the memory of the Great Fathers of the Revolution must be outraged more and more, in the bad life of their degenerate child.

Among the herd of journals which are published in the States, there are some, the reader scarcely need be told, of character and credit. From personal intercourse with accomplished gentlemen connected with publications of this class, I have derived both pleasure and profit. But the name of these is Few, and of the others Legion; and the influence of the good is powerless to counteract the mortal poison of the bad.

Among the gentry of America; among the well-informed and moderate: in the learned professions; at the bar and on the bench: there is, as there can be, but one opinion, in reference to the vicious character of these infamous journals. It is sometimes contended—I will not say strangely, for it is natural to seek excuses for such a disgrace—that their influence is not so great as a visitor would suppose. I must be pardoned for saying that there is no warrant for this plea, and that every fact and circumstance tends directly to the opposite conclusion.

When any man, of any grade of desert in intellect or character, can climb to any public distinction, no matter what, in America, without first grovelling down upon the earth, and bending the knee before this monster of depravity; when any private excellence is safe from its attacks; when any social confidence is left unbroken by it, or any tie of social decency and honour is held in the least regard; when any man in that Free Country has freedom of opinion, and presumes to think for himself, and speak for himself, without humble reference to a censorship which, for its rampant ignorance and base dishonesty, he utterly loathes and despises in his heart; when those who most acutely feel its infamy and the reproach it casts upon the nation, and who most denounce it to each other, dare to set their heels upon, and crush it openly, in the sight of all men: then, I will believe that its influence is lessening, and men are returning to their manly senses. But while that Press has its evil eye in every house, and its black hand in every appointment in the state, from a president to a postman; while, with ribald slander for its only stock in trade, it is the standard literature of an enormous class, who must find their reading in a newspaper, or they will not read at all; so long must its odium be upon the country's head, and so long must the evil it works be plainly visible in the Republic.

To those who are accustomed to the leading English journals, or to the respectable journals of the Continent of Europe; to those who are accustomed to anything else in print and paper; it would be impossible, without an amount of extract for which I have neither space nor inclination, to convey an adequate idea of this frightful engine in America. But if any man desire confirmation of my statement on this head, let him repair to any place in this city of London, where scattered numbers of these publications are to be found; and there, let him form his own opinion.

It would be well, there can be no doubt, for the American people as a whole, if they loved the Real less, and the Ideal somewhat more. It would be well, if there were greater encouragement to lightness of heart and gaiety, and a wider cultivation of what is beautiful, without being eminently and directly useful. But here, I think the general remonstrance, "we are a new country," which is so often advanced as an excuse for defects which are quite unjustifiable, as being of right only the slow growth of an old one, may be very reasonably urged: and I yet hope to hear of there being some other national amusement in the United States, besides newspaper politics.

They certainly are not a humorous people, and their temperament always impressed me as being of a dull and gloomy character. In shrewdness of remark, and a certain cast-iron quaintness, the Yankees, or people of New England, unquestionably take the lead; as they do in most other evidences of intelligence. But in travelling about, out of the large cities —as I have remarked in former parts of these volumes—I was quite oppressed by the prevailing seriousness and melancholy air of business: which was so general and unvarying, that at every new town I came to I seemed to meet the very same people whom I had left behind me, at the last. Such defects as are perceptible in the national manners, seem, to me, to be referable, in a great degree, to this cause: which has generated a dull, sullen persistence in coarse usages, and rejected the graces of life as undeserving of attention. There is no doubt that Washington, who was always most scrupulous and exact on points of ceremony, perceived the tendency towards this mistake, even in his time, and did his utmost to correct it.

I cannot hold with other writers on these subjects that the prevalence of various forms of dissent in America, is in any way attributable to the non-existence there of an established church: indeed, I think the temper of the people, if it admitted of such an Institution being founded amongst them, would lead them to desert it, as a matter of course, merely because it *was* established. But, supposing it to exist, I doubt its probable efficacy in summoning the wandering sheep to one great fold, simply because of the immense amount of dissent which prevails at home; and because I do not find in

America any one form of religion with which we in Europe, or even in England, are unacquainted. Dissenters resort thither in great numbers, as other people do, simply because it is a land of resort; and great settlements of them are founded, because ground can be purchased, and towns and villages reared, where there were none of the human creation before. But even the Shakers emigrated from England; our country is not unknown to Mr. Joseph Smith, the apostle of Mormonism, or to his benighted disciples; I have beheld religious scenes myself in some of our populous towns which can hardly be surpassed by an American camp-meeting; and I am not aware that any instance of superstitious imposture on the one hand, and superstitious credulity on the other, has had its origin in the United States, which we cannot more than parallel. . . .

The Republican Institutions of America undoubtedly lead the people to assert their self-respect and their equality; but a traveller is bound to bear those Institutions in his mind, and not hastily to resent the near approach of a class of strangers, who, at home, would keep aloof. This characteristic, when it was tinctured with no foolish pride, and stopped short of no honest service, never offended me; and I very seldom, if ever, experienced its rude or unbecoming display. Once or twice it was comically developed, as in the following case; but this was an amusing incident, and not the rule or near it.

I wanted a pair of boots at a certain town, for I had none to travel in, but those with the memorable cork soles, which were much too hot for the fiery decks of a steam-boat. I therefore sent a message to an artist in boots, importing, with my compliments, that I should be happy to see him, if he would do me the polite favour to call. He very kindly returned for answer, that he would "look round" at six o'clock that evening.

I was lying on the sofa, with a book and a wine-glass, at about that time, when the door opened, and a gentleman in a stiff cravat, within a year or two on either side of thirty, entered, in his hat and gloves; walked up to the looking-glass; arranged his hair; took off his gloves; slowly produced a measure from the uttermost depths of his coat pocket; and requested me, in a languid tone, to "unfix" my straps. I complied, but looked with some curiosity at his hat, which was still upon his head. It might have been that, or it might have been the heat—but he took it off. Then, he sat himself down on a chair opposite to me; rested an arm on each knee; and, leaning forward very much, took from the ground, by a great effort, the specimen of metropolitan workmanship which I had just pulled off: whistling, pleasantly, as he did so. He turned it over and over; surveyed it with a contempt no language can express; and inquired if I wished him to fix me a boot like *that?* I courteously replied, that provided the boots were large enough, I would leave the rest to him; that, if convenient and practicable, I should not object to their bearing some resemblance to the model then before him; but that I would be entirely guided by, and would beg to leave the whole subject to, his judgment and discretion. "You an't partickler, about this scoop in the heel I suppose then?" says he: "We don't foller that, here." I repeated my last observation. He looked at himself in the glass again; went closer to it to dash a grain or two of dust out of the corner of his eye; and settled his cravat. All this time, my leg and foot were in the air. "Nearly ready, sir?" I inquired. "Well, pretty nigh," he said; "keep steady." I kept as steady as I could, both in foot and face; and having by this time got the dust out, and found his pencil-case, he measured me, and made the necessary notes. When he had finished, he fell into his old attitude, and taking up the boot again, mused for some time. "And this," he said, at last, "is an English boot, is it! This is a London boot, eh?" "That, sir," I replied, "is a London boot." He mused over it again, after the manner of Hamlet with Yorick's skull; nodded his head, as who should say, "I pity the Institutions that led to the production of this boot!"; rose; put up his pencil, notes, and paper—glancing at himself in the glass all the time—put on his hat; drew on his gloves very slowly; and finally walked out. When he had been gone about a minute, the door reopened, and his hat and his head reappeared. He looked round the room, and at the boot again, which was still lying on the floor; appeared thoughtful for a minute; and then said "Well, good afternoon." "Good afternoon, sir," said I: and that was the end of the interview.

There is but one other head on which I wish to offer a remark; and that has reference to the public health. In so vast a country, where there are thousands of millions of acres of land yet unsettled and uncleared, and on every rood of which, vegetable decomposition is annually taking place; where there are so many great rivers, and such opposite varieties of climate; there cannot fail to be a great amount of sickness at certain seasons. But I may venture to say, after conversing with many members of the medical profession in America, that I am not singular in the opinion that much of the disease which does prevail, might be avoided, if a few common precautions were observed. Greater means of personal cleanliness, are indispensable to this end; the custom of hastily swallowing large quantities of animal food, three times a-day, and rushing back to sedentary pursuits after each meal, must be changed; the gentler sex must go more wisely clad, and take more healthful exercise; and in the latter clause, the males must be included also. Above all, in public institutions, and throughout the whole of every town and city, the system of ventilation, and drainage, and removal of impurities requires to be thoroughly revised.

Dickens, *American Notes*.

10

EVERY AMERICAN IS AN APOSTLE OF THE DEMO-CRATIC CREED

ALEXANDER MACKAY

OF European visitors to the United States before the Civil War, only Tocqueville was at once more perspicacious and more sympathetic than the Scotsman, Alexander Mackay. A journalist, Mackay early edited a newspaper in Toronto, and then joined the staff of the London *Chronicle*, for which he reported the Congressional debates on the Oregon question in 1846. His *Western World*, published in 1849, was designed to "comprehend the social life of America, the working of its political institutions, and the bearing of its policy upon its moral development." His views were liberal and tolerant, and no other English observer before Bryce was more favorably disposed toward the United States than this Scotsman who resigned his position on the *Chronicle* because of that paper's attitude toward Canada and who warned Britain that the United States would eventually usurp leadership among English-speaking nations. In 1851 Mackay was sent to India to investigate labor conditions and the prospect for cotton in that country, and died at sea on the way home.

MANY Europeans quit the shores of the Republic with unfavorable impressions of American character, in the broadest acceptation of the term. But in the majority of instances, those who do so enter the country with preconceived notions of it, and leave it ere they have learnt to discern objects through the right medium. The Americans as a people, for instance, are characterized by some as gloomy and reserved; whereas, if properly approached, they are frank, communicative, and not unfrequently even mercurial in their dispositions. Anyone who has mingled much in American society must have seen that gloom was far from being its predominant characteristic, at least in the case of American women. If they have any fault in this respect as a class, it is not that of coldness and reserve, but of over-vivaciousness, and a tendency to the frivolous and amusing. In parts of the country, where fanaticism in religion has for some time prevailed, a settled gloom may be discerned on the majority of countenances; but it does not so much indicate a morose spirit as a real or affected habit of looking serious. . . .

The Americans are almost universally known to be a sensitive people. They are more than this; they are over-sensitive. This is a weakness which some travelers delight to play upon. But if they understood its source aright, they would deal more tenderly with it. As a nation, they feel themselves to be in the position of an individual whose permanent place in society has not yet been ascertained. They have struggled in little more than half a century into the first rank amongst the powers of the earth; but, like all new members of a confined and very particular circle, they are not yet quite sure of the firmness of their footing. When they look to the future, they have no reason to doubt the prominency of the position, social, political, and economical, which they will assume. But they are in haste to be all that they are yet destined to be; and although they do not exact from the stranger a positive recognition of all their pretensions, they are sensitive to a degree to any word or action on his part which purports a denial of them. It must be confessed that this weakness has of late very much increased. A sore that is being constantly irritated will soon exhibit all the symptoms of violent inflammation. The feelings of the American people have been wantonly and unnecessarily wounded by successive travelers who have undertaken to depict them, nationally and individually, and who, to pander to a prevailing taste in this country, have generally viewed them on the ludicrous side. It is a mistake to fancy that the Americans are impatient of criticism. They will submit to any amount of it that is fair, when they discover that it is tendered in an honest spirit. What they most wince at is the application to them and their affairs of epithets tending to turn them into ridicule. You may be as severe as you please with them, even in their own country as well as out of it, without irritating them, provided it appears that your intention is not simply to raise a laugh at their expense. . . .

The Americans are much more sensitive at home than they are abroad. Their country is but yet young; and when they hear parties abroad who have never seen it, expressing opinions in any degree derogatory to it, they console themselves with the reflection that the disparaging remark has its origin in an ignorance of the country, which is judged of, not from what it really is, but simply as a State of but seventy years' growth. Now in Europe it is but seldom that seventy years of national existence accomplishes much for a people. It is true that more has been done for mankind during the last seventy than perhaps during the previous 700; but the development of a nation in Europe is a slow process at the best, as compared with the course of things in this respect in America. The American, therefore, feels that, if the European would suspend his judgment until he saw and heard for himself, it would be very different from what it is when begotten in prejudice and pronounced in ignorance. This takes the sting from such disparaging criticism abroad as he may chance to hear. But if it is offered at home, unless it is accompanied with all the candor and honesty in which such criticism should alone be indulged in, he has no such reflection to take refuge in, and it wounds him to the quick.

If, notwithstanding all the evidences which the country affords of unexampled prosperity, universal contentment, social improvement and material progress, the foreigner still speaks of it, not in terms of severity, but in those of contempt—in terms, in short, which the American feels and knows are not justifiable—he can only refer the criticism to a predetermination to turn everything into ridicule, and is consequently not unjustly offended. . . .

If the Americans are more sensitive at home than they are abroad, they are more boastful abroad than they are at home. The one is a mere weakness, the other frequently an offense. Many in Europe judge of the American people from the specimens of them who travel. There are, of course, many Americans who travel, who, if they partake largely of the national vanity attributed to them all, have the tact and the courtesy to conceal it. Indeed, some of the best specimens of Americans are, for obvious reasons, those who have traveled much from home. But the great mass of American travelers enter foreign countries with as thick a coat of prejudice about them as Englishmen generally wear in visiting America. The consequence is that they commit the fault abroad, at which they are so irritated when committed in regard to themselves by the foreigner in America. With the American abroad, however, this fault assumes the reverse phase of that taken by it when committed by the foreigner in America. . . .

It would be erroneous to suppose that the national vanity which so many Americans exhibit abroad is prominently manifested at home. At all events it is not obtruded upon the stranger. The evidences of the country's greatness, both present and prospective, are before him when in the country; and to recapitulate them to him under these circumstances would be but to tell a tale twice over. If he does not draw favorable conclusions from what he sees, it is hopeless to expect him to do so from anything that he could hear. The American may be amazed at his real, or annoyed at his wil-

ful, blindness, but he generally leaves him to his own in-
ferences. It is only abroad, and when in contact with those
who have not had ocular demonstration of it, that he is
prone to dwell in a vaunting spirit upon his country's greatness.

Some allowance, however, should be made for the American, even in his most boastful humor. If he has nothing in a
national point of view to be vain of, he has certainly much
of which he can and should feel proud. There is no other
country on earth which in so short a time has accomplished
so much. It has but just passed the usual term allotted as the
period of life to man, and yet it takes rank as a first-rate
power. But let it not be supposed that all this has been
achieved in seventy years. The American republic has never
had a national infancy, like that through which most European nations have passed. The colonies were, in a measure,
old whilst they were yet new. They were as old as England
herself in point of moral, and new only in point of material,
civilization. They were not savages who laid the foundations
of our colonial dominion in America, but emigrants from a
highly civilized society, carrying with them all the moral
results of centuries of social culture. . . .

Intimately connected with the pride of country which
generally distinguishes the Americans is the feeling which
they cherish toward their institutions. Indeed, when the national feeling of an American is alluded to, something very
different is implied from that which is generally understood
by the term. In Europe, and particularly in mountainous
countries, the aspect of which is such as to impress itself
vividly upon the imagination, the love of country resolves
itself into a reverence for locality irrespective of all other
considerations. Thus the love which a Swiss bears to his
country is attached to the soil constituting Switzerland, without reference to the social or political institutions which may
develop themselves in the cantons. And so with the Scottish
mountaineer, whose national attachments center upon the

rugged features of his native land. It is seldom that the national feeling exhibits itself to the same extent in the breast of one born and bred in a country surpassingly rich, perhaps, in all the productions which minister to the comforts of life, but destitute of those rough and stern features which so endear his country to the hardy mountaineer. It is quite true that inspiriting historic associations may frequently produce feelings of national attachment similar to those inspired by a grand and imposing development of external nature: it is thus that some of the most patriotic tribes on earth are the inhabitants, not of the rugged mountain defile, but of the rich and monotonous plain. But the American exhibits little or none of the local attachments which distinguish the European. His feelings are more centered upon his institutions than his mere country. He looks upon himself more in the light of a republican than in that of a native of a particular territory. His affections have more to do with the social and political system with which he is connected than with the soil which he inhabits. The national feelings which he and a European cherish being thus different in their origin and their object are also different in their results. The man whose attachments converge upon a particular spot of earth is miserable if removed from it, no matter how greatly his circumstances otherwise may have been improved by his removal; but give the American his institutions, and he cares but little where you place him. In some parts of the Union the local feeling may be comparatively strong, such as in New England; but it is astonishing how readily even there an American makes up his mind to try his fortunes elsewhere, particularly if he contemplates removal merely to another part of the Union, no matter how remote, or how different in climate and other circumstances from what he has been accustomed to, provided the flag of his country waves over it, and republican institutions accompany him in his wanderings.

Strange as it may seem, this peculiarity, which makes an

American think less of his country than of the institutions
which characterize it, contributes greatly to the pride which
he takes in his country. He is proud of it, not so much for
itself as because it is the scene in which an experiment is
being tried which engages the anxious attention of the world.
The American feels himself much more interested in the success of his scheme of government, if not more identified with
it, than the European does in regard to his. The Englishman,
for instance, does not feel himself particularly committed to
the success of monarchy as a political scheme. He will support it so long as he is convinced that it conduces to the general welfare; and, judging it by this standard, it is likely that
he will yet support it for a long time to come. He feels his
honor to be involved in the independence of his country, but
does not consider himself to be under any obligations to
prove this or that political system an efficient one. The political scheme under which he lives he took as part and parcel
of his inheritance in a national point of view, and his object is
to make the best of it. It is very different, however, with the
American. He feels himself to be implicated, not only in the
honor and independence of his country, but also in the success of democracy. He has asserted a great principle, and
feels that, in attempting to prove it to be practicable, he has
assumed an arduous responsibility. He feels himself, therefore, to be directly interested in the success of the political
system under which he lives, and all the more so because he
is conscious that, in looking to its working, mankind are
divided into two great classes—those who are interested in its
failure and those who yearn for its success. Every American
is thus, in his own estimation, the apostle of a particular
political creed, in the final triumph and extension of which
he finds both himself and his country deeply involved. This
gives him a peculiar interest in the political scheme which he
represents; and invests his country with an additional degree
of importance in his sight, as in that of many others, from
being the scene of an experiment in the success of which not

only Americans but mankind are interested. Much, therefore, of the self-importance which the American assumes, particularly abroad, is less traceable to his mere citizenship than to his conscious identification with the success of democracy. Its manifestation may not always be agreeable to others, but the source of his pride is a legitimate and a noble one. It involves not only his own position, but also the hopes and expectations of humanity.

It is this feeling which renders the establishment of monarchy an impossibility in the United States. The American not only believes that his material interests are best subserved by a democratic form of government, but his pride is also mixed up with its maintenance and its permanency. It is a common thing for Europeans to speculate upon the disintegration of the Union, and the consequent establishment, in some part or parts of it, of the monarchical principle. These speculations are generally based upon precedents, but upon precedents which have in reality no application to America. The republics of old are pointed to as affording illustrations of the tendencies of republicanism. But the republics of old afford no criterion by which to judge of republicanism in America. The experiment which is being tried there is one *sui generis*. Not only are the political principles established different from those which have heretofore been practically recognized; but the people are also in a better state of preparation for the successful development of the experiment. . . .

The American Republic, in the first place, differs essentially from all that have preceded it in the principles on which it is founded: it is not a republic in simply not being a monarchy: it is a Democratic Republic, in the broadest sense of the term. If it is not a monarchy, neither is it an oligarchy. It is the people in reality that rule; it is not a mere fraction of them that usurps authority. The success of the American experiment depended, as it still depends, upon the character of the people. As already shown, the stability of the republic is intimately identified with the enlightenment of the public mind—in other words, with the great cause of popular education; it is to the promotion of education that it will in future chiefly owe its success. But its maintenance at first was mainly owing to the political antecedents of the people. It is quite true that they were converted in a day from being the subjects of a monarchy into the citizens of a republic. But let us not overlook the long probation which they underwent for the change. . . .

The political transition, therefore, which took place in 1776, so far from being a violent one, was but the natural consequence of the political education to which the American colonists had been subjected for a century and a half before. The moment they separated themselves from the imperial crown, they assumed the republican form of government, not from impulse or enthusiasm, but from the very necessity of the case. They had been long taught the lesson of self-reliance and self-control; and if, so long as they were colonists, they remained monarchists, it was more from old associations and ties than from not being ripe for a republic. The establishment of the Republic in America in 1776, then, was not a violent act, but a necessary one, after the disruption between the colonies and the mother country. This is what those forget who predict that the Republic will speedily relapse into monarchy. But it is in this that consists the essential difference between the American Republic, and the European republics of a modern date. Had the establishment of the Republic in 1776 warred with the habits or done violence to the feelings of the people, its overthrow might have been speedily looked for. But so far was this from being the case, that no other form of government could have been instituted that would have outlived a lustrum. . . .

Republicanism alone was suited to the character of the people and the exigencies of the country. Republicanism alone, therefore, was possible.

It is equally so at the present day. Consider the Americans

now—and what is there in their character, feelings, or circumstances to lead them back to monarchy? Everything connected with them tends the other way. Their associations are all republican—their principles and practice have ever been so—their interests have been subserved by republican institutions, and their pride is now involved in their maintenance and extension. The circumstances of the country, and the character and genius of the people, are as much now as in 1776 inimical to monarchy. On what, therefore, rests the supposition so often hazarded by parties in this country, that violence will be done, and that ere long, to the Republic in America? Unless the people can be persuaded to do violence to their feelings, tastes, habits, and associations, and to adopt institutions incompatible with their position and circumstances, there is no fear of democracy in America.

Many point to the accumulation of wealth as that which will work the change. It is quite true that some of the millionaires of America would have no objection to the establishment of a different order of things. But both in numbers and influence they are insignificant, as compared with the great mass even of the commercial and manufacturing communities, who are staunch democrats at heart. Much more are they so when we take the great agricultural body of America into account. Here, after all, is the stronghold of democracy on the continent. However it may be undermined in the town, its foundations are deeply and securely laid in the township. No one who has mingled much with the American farmers can entertain any serious doubts of the stability of democracy in America. Even were the entire commercial and manufacturing community otherwise disposed, they could make no impression against the strong, sturdy, democratic phalanx engaged in the cultivation of the soil. But the great bulk of the commercial and manufacturing classes are, as already intimated, as devoted to the republican system as any of the farmers can be. During the whole of my intercourse with the Americans, I never met with more than two persons who expressed a desire for a change. One was an old lady who had got a fright at an election, and the other was a young lieutenant in the army, who lisped, through his moustache, his preference for a military despotism to a republican government. It was very evident that he understood neither the one nor the other.

The following will serve to illustrate how deeply the republican sentiment has infused itself into the minds of all classes in America. On my return to Liverpool I visited Eaton Hall, near Chester, in company with some Americans who had been my fellow-voyagers. After inspecting the interior, we strolled along the magnificent grounds which enclose that noble pile. One of the company was a retired merchant of New York, who had amassed a large fortune, and occupied a fine mansion in the upper and fashionable part of Broadway. After waiting until he had seen all, I asked him what he thought of it. He replied that he would give me his opinion when we were in the streets of Chester. I understood his meaning, and asked him if he did not think that the same diversities of light and shade would soon be exhibited in his own country. He replied that it was possible, but that he would shed the last drop of his blood to prevent it, and impose it as a sacred obligation upon his children to do the same. This was not said in vulgar bravado, but in unaffected earnestness. But it may be said that this is but one example. True, it is but one example, but I can assure the reader that it illustrates a universal sentiment.

It may be considered a little singular, but if the love of democracy admits of degrees in America, the ladies cherish it to the greatest extent. Could there be a better guarantee for its continuance? . . .

Many of what some regard as the more inflated peculiarities of the American character may be attributed to the faith which Americans cherish in the destiny of their country. Whatever may be its future social and political influence, they have no doubt that, as regards territorial extension, it will yet embrace the continent. The issues which such a consummation involves are enough to make a people feel proud of their country. The realization of their hopes in this respect, they regard as a mere question of time. They feel that there is, in reality, no power on the continent that can ultimately resist them. . . .

The Americans are charged by some as being guilty of inconsistency in the fondness which they manifest for titles. But those who make this charge do so without reflection. The Americans are fond of titles, but that does not argue that they are inconsistent republicans. The fondness for titles which they display is but a manifestation of the fondness for distinction natural to the human mind. And what sane man ever inculcated the idea that republicanism was inconsistent with the love of distinction? Constitute society as you may, there must be posts of honor, power, influence, dignity, and emolument, to strive for. These exist in republics as well as under any other form of government. Are they not to be striven for without compromising one's political creed? And if the office is obtained, why not be called by its name? The Presidency of the republic is an office—he who obtains it is called the President. Does a man cease to be a republican because he aspires to both? Is it not rather a laudable ambition that prompts the aspiration? Or should he who obtains the office drop the title? As it is with the title of President, so it is with all other titles in America. A judgeship is a distinction. On him who obtains it, it confers the appellation of Judge. A governorship of a State is a distinction. He who is appointed to it is called the Governor. And so on through all the offices in the State, civil and military. There is this broad and essential difference, however, between titles as coveted in America and titles as existing in Europe. There the title pertains to a distinction acquired by the individual himself, for himself, and has always connected with it some office of trust or responsibility. Here we have similar titles, but we have others also which spring from the mere accident of birth, which are connected with no duties, and which do not necessarily indicate any merit on the part of those possessing them. The time was in England when Marquis, Earl, and Viscount indicated something more than mere arbitrary social rank. There are in America no titles analogous to these. There duties are inseparable from titles. So long as there are offices in the Republic to be filled, and so long as republicans may legitimately aspire to fill them, so long may they, without sacrificing their consistency, assume the titles of the offices to which they are appointed.

The love of money is regarded by many as a striking trait in the American character. I fear that this is a weakness to which humanity must universally plead guilty. But it is quite true that it is an absorbing passion with the Americans. This cannot be denied, but it may be explained. America is a country in which fortunes have yet to be made. Wealth gives great distinction, and wealth is, more or less, within the grasp of all. Hence the universal scramble. All cannot be made wealthy, but all have a chance of securing a prize. This stimulates to the race, and hence the eagerness of the competition. In this country, however, the lottery is long since over, and with few exceptions the great prizes are already drawn. To the great bulk of the people wealth is utterly unattainable. All they can hope for is competency, and numbers fall short even of that. Men soon flag in a hopeless pursuit. Hence it is that, in this country, the scramble is neither so fierce nor universal.

The American people discover an extraordinary talent for invention. The Patent-office in Washington is a most creditable monument to their inventive powers. They are also quick in the adoption of an improvement, no matter from what source it proceeds.

They are excessively fond of being well dressed. The artisans amongst them are particularly so, not so much from personal vanity, as from the fact that they make dress a test of respectability. Almost every man who is not an emigrant wears superfine broad-cloth in America, if we except the hard-working farmer, who generally attires himself in home-spun. You seldom meet with a fustian jacket, except on an emigrant's back, in an American town.

This leads me, in concluding this chapter, briefly to glance at the physical condition of society in America. If the social structure in the Republic has no florid Corinthian capital rising into the clear air above, neither has it a pedestal in the mire beneath. If it is devoid of much of the ornamental, so is it also wanting in much of the painful and degrading. It may not be so picturesque as many of the social fabrics which have sprung from chivalry and feudalism, but it is neverthe-less compact, elegant, symmetrical, and commodious. It is to English society, what a modern house is to an Elizabethan mansion—it is not built so much to attract the eye as to ac-commodate the inmates.

The most important feature of American society, in con-nection with its physical condition, is that competence is the lot of all. No matter to what this is attributable, whether to the extent and resources of the country, or to the nature of its institutions, or both, such is the case, and one has not to be long in America to discover it. It is extremely seldom that the willing hand in America is in want of employment, whilst the hard-working man has not only a competency on which to live, but, if frugal, may soon save up sufficient to procure for himself in the West a position of still greater comfort and independence. There are paupers in America, but, fortunately, they are very few. They are generally con-fined to the large towns; nor need they subsist upon charity, if they had the energy to go into the rural districts and seek employment. This, however, is not applicable to the ma-jority of them, who are aged and infirm. It may be laid down as a general rule, without qualification, that none are deprived of competency in America except such as are negligent, idle, or grossly improvident. The general effect of this upon society has been already considered. Both in their social and political relations, all classes are thus able to act an independent part—an important consideration in connection with the peculiar polity of America.

This being the broad and wholesome basis on which society, so far as regards its physical condition, rests, the character of the superstructure may easily be inferred. Where all classes have a competency, no class demurs to the luxuries enjoyed by another. There is but little jealousy of wealth in America, for reasons already explained. It is but in extremely rare instances that gigantic accumulations have as yet been made. Nor are they likely to be speedily multiplied, the whole spirit of legislation being against them. There is no legislation against accumulations of personal property, for the very good reason that it would be difficult to prevent its distribution. It is sure to circulate through the community, so that all, by turns, can have the advantage of it. But the whole spirit of American legislation is decidedly averse to accumulations of landed property. Such the people conceive would be incompatible with the safety of their institutions. They have accordingly removed all restrictions upon its alienation, and land is now as marketable a commodity as the wheat that is raised upon it.

It is seldom indeed that you find a native American, or the descendant of an emigrant, occupying a lower position than that of an artisan. Those who are mere laborers are almost exclusively emigrants, and in nineteen cases out of twenty, Irish emigrants. Such as emigrate from England, Scotland, or Germany, are soon absorbed into the rural population, and become, by-and-by, proprietors of land themselves. But the Irish congregate in masses in the large towns, as they do here, to do the drudgery of the community. It is thus that, if a canal is being dug, or a railway constructed, you meet with bands of laborers almost entirely composed of Irishmen. Their descendants, however, become ambitious and thrifty, and form the best of citizens.

Enough has here been said to show that America is the country for the industrious and hard-working man.

Mackay, *The Western World, or Travels in the United States in 1846–47.*

SOCIAL LIFE AND
CUSTOMS OF THE
FRONTIER

OLE MUNCH RAEDER

MOST of the visitors who came to the United States during
the Middle Period were impelled by curiosity or by financial
considerations. Raeder, like Tocqueville, came on a government mission. One of the most distinguished of Norwegian
scholars and civil servants, Raeder had studied at the Universities of Christiania and Copenhagen, and in France and
Germany. In 1847 he was sent, by his government, to make
a study of the jury system in America. After his return to
his native land he published a three-volume work on the
jury system in the United States, Canada, and Britain which
served as the basis for legislative discussions and reforms for
years to come. While Raeder traveled over the whole of
the United States, he was particularly interested in the
Scandinavian communities of Wisconsin, and other parts of
the old Northwest, and his letters give us some of the liveliest pictures of life along the farmer's frontier that we have
in our literature. After a long career in politics and diplomacy, Raeder died in 1895, in the eightieth year of his life.

❖❖❖❖❖❖❖

DURING my sojourn in Wisconsin I had a pretty good opportunity to become acquainted with the state of affairs and to admire the earnestness and the intelligence with
which people strove to better their conditions. Very little

can be said about the customs of the people that will apply to all, because in a group so recently thrown together from all parts of the earth, there are not as yet any distinct group characteristics. Because in most places there is not a single grown man or woman native to the place or, indeed, to the territory; there is not, of course, a great deal of local attachment such as that which in Norway binds a person to one particular locality. Wisconsin has become their home simply because, after weighing the arguments pro and con, they have decided that they probably can get along better there than where they have been before. Many of them have moved a number of times, always farther west, and they will very likely do so again. There is nothing narrowly local about either their patriotism or their plans and enterprises. Their sentiments have been subjected to their reason and as a result have become clearer and broader; they have become helpful instead of harmful. All are Americans and their nationalism is constantly increasing as they become more conscious of a common history, with memories of common enterprises and common glory. This patriotism is more concentrated and therefore stronger than it would be if people also bestowed their affection upon some particular state or community as the best spot in the Union and the universe. It might seem as though the rather glowing accounts an American sometimes gives about his home community bear evidence of rather strong local feeling, but the main explanation is simply that those things which are close at hand have impressed him more than those which are more distant. It is not so much a sentimental liking for one spot as an evaluation of its natural resources, the progress that has been made there, and so on. Furthermore, it is to his interest to attract as many people as possible to his community, and all sorts of "puffs" have become, as it were, a part of Brother Jonathan's speculative business sense.

People living on the western frontier, many of whom have gone there to make up for failures or misplaced investments

in the East, quite generally give up for the time being those
pleasures and social observances which usually accompany
a higher civilization. Some of them take a liking for the
simple life which they have been obliged to adopt, and allow
their suspension of luxuries of every kind to continue "without day," but others introduce their accustomed refinements
as soon as they are able. In a number of homes at Madison,
Elkhorn, and Janesville, I found all the comforts and all the
elegance that we generally associate with the upper classes in
Europe. In some of these homes I even saw candle-snuffers
and handkerchiefs in use. People no longer sit around spit-
ting at the stove as is the fashion out here in the West; tobacco chewing is restricted if not altogether outlawed, and
cuspidors protect the floor and the carpets. What I have
said about the use of handkerchiefs must not be taken to
mean that such articles are an unknown commodity out
here, but only that they are used rather economically, after
the major operation has been performed with the fingers.
Women are not guilty of such a practice, but even the most
elegantly attired gentlemen are often very proficient at it.
As far as the absence of candle-snuffers is concerned, I must
admit that I first thought it was total and I was very agreeably surprised when I found one at Jefferson. One learns to
appreciate the value of such things after he has had to get
along without them for some time, as I had. Although the
specimen I found at Jefferson was in such shape that it took
two men to repair it, I could not help regarding it as one of
the masterpieces of modern civilization. Here along the Mississippi there are candle-snuffers, but their form bears evidence of the fact that their manufacture and use have long
been forgotten arts and have but recently been revived.

As a final evidence of the extent to which gentlemen of the
higher classes have been able to break away from the current
practices may be mentioned the fact that some of them no
longer polish their own shoes. Skill in this art, indeed, is generally regarded as one of the essentials of a true gentleman, as

was most natural in a country where one could not wear nicely polished shoes unless he did the polishing himself. But now, thanks largely to the stream of Norwegian and German immigrants, people are beginning to keep servants; and consequently this standard as to what constitutes a gentleman no longer applies, since its neglect no longer necessitates the wearing of disreputable shoes. So much progress has been made that on special occasions, such as the court sessions, when a large number of distinguished gentlemen are gathered, it often happens that some ambitious individual offers his services as bootblack and puts up announcements at public places, for the benefit of those who feel that they have not time to do the job themselves.

Generally speaking, I believe that Wisconsin has acquired more European flavor than most of the other districts in the West. This is due partly to the fact that the Norwegian, German, and Irish immigrants provide a class of servants more obedient and less exacting than the Yankees, but not servile and thoughtless as the Negroes. Furthermore, most of the Americans here have come from New England and New York, where the greatest culture and refinement is to be found. Among these people there is none of that coarseness which one meets so often in the southwestern states, in spite of the smooth, polished exterior; it finds abundant nourishment there in the slavery system, at all times and all places an abomination, despite all arguments to the contrary.

One of the finest features of life in Wisconsin is the general moderation in the use of strong drink. Although I spent over a month in the company of such men as one would generally expect to lead a somewhat merry life, and under circumstances that offered special temptations in this direction, I never saw anything that could have offended even the strictest temperance man. Wine was never served with meals or in the evening. At most a glass of beer in the evening was considered a luxury. On one occasion a young lawyer just admitted to the bar wanted to establish himself by a general treat, and he invited me and the others who were present to accompany him to the bar-room of his hotel. On the way I asked someone what happened on such occasions and was told that one could have his choice of all sorts of good things, in addition to cigars. I was looking forward to a real celebration, but alas! the only choice was between "brandy and water" and "whisky and water." That rather robbed the treat of its pleasure as far as I was concerned.

And what a difference there is between an American and an English court dinner! As far as the food itself is concerned, the difference is evident from the fact that the former costs about a Norwegian mark and the latter more than two specifer, not including the cost of wine. In England the party is made up of the counsellors alone, as the judges generally eat by themselves, and the attorneys as well as clerks and other officers of the court are excluded. Here in Wisconsin all without exception, jury, witnesses, defendants, and so on, gather about the dinner-table at the hotel while court is in session. The English counsellors eat their dinner in the evening, after the toil of the day is over, while the Americans take an hour and a half at noon, but they devote only a small part of it to gulping down their dinner. The Englishmen enjoy their dinner; the Americans just eat it. The Englishmen lay aside their professional dignity together with their gowns and wigs in order to drown their cares in champagne and burgundy with song and merriment. The Americans change neither their clothes nor their manners, drink their water in silence and consider how they are going to tackle the case that comes on at 1:30. In England, not only does the exclusive flavor that attaches itself to such a small, select group tend to give it a somewhat higher tone, but the knowledge of the strict code of honor that prevails among them, as well as their broad general culture and the outstanding abilities that have elevated them to positions of trust and honor—all these factors tend to purify the atmosphere about them, so to speak, and give a visitor the agreeable sensation of being in particularly good company.

Here, in this section of America especially, there are many of the lawyers who do not particularly command one's respect, either for their natural abilities or for their culture and training. When a lawyer in the East finds the competition too sharp for him he generally goes west. The same is true of many young men who hesitate to begin their careers too close to their home communities, where everyone knows them. I have spoken with some lawyers of this kind, who knew so little about European conditions even in their own special field that they thought the English common law was in force in Norway. One of them was greatly surprised when I told him that we not only had our own laws but our own government as well; he had the impression that we were subjects of Queen Victoria! The lawyers out here do have their merits, however. They certainly are kind and obliging to strangers. Furthermore, many of them play trumpets, trombones, flutes, or other musical instruments; these come together and organize bands which enliven things very considerably as the court visits the different towns. One of my good friends is an excellent piccolo player.

Raeder, *America in the Forties.*

12

AMERICAN NOTIONS
OF ARISTOCRACY

THOMAS COLLEY GRATTAN

THOMAS GRATTAN'S *Civilized America* (1859) has long enjoyed a somewhat unmerited distinction among English interpretations of America. For ten years the British consul at Boston, Grattan knew the United States rather better than most of those who wrote books about it, but his knowledge was pretty much limited to the East and to the upper classes. Though he sneered at the pretensions of the American "aristocracy," he himself was something of a pretender, both in society and in literature. Born in Dublin, in 1792, and trained to the law, Grattan preferred a career in society and letters. On his way to South America to participate in the wars of independence then raging, Grattan stopped off in France, married there, and settled down in Paris, where he met Thiers, Lamartine, and other literary figures like Washington Irving and Thomas Moore. He tried his hand at poetry, edited a literary review, published three volumes on the "Highways and Byways" of France, attached himself to the Prince of Orange, and wrote a history of the Netherlands, and eventually landed the consulship at Boston, in 1839. During the next decade he gathered material for his *Civilized America*, then handed his job over to his son and returned to London, where for the next fifteen years he wrote articles on the United States for the British journals. Where visitors like Mackay were impressed with the genuine democracy of America, and where others like Dickens were affronted by the leveling character of American society, Grattan chose to notice the yearning for aristocracy and class distinctions.

Among the many words misunderstood or misapplied throughout the United States, there is not one more frequently used, or in its application more thoroughly abused, than the word "aristocracy." It is one of those which are in common usage in England, with a distinct and specific meaning, but which, when they enter into American discourse, seem totally devoid of the sense an Englishman gives them. I cannot here attempt to enumerate all those which are applied so differently in the two countries, expressing qualities in individuals or in things. But I may mention, as an example, another word of the same genus as that now in question: that is, "gentlemanly," and it shares the same fate, of being, as I have elsewhere remarked, quite misunderstood on the American side of the Atlantic. This latter word is almost invariably employed there to designate the manners of hotel keepers, the persons serving at the bar of a public-house, the box-keeper at a theatre, conductors of railroad cars, or other individuals of that class, who have opportunities of being civil and accommodating to customers. The meaning which we attach to it, as implying well-bred or courtly demeanor, is quite unknown. Anyone possessing this engaging quality is distinguished in America by some other epithet, as "a fine man," "one of the upper crust," etc., while the newspapers teem with compliments to the "gentlemanly" mixers and vendors of mint juleps, gin slings, or snake-root bitters. The profuse repetitions of the word in this way naturally make an Englishman smile, merely because they are to him indicative of vulgarity.

To meet anything quite coming up to English notions of a finished gentleman is scarcely to be expected. The difficulty can be proved on a perfectly (popular) heraldic principle. Everyone knows that it takes three generations to make a gentleman. And as that implies three generations of liberal education and all the appliances of gentility, ergo, it is very rare, if to be found at all among Americans; for such a thing as grandfather, father, and son in one family preserving their fortune and station is almost unheard of. The fluctuations of property are sure to reduce one generation out of three to a low level; and thus it is that we see so many persons of respectable manners just bordering on good-breeding, and so few that are thoroughly well-bred.

This subject of American gentlemen is one of so much difficulty—I might say delicacy, in as far as the feelings of many are concerned—and it rises up in so many forms that I must revert to it in a desultory way, instead of having made it a topic to be treated under one distinct head, and standing, like any abstract question, by itself.

Laws, institutions, and principles are independent facts, established and, comparatively speaking, of fixed tenure in the country. They are things to be referred to as precedents, apart from the everyday pursuits of the population. But manners are mixed up with every movement of the social system. We are in unceasing contact with them, in every situation of life. Their varieties surround us; we meet them at every turn, and see them in ever-shifting aspects. It is, therefore, that we may be deceived by impressions strictly just in themselves, but which some new position may throw into totally opposing combinations, as a shake of the kaleidoscope changes its commingled atoms into forms directly different, though the materials are always the same.

Manners in the United States are of this nature. There is no standard for them from the want of a permanent class in society to be looked up to and imitated. As the whole of its ingredients are mixed and incongruous, almost each individual follows his natural bent; and we find in the same circles most striking contrasts of style, "everyone" being, as might be said, "his own gentleman." Persons are to be found in America of really good *ton*, even according to the European estimate, but they are infrequently met with in the business or political world. You must look for them on the banks of the Hudson, the Delaware, or the Ohio, in villas with the appurtenances of refinement; in the remote valleys of New

England; or on the plantations of the Southern States—and there surrounded by the repulsive associations of slavery, which neutralize the graces to whose culture they administer. All the men of that superior stamp, to mix with whom it was occasionally my good fortune, were (with rare exceptions) out of the whirl of politics, and what is called in the phraseology of the cities "high life." They do not come into contact with the pushing inelegancy of the mass from which the leading party-men and the highest functionaries, whether state or federal, are chosen. Many of the secluded gentry of whom I speak have been partly educated in Europe, or have extended their adult experience there long enough to appreciate the tastes and habits of the Old World; and they do not hesitate to choose between the obscure enjoyments of their country homes and the ambitious vulgarity of public life. It was most gratifying to join those delightful circles. But it was not in them that I was to find materials for a book on the general characteristics of civilized America. It was among the motley crowd of the millions that I had to make my way, and among whom my temporary lot was cast.

Admitting, then, that those millions have no available resource in which to find models of refined behavior, it is no blame to them if the system under which they live and thrive should be the foundation of a somewhat inelegant superstructure. It is, on the contrary, in my opinion, well adapted to their whole scheme of polity; and it is much to be lamented that they are not satisfied to conform to it. I might accumulate proofs, extracted from the public papers, of the generally ignoble notions they form of "high" and "fashionable" life, as well as the meaning they attach to the word "gentlemanly"; but I will confine myself to a few.

In the columns of a New York paper, I find the following obituary notice of a gentleman whom I had frequently met in that city and elsewhere, without being at all aware of his antecedents or pretensions:—

Mr. Hone has long occupied a prominent position in our social, commercial, and political circles. He was of humble origin, being the son of a baker. In early life, he entered into the mercantile profession in Maiden Lane, and afterwards engaged in the auction and commission business in Pearl Street, always standing at the head of the auctioneers. In the fashionable world Mr. Hone always held a high rank, being always considered a leader of the *ton*. Indeed, it has been said that if an order of nobility had existed in this country, Mr. Hone would have claimed the right of being numbered in their ranks. His bearing, though courteous toward his fellow-citizens, was aristocratic and self-confident; and when any of the foreign nobility visited our shores they received his hospitality, while he was personally but little known to the mechanics and other middle classes of American society.

This fluent and clever auctioneer might possibly have had the patrician contempt for the class he sprang from which is here ascribed to him; and he was perhaps a Coriolanus in pride, though not in bearing; but the thing to remark in relation to him is that he is here held up as a model aristocrat and a ready-made nobleman.

Flying to a higher altitude, that of the White House itself, and without reverting to its past distinguished occupants, the *Baltimore Sun,* of the month of August, 1858, gives the following anecdote of the present incumbent, Mr. James Buchanan. It has nothing to do with his political position. It is given merely as an illustration of manners among the highest politicians and statesmen of the United States, whose habits are, no doubt, formed from those of early youth, the boy being, more particularly in such matters, the father of the man. The Presidents have not been uniformly models of good breeding or good taste. Readers may remember the mention of Sir Augustus Foster, of Mr. Jefferson having told him rather exultingly that "he was in the habit of washing his feet

every morning," implying that it was an unusual thing even
with persons of his station. I myself can truly record that on
being presented to another occupant of the White House,
he, previously to shaking hands and giving me welcome, took
a quid of tobacco from his mouth, and threw it behind one
of the gilded and satin-covered sofas; and a good deal of
notoriety was about the same time given to the fact of the
same gentleman having, not merely "roomed" with, but
actually slept with a member of the Federal Senate, who
proved himself to have been a very "strange bedfellow" indeed. With these homely examples before him, Mr. Buchanan
may be fairly cited as another, in the following free and easy
sketch, which I give in its entirety:—

Familiar as our people are generally with the unostenta-
tious habits of the chief officers of our government, one
cannot witness them, with the knowledge of the pomp and
show of royalty to invite the contrast, without involuntarily indulging it. On Saturday last President Buchanan
arrived at the Relay House, or Washington Junction, as it
is more properly called, en route for Washington city.
There was a rumor abroad that he was to arrive, and the
visitors had consequently grouped about the house when
the train came along. We soon perceived the President
coming from the cars to the platform, looking heartily, but
thoroughly travel-soiled, smiling and cheerful. By his side,
and evidently offering with gentlemanly deference the
courtesy of attention, was a rather rough-looking individual, whom we took for a conductor or brakesman.
The gentleman will excuse our blundering in such a matter; but, upon inquiry, we were informed he was Sir William Gore Ouseley. On passing into the bar-room the
President threw off his coat and his white neckcloth, care-
lessly pitching them over a chair, opened his shirt-collar,
and tucked up his sleeves for a wash, conveniences for
this purpose being in the apartment. At the time, however,
both basins were occupied by two young men, neither of
whom seemed to be aware that the President was about.

He waited patiently some time when some one spoke and invited him upstairs. He declined, however, quietly remarking that he would wait for his turn. And as soon as the basins were vacated he "took his turn" in a jolly good wash in the public bar-room. This done, he seemed rather perplexed about the arrangement of his neckcloth, and seemed likely to tie his nose and mouth up in it. Somebody just then offered assistance, and the President was briefly equipped. At about this time, a person who had come into the room sang out pretty near to him, "Look here, I thought the old Pres. was to be here to-day—" The speech was cut short by a nudge, while a momentary comical expression passed across the face of that same "old Pres." A cigar was handed to him by a friend; he took a good satisfying drink of—not "old rye," which he is said to affect, when prime—but ice-water, had barely fired up his cigar, when the bell rang, and "all aboard" summoned the chief magistrate of the United States to his seat in the cars, and away they went to Washington. We took our admiration of this scene of republican simplicity quietly with us into the cars for Baltimore, and mused with some complacency over the sterling honor of being an American citizen.

I record these small matters to show that I have good reasons for saying that American ideas about gentleman-like manners and habits are different from ours. No one more despises instances of over-fastidious coxcombry. All who, like me, have seen a good deal of the rough work of life in various countries, have often been reduced to far greater straits than that which the President of the United States here voluntarily chose for himself. In his case it was matter of taste, not necessity, and he had a perfect right to indulge it. But the striking moral of the story is contained in the concluding words of the foregoing article. Here we find the editor of an American newspaper of well-established credit, and to a certain degree (like all persons of his profession) a censor, or at least a critic of manners as well as morals, glorifying himself for "the sterling honor of being an American citizen," not from pride in the greatness of his country or the virtue of its people; not from the contemplation of any deed of heroism, piety, or benevolence, on the part of a compatriot; but simply because President Buchanan, in preference to decently performing his ablutions in a private room, chose to take "a jolly good wash" in a public bar, out of a basin recently used, and in all probability imperfectly rinsed.

Can any American of any grade, who knows anything of English habits, complain after this so recent instance, of my saying that their general notions of gentlemanly bearing are different from ours? I was glad to find on reading the anecdote that there was no intimation of Sir William Ouseley, our special Minister to Central America, having followed the President's example (much as his appearance seemed to require it) in making use of the other utensil in a similar manner; though it might have increased his popularity, and given him some advantage in conducting his negotiations. . . .

But, however we may smile at the way in which gentlemen, servants, lords, merchants, bankers, inn-keepers, and grocers are jumbled together in the American nomenclature, the misapplication of the important word which furnishes the heading for this chapter must excite most unpleasant feelings in all who observe the source from which the fondness for it springs. . . .

But the yearnings in the United States for the vague aristocracy thus dreamt of is not unnatural, nor inconsistent with republican ideas. Almost all the great writers of antiquity, expressing no doubt the prevalent feeling of their times, were more inclined to aristocracy than democracy; and even Harrington, in (comparatively speaking) our own days, says, that "If any man founded a commonwealth, he was first a gentleman," which, he adds, that Oliver Cromwell was; showing, at any rate, his own fitness (or unfitness) for judging what constitutes a gentleman according to a high standard.

No family, as far as I can learn, has yet taken root in the public heart of America. No descendants of the heroes or sages of the Revolution, of the various Presidents, or other leading men are now looked up to in honor of their name; nor are the sons or brothers of living nobilities considered as entitled, as a matter of course, to a preference for official station, or treated with any peculiar distinction. There is rather a prejudice against such nominations and such indications, and they are rarely heard of. A needy adventurer, in power himself, may now and then venture to give a post to one of his family, but his doing so rather tells against both the patron and the nominee.

It must be, on the other hand, remarked, that the children of a disreputable parent do not suffer in the public estimation from that cause. It is no bar to a man's preferment that his father was unworthy. This would seem to argue a generous forbearance in the public mind; but I regret to say I cannot trace it to that cause. I am rather inclined to attribute it to an indifference to disrepute, parallel to the evident want of appreciation of virtue. The natural repugnance to dishonor, any more than the instinctive veneration for respectability, which leads European minds to give credit for the merits, as well as to visit the sins of the fathers on the children, are no part of the good or the evil of American character. They seem to me essentially results of the spirit of feudalism; and they must, therefore, be co-existent with aristocratic tendencies. I am not, in stating these particulars, giving either blame or praise to the strong anti-aristocratic leaning which prevails, even in the minds of those who are very glad to consider themselves "American aristocrats." They are, in fact, altogether unaware that the pride of birth is the fundamental basis of an aristocracy; and if they hope to establish such an institution, at however remote an epoch, they must begin by encouraging feelings of liberal respect for the inheritor of an honorable name, and proving them by according him more consideration than they show for the tradesmen whose wealth places them in the front ranks of their "first men."

Large landed possessions, with a train of dependent serfs or tenants, another absolute element of stability in the formation of an aristocracy, exist not at all in the northern or eastern portions of the United States; and are, in the west, coupled with certain drawbacks of inelegance in the possessors, that neutralize this effect. The rough work of forest-clearing, or prairie-planting, brings all those western men to a level, which their particular number of acres does not at all affect. The coarse-clad settler who oversees his workmen differs little in the eyes of the latter from themselves. And the squatter who claims a patch of land considers himself as well worthy of regard as the purchaser of a district. Aristocratical institutions are altogether incompatible with such a state of feeling in the majority of the community, and the mere ambition of a few wealthy individuals, who wish to consider themselves better than their fellows, is the only approach that can be found to the much envied gradation of rank which that minority longs for. . . .

And where—north, east, west, or south—may we look for that proud peculiarity of aristocracy, the large encouragement given to literature, art, and science? What individual in the whole Union fosters talent for its own sake, and is prodigal of his money in the purchase of its chefs-d'oeuvre? A wealthy banker or broker may order his portrait or his bust, but which of them subscribes for a great national picture, or sends a promising artist at their expense to Rome, or pays a liberal price for a group of statuary? If those persons exist, I know them not; and if individual exceptions to the general ignorance of art, and niggard indifference to artists, are to be here and there found, most assuredly they would not, if united in any one American city, be enough to form a class.

Wanting everything that really constitutes an aristocracy, how absurd is the application of the epithet to any portion of the citizens of America! Such an institution is essentially permanent, privileged, and powerful. No individual portion of the American institutions possesses per se permanency, privilege, or power. Their force and their stability exist only in union. Not one of the component parts of their constitution taken singly could stand alone for a day. An oligarchy might be claimed as their birthright by a clique, with just as much justice as an "aristocracy," founded merely on purse-right, can be asserted to exist in any country on earth. Let the citizens of the United States mark it specially in their vocabulary, as being a term that cannot bear any possible application to themselves. And, for the happiness of the masses which are spreading so fast over the immense Republic, let it be hoped that the thing which the word really designates may never be transplanted thither from Europe, where it is indigenous and congenial. . . .

The error most manifest at both sides of the Atlantic with respect to America is that of viewing its institutions in comparison with those of England. None of the hasty travelers from the Old World seem capable of looking at the New in an aspect of separate existence. They seem to consider both as parts of the same system, political and social. This would be all very well if they bent their thoughts to the examination of mere character, for human nature everywhere presents certain characteristics in common. But although the same kind of human beings are to be found in the Old and New World, the systems which they have formed for themselves, and which in their turn tend to fix, if not actually to form, their characters, are totally different. Yet the American seems at times as much at fault as the European in this respect. If the latter sees in American civilization only its discrepancies compared with that which he left at the other side of the ocean, the former too often considers it as susceptible of the same regulations, while in fact it is utterly distinct, and as opposite as it is distinct. A totally different order of things is produced from two separate stocks having many resemblances, but not more than varieties of fruits or flowers of a different species, agreeing in certain generic elements with those on which they are artificially grafted.

Europeans who would rightly judge the working of things in America should look at it as though they had never seen Europe, and Americans should manage their country as though Europeans never could come to look at it. Invidious comparisons on the one hand, and a servile emulation on the other, are the consequences of an impracticable standard being set up. But, erroneous as this general method of judging undoubtedly is, it is more pardonable in the man born and bred in European habits of thought and feeling than in him who knows nothing of those habits but from reading or hearsay, and who ought to be superior to a paltry imitation. The great mass of the American people are, no doubt, free from the reproach I would convey to still a large minority, and one unluckily formed of individuals filling the foremost ranks among the intellect and influence of the country. That the leading classes in social position, as well as the chief leaders in political life, are infected deeply with this disease of European tendencies is a truism established and admitted. Very lamentable is it that it should be so; for, by setting up a model they can so poorly imitate, and measuring themselves by a standard disproportioned to their growth, they make the most awkward mistakes, and cut the most outré figure. This argues a great want of independence, and it proves the scarcity of original minds in the wealthier orders throughout the country.

Were a well-established national self-reliance felt among the leading men in the United States, there would be none of the melancholy parodies of "High Life," none of the yearnings after aristocratical distinctions, which are now so flagrant. Men would then strike out some new plan of social organization, and act up to it, even though it clashed with the scheme of polity in force elsewhere. However defective that plan might be, it would be, if it were only consistent with existing institutions, better for the country than the best of any other country which was adopted at second hand, and forced into a system with which it had no fitness. . . .

There are two facts to which the wealthier portion of the wealthy class of America seems to be blind. First, that there exists a high order of civilization and even "fashion" (their darling word) easier of adoption than the fastidious elegance of English high life; and that this is to be found in the manners and habits of the upper circles in France, Germany, and the other countries of Europe. Secondly, that even if it were possible to establish an aristocracy in America, it would be incompatible with the existence of the Republic. Exotic plants can grow only in a hot-house. A lord could not live long without a congenial atmosphere. And to enable an order of nobility to exist, there must be not only an ambient air of popular homage, but a vivifying source of light and heat above, to draw up the dews, that come down again in fertilizing showers of dignity and honor.

If some of the American aspirants for aristocratic station would strip this metaphor into plain sense, and ponder over the truth it is meant to illustrate, their yearnings might be modified into simple regret. Admitting their hopes to be impossibilities, they might in time become satisfied that what is must be. And viewing the state of things in England, rather as warnings than examples, be content to enjoy in their own country a system of equalized well-being that has no parallel on earth.

Grattan, *Civilized America*.

13

THE BRITISH AND AMERICAN
CHARACTERS COMPARED

FRANCIS AND THERESA PULSZKY

IN 1852 Louis Kossuth, hero of the Hungarian struggle for independence, came to America, and in his entourage were the Pulszkys. Kossuth, as leader of Hungarian liberals and dictator of Hungary, had fought an heroic and, on the whole, successful war against Austria, but the intervention of Russia forced his abdication and drove him into exile. In 1851 he was liberated from his confinement in Asia Minor, and on an American man-of-war made his way to England. After an ovation there, he turned to America, and his visit was the occasion for an outpouring of enthusiasm and chauvinism. Of his companions little is known, except that Francis Pulszky later wrote an autobiography which told the story of the war for independence. What interested the Pulszkys most in the United States was the relation of the white, black, and red races to each other, but their observations on this question are less interesting to us than their comparison of English and American civilizations.

THE Americans, unlike their English brothers, take care of the education of all the white children of the free States, and endeavor to do the same in the South, and not only in the cities, but also in the rural districts. The American government in the States and in Washington does not rest on the exclusive influence of the wealthier classes, but on the education of the people at large. Contrary to English custom, it is the State, not the Church, which provides for the schools; yet secular education has not impaired the religiosity of the people.

As the English, the Americans are chiefly a commercial people; dollars and cents influence them in the same way as pounds, shillings and pence influence the English. Wealth, and not the enjoyment of wealth, is, in the old and new country, the principal aim of the life of the many. But with the English there is a class less intent on making money, and sometimes generous in spending, viz., the old aristocracy, which has inherited the accumulated riches of many generations. In America there is no such class; to favor the eldest son is not countenanced either by laws or by customs of the people; equal partition amongst the children is the law and the habit of the country. Wealth, therefore, changes hands rapidly. And yet the great bulk of Americans, though covetous of gain, are, on the whole, more generous than the English. To those who doubt this fact we point to the enormous amount of the numerous and continuous gifts and contributions for churches, hospitals, colleges, libraries, and charitable institutions of every description. The lower classes in America are better educated than in England; they are better off, and kind-heartedness and generosity are always characteristic with those who earn their livelihood by their labors and not by their capital. Moreover, the democratic institutions of universal suffrage and the frequent elections make the wealthy classes dependent on the working people for attaining honors; with universal suffrage individual liberty is impossible; one way, therefore, to get popularity is the establishment of institutions for the public.

The Englishman is proud; he does not care whether he is liked or disliked by other nations, satisfied that he must be respected. The social world for him does not extend beyond his island, and he keeps aloof from foreigners. Clinging to his own manners and customs, and mode of thinking, he is exclusive and conservative. His self-confidence is too great to be disturbed in any way; he therefore does not care for ridicule; he laughs heartily when his follies are caricatured, he never fears that foreigners could influence his turn of mind, and he allows therefore, without restraint, all the exiles of Europe, however he may detest their principles, to live upon their own means and exertions on English soil. He occasionally gives them alms, but seldom stretches out his hand to put them in the way of helping themselves; few only take the trouble of sparing time and thought to a foreigner, in the country where the pressure of applicants for every sort of employment is so strong. Whatever may be the talent or distinction of the alien, he never can be wholly naturalized in the society of England. The higher classes are disposed to regard him with kindness and interest, though never with the feeling of full equality; but the working classes dislike the immigrant, as a rival on the field of competition. Even the law naturalizes him but partially; he can become a voter or a municipal officer, but neither a judge nor a representative. Yet that which the habits of the most refined society do not concede to rank, talent and distinction, and what the law of the first country of Europe does not grant, *equality*, can be got by wealth acquired in the manufacturing and commercial line. The foreign-born wealthy banker, manufacturer and merchant, is considered the equal of the English banker, manufacturer and merchant; they require one another.

In the United States all this is different. The American has not the pride of exclusiveness. Well aware that he is the son of a young and growing country, his ambition is to see it radiant with the concentrated glory of the whole world. For him, every accession of power is welcome, from wheresoever it comes. The immigrant is, therefore, no stranger to him; he does not feel his rivalry; it is a fellow-workman for American greatness. From the moment of landing, the foreign-born is, in every respect, socially the equal of the native. After a short residence, the law opens to the new citizen every career of honor, and withholds but one post from him, that of President of the United States. The manners and customs of the United States give life to the law, and in the Senate at Washington we see Irish, French and Germans, sent by the confidence of the native citizens to the highest council of the nation. The adopted son of the country shares all the rights and advantages of the son of America. But the same ambition which renders the American so liberal toward the newcomers, makes the intercourse with him often unpleasant to the European. Many of the citizens of the United States really believe that they have already attained the perfection at which they aim; they, in consequence, are boasting and bragging, and mention the greatness of their country, and the superiority of their institutions, so often and on such petty occasions, that they become ludicrous, and convey the impression as if it were vanity and not ambition which ruled them. They are touchy in the highest degree; they can bear earnest reproach, but never ridicule; and in this respect it is worthy to be remarked that all over the Union there is not one single satirical paper, like the English *Punch* or the French *Charivari*. Their political caricatures are few, circulated almost exclusively amongst the higher society in the large commercial cities. Wit and criticism are not the endowments of a young people; they flourish only in old communities when the creative genius begins to decline, when knowledge has accumulated and taste has become fastidious.

The eloquence of the two countries bears the same stamp of their age. In the palace of Westminster the palm of oratory is given to those who make clear and logical statements, in which cool reason analyzes concisely the facts of the case, its causes and consequences. The next effort is to unveil the errors of the opponent, and to cover him with ridicule. Wit, irony, and sometimes invective are the most usual weapons employed in Parliamentary struggle. Appeals to the feelings or to the passions are rare; adorned eloquence is not congenial to the English taste of the present age, which is evi-

dently that of criticism. Gradual reform of abuses is its
watch-word; constructiveness, genius, and freshness of mind
seem to have passed away from the English statesmen. They
are men of *routine*, and they snub and put down men of new
ideas. Therefore, whenever new institutions are to be introduced, either because the old ones are too rotten in their
foundations to be mended—as in Ireland; or because new
communities have grown up with new wants—as in the
Colonies; parliamentary wisdom is always blundering, in
spite of its omnipotence.

America, on the contrary, is a young country; reform cannot yet be the principal object of her policy, because abuses
have not yet had time to grow. The gigantic expansion of
the country; the growth of new Commonwealths under the
most different circumstances; the complications with foreign
governments, unavoidable in an enterprising Democratic
community; the antagonism of the white, red, and black races
within the territory of the Union; and the difference of interests among the commercial, agricultural, planting, and
mining States, give an immense field to the creative genius,
and call it forth from amidst all classes of the young and
vigorous nation. American eloquence bears, therefore, a
peculiar stamp. Even the coolest reasoner often appeals to
the passions; the Northern Free Soiler hurls his defiance
against the written law, and points to the law of God; the
Southern slaveholder thunders forth the threat of secession;
the States of the Mississippi Basin accuse the sea-coast States
—the Old Thirteen—for their exclusive commercial policy,
which leaves the resources of the West undeveloped; and the
facility with which a community like that of the Mormons
has increased and nearly grown into a sovereign State, would
appal every nervous statesman. Vital interests are at stake in
the Capitol at Washington, and great occasions engender
great men; they never lack the opportunity for displaying
their talents. But the crowd of their numerous imitators,
anxious to rival them, sink into the bottomless sea of verbiage

and false pathos; unable to grapple with the difficulties, they describe them with exaggerating grandiloquence, and hide with flowers of oratory the shallowness of their ideas.

The English nation is eminently conservative. It has attained the highest position to which it has aspired; it has now only to maintain it, in politics and in literature. New ideas, and even new words, are disliked in England; society is settled, and fears to be disturbed; the most necessary reforms are carried slowly, and with timorous hands. In America, the spirit of progress is bold, and often encroaching; with the exception of the Southern society, it changes its aspect incessantly; new ideas easily get a fair chance of being practically tried; the public at large does not shrink from testing at once different solutions of a political problem, and the sovereignty of the States affords great opportunity for it. New words are coined by the dozen; the old oak of the Anglo-Norman language still sprouts here as sprightly as it did in England three centuries ago, and though many of the leaves will soon wither and fall, others will remain as verdant as those which adorn the cisatlantic branches of the mighty stem.

The English nation has controlled its fighting propensities by its financial prudence—though in India, China, or Kaffraria they plunge sometimes into war, yet it is always unpopular. Nothing short of an actual attack could induce England to go to war against any first-rate European power, though the army and navy is considerable, and the expenditure for it more than considerable.

The Americans give vent to their fighting propensities; no large national debt deters them from war; their army is small, not exceeding 11,000 men, the officers included; just as many as are required for the defense of Texas, New Mexico, California and Oregon against the Indians. Yet the nation is warlike; in case of emergency hundreds of thousands of volunteers are ready to encounter the perils of a campaign. War is popular with the great bulk of the nation.

In England the people is divided into classes, almost into castes. Political equality is unknown there, and though the younger sons of the aristocracy often descend to the grade of professional men, yet the hierarchy of rank and classes is never disturbed by these changes. Every individual divests himself of his former caste by entering the higher one. The traditional reverence for social rank and station without regard to the individual who holds them has become one of the principal features of English life. Equality is the lifeblood of American society. Every attempt of the Whigs to establish a social aristocracy of birth and wealth has always failed. Society is not divided into classes, but only into coteries. The family of the wealthy naturally associate with their equals in wealth, the poor with the poor; yet the political dependency of the rich on the working men makes all exclusiveness impossible.

The steadiness of English society, a necessary consequence of aristocratic institutions and habits, makes the English generally reserved and not easily excitable. The same cause gives stability to their views and inclinations. They are slow to promise, but you can depend upon them, they generally keep their word. It is difficult to get an English friend, but he remains a friend for life. The American character is more amiable, though often less reliable. The Americans are cordial, frank, anxious to oblige, and ready to make friends. In the fulness of their heart, they generally promise more than they can keep. Easily excited, they are not seldom deceived by their impressions, which, therefore, are often only transient.

The English bear the stamp of the ancient Doric tribe, the Americans that of the Ionian.

The danger of England is principally her pedantry and her materialism, which threaten to stifle the higher sentiments of morality and patriotism. She has become demoralized by her own conquests to such a degree that she does not know how to appreciate political right and wrong, except by the gross standard of energetic administration. . . .

The Americans are in a similar danger by their vanity. The watch-word, "Our country, our State, right or wrong," this baneful word, borrowed from the French, has been carried across the Atlantic, and threatens to confuse their notions of right and wrong. The fabric of their institutions was founded on the rock of religious principles and self-denial; the patriotic devotion of their revolutionary fathers, and the unselfishness of Washington has raised it to commanding grandeur. Let the Americans beware, lest obstinate ambition and misunderstood patriotism, which disregard moral right and wrong at home and abroad, undermine the foundations of the noble temple of their liberties. May both nations remember that the buyers and sellers and money-changers belonged to the market, and were driven from the temple.

Francis and Theresa Pulszky, *White, Red, Black.*

14

OVER DIVERSITY
THERE BROODS A
HIGHER UNITY

PHILIP SCHAFF

PHILIP SCHAFF, like Lieber, belongs to the New World
rather than the Old, but the interpretation of the United
States which he wrote in 1855, and from which this chapter
is taken, was addressed originally to a German audience and
represents what was still an immigrant's point of view. Born
in 1819 in the Swiss canton of Grisons, Schaff studied at
Tübingen, then the greatest center of theological studies on
the continent, and later at Halle and Berlin. In 1844 he was
called to a professorship at the German theological seminary
at Mercersberg, Pennsylvania, and thereafter attached himself permanently to America. Editor of the first German
theological magazine in the country, Schaff was a leader in
the movement to Americanize the German church. In 1870
he was appointed Professor at the Union Theological Seminary in New York, and subsequently became President of
that famous institution. During a long career devoted to
scholarship he wrote widely on theology and church history; his most valuable work was a seven volume *History
of the Christian Church* which commanded international
fame.

❖❖❖❖❖❖❖

THE United States present a wonderful mixture of all
nations under heaven. . . . Not only the nationalities
of the Old World, however, but even the national peculiarities of condition, manners and habits, obsolete in their na-

tive lands, there perpetuate themselves to this day in many instances with remarkable tenacity. In Virginia you meet the English gentleman of the age of Elizabeth and the later Stuarts; in Philadelphia, the Quaker of the days of George Fox and William Penn; in East Pennsylvania, the Palatine and the Swabian of the beginning of the last century; in New England, the Puritan of the times of Cromwell and Baxter; on the banks of the Hudson and in New Jersey, the genuine Hollander; on the shores of the Northern lakes hundreds of Scotch, so that a traveler from the country of Burns "at the Kirk on Sabbath would hardly ken he were frae hame"; in South Carolina, the Huguenot and French nobleman of the seventeenth century, or at least very striking traces of their character, which in Europe are even far more obliterated. This fact, itself, shows how cautiously one must receive the accounts of so many European tourists, which take some single element by itself, and make it the standard for the whole; thus producing the most contradictory representations.

But now, what is most remarkable is that over this confused diversity there broods after all a higher unity, and that in this chaos of peoples the traces of a specifically American national character may be discerned. Those who find in the United States only the faint echo of European nationalities, and so feel obliged to deny that country an independent future in history, are very much mistaken. Whoever treads the soil of the New World with open eyes perceives at once a thoroughly fresh and energetic national life, which instantly takes up and assimilates all foreign elements, excepting only the African and the Chinese. The American's digestive power is really astonishing. How many thousands and millions of Europeans has his stomach already received! And yet he has only grown firmer and healthier thereby.

The basis of the American nationality is undoubtedly English, though unquestionably a peculiar modification of it, possessing much greater capacity than the original for receiving and working up foreign material. To gain a clear conception of the Anglo-Saxon race one must travel to England, Scotland, and North America. If he sees the Englishman only abroad, he meets him in the most unfavorable circumstances. . . . The like is true, though not so strikingly, of the American. But what seems their weakness abroad— seems, I say, for with all their stiffness and strangeness one cannot help respecting and admiring them on other accounts —that very thing is their strength at home. The Anglo-Saxon and American, of all modern races, possess the strongest national character and the one best fitted for universal dominion, and that, too, not a dominion of despotism but one which makes its subjects free citizens. For they are at once liberal and conservative. In them—and this is the secret of their national greatness and importance—the impulse toward freedom and the sense of law and order are inseparably united, and both rest on a moral basis. Conscience and the sense of duty are very strongly marked in them, and I doubt whether the moral influence of Christianity and of Protestantism has more deeply and widely affected any nation than it has the Anglo-Saxon. . . .

The American has the same organizing talent, the same self-control, the same practical energy, the same business faculty, as the Englishmen. His spirit of enterprise is still stronger, and not rarely degenerates even into foolhardiness and the most reckless disregard of human life, fearfully manifest in the countless conflagrations in cities, and disasters on steamboats and railroads.

The American, I grant, has less solidity than the much older Englishman. But he makes up for this in vivacity, elasticity, and capacity for improvement. The Englishman, too, is shut up on his island; the American moves on a great continent and between two oceans. The former has not yet been able to assimilate to itself the Celtic Irishman in his immediate neighborhood, nor thoroughly to redress his grievances;

the latter at once infuses into the immigrant the common feeling of the American.

But though the main features of the American national character may be already quite plainly discerned, and reveal themselves as predominantly Anglo-Saxon; yet it is only in its formative state; and the more it develops, the more sensibly do the un-English elements, favored by the increasing emigration from the continental countries of Europe, modify the whole. In New York the Hollanders—the first settlers—in Louisiana the French, can never be wholly obliterated. Least of all, the Germans, who, with their descendants, must already number four millions and upwards. Even now, the Middle and Western States, in which most of the Germans have settled, differ very perceptibly in character, from New England and the Southern States. As they lie between the two geographically, so they hold a middle place also in a natural and social point of view. . . .

Many of the larger cities even, as New Haven and Cleveland, are charmingly arranged, almost every house having an inclosed green in front, planted with trees and flowers, so that the streets present the delightful aspect of a garden promenade. The smaller towns are, in general, much handsomer, the streets wider and straighter, the houses more inviting and convenient, than in Europe. And in the principal cities, New York, Philadelphia, Boston, Baltimore, Washington, Cincinnati, New Orleans, all European luxury is making only too rapid and perilous progress. Had not New York so many churches and Christian societies, and so strictly kept Sundays, it might already be called a second Paris, which it will soon be also in point of population.

In the lead of this luxury stand sometimes the most disgusting forms of mushroom aristocracy, which rests upon nothing but the dust of gold. These American fops and quack aristocrats, who, void of all true nobility, have no sense for anything but outward show are not rarely met, to

our shame, in European capitals and watering places, striving
to outdo the polite world in vanity and folly. . . . It is
characteristic that the two largest and most princely mansions in New York and Philadelphia were built by quacks
out of the proceeds of their sarsaparilla. Whether the enormous increase of luxury and worldly pomp and splendor
will gradually undermine the Republic, whose proper foundation is the patriarchal style of simplicity and honesty, time
must tell. At any rate the flourishing commerce and growing
wealth of the country involves great danger of a bottomless
materialism and worldliness; and I see in Christianity alone
the powerful corrective, which has thus far saved the higher
intellectual and moral interests, and which will secure to
them in future the predominance over the "almighty dollar."
It is a remarkable fact, however, that wealth hardly ever
continues to the third generation in the States, and that all
this artificial aristocracy soon runs out. The middle classes
are there, more than in any other country, the proper bone
and sinew of society and always restore the equilibrium.

Social life in America is in some respects freer, in others
stiffer, than in Europe. Much, that is not at all offensive
there, is rudeness to the European; and the American, in
turn, is greatly scandalized with things which in the Old
World are innocent customs. It were unjust and pedantic to
make such mere externals the standard of judgment respecting the people. The old proverb here holds true: So
many countries, so many customs. . . . There is more of a
kind of medium cultivation than in Europe, where accomplishment is aristocratic, or confined to certain classes. The
United States is the country for average intelligence, average
morality, and average piety. Republican institutions, as may
even be observed to some extent in Switzerland, tend to level
away social distinctions. In America, while there are not so
many towering heights of culture, there is, on the other hand,
no such widespread and degrading ignorance as in the masses
of Europe. There almost everyone tries to become a gentle-

man or a lady; that is, to attain the English ideal of outward and inward intellectual and moral culture, so far as his circumstances and position allow. Almost every man has some routine, at least outwardly; he can represent something; he reads gazettes and newspapers; knows how to talk sensibly about the general affairs of his country; and can, if necessary, make a speech, and generally turn his knowledge to good practical account. . . .

Domestic life in the United States may be described as, on an average, well regulated and happy. The number of illegitimate births is perhaps proportionally less than in any other country. Divorces are very rare, and are made by the laws far more difficult than, for example, in Prussia. This is the good effect of the laws of old England, which has practically made divorce almost impossible. . . . True, the American family life is not characterized by so much deep good-nature and warm, overflowing heartiness, as the German. But instead of this the element of mutual respect predominates. Husband and wife, parents and children, stand more independently toward one another, in a respectful dignity, and thus avoid many collisions. When the partners speak of each other in the third person, it is not commonly by the familiar names: my husband, my wife, but by the family name, with Mr. or Mrs. prefixed, or by the official title. In fact, even in direct address the wife not unfrequently gives her husband his title of Doctor, Professor, and so forth, particularly in company.

The American's profound respect for the female sex is well known. This old Germanic trait, celebrated so early as by Tacitus, has most fully developed itself in the Anglo-Saxon race under the influence of Christianity, and is very favorable to domestic and public morality. Whoever is acquainted with family life in England, knows how high and dignified a position woman holds there, and how much is comprehended in the term *lady*. America goes yet a step further. It is sometimes called a woman's paradise. . . . In the United States, woman is exempt from all hard labor (except perhaps among the immigrants, who keep their foreign customs, and in new settlements, say in Texas, or Wisconsin, or Oregon, where circumstances demand the strength of all hands); that she can travel unattended from one end of the vast country to another without being molested in the least; that in the steamboats, the great hotels, and public places, she finds her own saloons, sometimes extremely elegant, and all possible conveniences, and has the precedence in every company. It is characteristic also that in America one must address a mixed audience, not as "Gentlemen and Ladies," as in all other languages, but in the reverse order, as "Ladies and Gentlemen."

Schaff, *America*, A Sketch of the Political, Social, and Religious Character of the United States.

15

THE PRACTICAL GENIUS
OF THE AMERICAN

ADAM G. DE GUROWSKI

EVERY student of the American Civil War knows the venomous Gurowski *Diary*, but few are acquainted with the earlier and far more interesting study of the American character from which this selection is taken—*America and Europe* (1857). Count Gurowski—as he was always known—was born in the Palatinate of Kalisz in 1805, and before his twentieth year had been expelled from school for revolutionary activity. He studied for a time in Germany, but shortly returned to Poland to help organize the revolution of 1830 against Russian tyranny. On the failure of that uprising he fled to Paris, joined the National Polish Committee there, and had the gratification of being condemned to death *in absentia*. Thereafter his career was, for a short time, a checkered one. He wrote on Polish history, studied at Berlin and Heidelberg, lectured at the University of Berne, and in 1849 made his way to the United States. During the Civil War he served as translator in the State Department, and from this dubious vantage point watched what he considered the mismanagement of the war with malign dissatisfaction. But if Gurowski appears at his worst in his *Diary*, he appears at his best in his sober, judicious, and on the whole appreciative analysis of the distinguishing features of the American character in his *America and Europe*.

THE AMERICAN MIND

THE American mind tends pre-eminently toward the objective, at times however being given to the subjective, even to abstract speculation. It is singularly impulsive and receptive, seizes eagerly upon the most antagonistic objects, and embraces them with considerable elasticity. Expansive, and at times daring, it is less disciplined and subdued by routine, than is the case with the English mind. Hitherto the American mind has not reached the elevated standpoint of an absolute, intuitive individuality. Stimulated by the fulness and vigor of intuitiveness, but open to the breathing influences of outward nature, to the ever freshly pouring combinations of events, the mind ascends slowly, step by step, into the expanding region of normal self-consciousness. It is inquisitive, analytic, dismembering, and still eager often to discover, to comprehend a general law, to accept general formulas and axioms, and to submit to them. It grapples willingly with difficulties, but is not however always enduring or patient enough to overcome and subdue them, above all when the difficulties are founded in merely abstract, speculative combinations. Evoked to self-conscious activity, the American mind was thrown at the start into a stern and rough medium, and cut off from the motherland; it was obliged to direct all its intensity to struggles with nature, with destructive matter, was forced to choose and decide swiftly, to act, and not to remain in musing contemplation.

Immediate practical results are more attractive for the American mind, although not exclusively, than the charms of imagination. In its intellectual, positive turn, it yields easily to the pressure of outward events and combinations. Intellect finds more food, more stimulus, in externalities, and therefore it overpowers the spirit, the imagination, as well as the tendency to abstract, interior contemplation. Of great mobility, expansive but not deep, the American mind as yet seems unable to seize thoroughly and penetrate deeply into the infinity of intuitive ideas, engrossed as it has hitherto been by sensations. The social condition, the primitive state of nature, opening uninterruptedly her wider and wider circles before the American, challenge and attract the intellectual powers, carry away the activity into one general, explorative, mechanical, commercial current. But then even a certain inborn elasticity redeems and saves it from utter degradation. And so, notwithstanding this seemingly all-absorbing commercial propensity, the mind of the people at large does not become eaten up or narrowed, as is the case, for example, with the immense majority of the various commercial classes in Europe. The so-called petty shopkeeper spirit does not prevail in America to the same extent as in most of the European parent countries.

Excitability, omnipotent in the American character, scarcely affects the activity of mind. The keen internal perception of the object strongly resists excitability or nervousness, and dispels the mist that has been aroused. If the Americans do not resist but yield to the current of excitement, it is more from want of independence than from want of a sound, internal, mental judgment. Comparatively rapid and comprehensive in assimilation and combination—far more so than the English—the American mind seems to be indifferent to method; at the same time, by a striking contrast, the intellect is disciplined by it in most of its mechanical dealings with the realm of matter. Though not absolutely rigorous in its operations, the American mind is earnest, giving fixity and ballast, and forming a counterpoise to the often febrile unrest of character.

The various peculiarities of the American mind, the outbursts of its originality and independence, are manifested more generally and freely in the people at large, in its promptings and impulses, than in those which are commonly considered as the representative minds, the literary stars, or any other exponents of the spiritual or imaginative faculties. Among the people likewise, as for example among that of

New England, that of the West, gushes out and is domestic in the rich vein of humor, which constitutes a trait of originality, distinct from the English humor, and from that of other European nations.

Taken in the whole, in its substance, the American mind is eminently a progressive one. If it is as yet comparatively deficient in absolute philosophical comprehensiveness, if it assiduously elaborates the special and the single, by this process it gathers and prepares materials, to become coordinated, then fused together. The eternal spirit which watches over the progress and the development of mankind alternately evokes to prominent activity the various powers and attributes of the mind, bringing them into full play, and making them preponderate, the one over another, according to the given conditions and necessities. Observing in mankind the march of mental culture, there is clearly perceptible an alternated but uninterrupted putting out and holding back of the various mental powers, the intuitive and the intellectual playing into each other. This assimilation and fusion at the given moment of the life of individuals, as of a whole people, constitute a complete real progress and civilization. Almost every mental and intellectual phenomenon corresponds to a philosophical and social claim of our being, and solutions are obtained by their harmonious interweaving. Then again new problems arise, requiring new combinations and fresh efforts. Exclusive idealism and exclusive positivism, bear the mark of one-sidedness and uniformity, and are not virtually progressive. A wheel can stand still, can turn backwards, but its normal function is to move onward, and carry onward all its composing atoms. So it is with the mind; it embraces subject and object and moves on, because movement and progress are the sole conditions of life and of development; they alone are creative.

The powers of the intellect have been exclusively put into requisition and taxed from the first signs of vitality made by American society. As a people, as a nation, the Americans have not traversed the same successive stages as other peoples and nations. It can be said that America has had no childhood, no juvenility. She was not lulled at the cradle with the legend, with the mythic song, with the murmur of tales. The Americans matured at once, and at once wrestled with stern reality.

CHARACTERISTICS

Political and social institutions often give an indelible mark to the character of a people, and as often again they are its reflection. History is full of the evidences of this fact. In America the character of the people and the institutions have acted reciprocally on their development: a case of very rare occurrence in the history of nations and of their political and social evolutions. No nation, no people now existing, is so thoroughly and intensely identified with its institutions as is the American people.

With sacred jealousy the American people watches over the national honor, over its relations with other States, over national independence. Being in possession of the highest goods, no sacrifice can be too great for their defense and preservation. No invasion from whatever quarter, no conquest, no overthrow of the existing order, could ever be successfully carried out. Not the presumed Anglo-Saxon blood, but the genuine American feeling, pouring out from constitutive principles as from a fountainhead, is the repelling force. Patriotic, exalted devotion is not an effort, but a natural lineament of character, a simple but inherent element of national life.

The love of social independence, of domestic liberty, and their fullest enjoyment, produces in the American character that unbending quality which disables the individual from becoming a permanent denizen of other powers, of other States. There may be a few rare exceptions. It is almost impossible to imagine an American becoming a servant of kings, subservient forever to social caste. Soon his better nature must revolt; but numbers of Europeans, from all social orders and positions, assimilate themselves easily and in a short time to the state of things prevailing here; they become identified with it to the core. To an Americanized, and therefore a reinvigorated European, a return to the past worn-out conditions of existence would prove unbearable. . . .

Not less salient and peculiar than the public spirit, and created by the same or similar causes, is the characteristic of the American mind manifested in the thirst for knowledge, for information. It imperatively urges the individual with a pertinacity and generality not to be met with in any other nation on the globe, to satisfy this noble mental irritation, to satisfy it by sacrifices of the time and means, whether large or small, at his disposal. It is thus the most brilliantly projecting feature, and an individual property of this people. Not the wealthy, not the better circumstanced are principally the expression of these urgings, but it is rather special to the laborious masses. Not outward worldly leisure produces or evokes it, but an inward impulse. That is one of the cardinal differences between American and European populations. This craving results from the radical recognition of equality of rights in every individual, inspiring him with self-consciousness, with self-respect, and opening before him the bright horizon of nobler purposes and aims. It is not a transmission by blood, nor the result of certain liberal concessions, called in Europe liberal institutions. In the English people, the nearest kindred to the majority of Americans, and living under liberal institutions, this spontaneity is not awakened, and the mass still gropes its way in a self-contented ignorance.

Neither is this craving incited by an admonition, exercised from above, by the efforts of a government, by the prevalent suggestions or example of a so-called superior stratum of society. This American phenomenon strengthens the faith that the human race is to bask in floods of light, that enlightenment is the essence of man's nature, although its effusion may have been benumbed for uncounted ages. This characteristic trait redeems at once the broadest and most truly democratic comprehension of a people from the cavils heaped on it by the apostles of an absolute supreme authority, which, according to their assertions, is to hover providentially above the masses, to take the initiative and to direct their mental development.

Extremes seemingly prevail in the American character. It is a combination of violent, nervous, feverish excitement and sturdy quietude, of calculation and daring, of cautiousness and swiftness in decision and action, of steadiness of purpose and recklessness in pursuits. It is stubborn and mobile, impressible and cold, cunning and straightforward. Often inflated with immense pride and self-conceit, now soundly appreciating one's powers, and then humbly underrating them.

Excitement is one of the most powerful springs in the American. It is so contagious that newcomers, after a comparatively short residence, are affected and carried away by it. Easily excited, the American cheerfully, nay, enthusiastically, greets the object which for the moment satisfies this necessity of his temper; and no efforts of his own invention are spared to endow this object for the moment with all imaginary attributes. Neither age nor sex is exempted from this intoxicating pleasure. He pays willingly and with the best grace for the moment of satisfaction, and raises the idol to the skies. But when the excitement is over, he lets it slide, unceremoniously, or often drops it roughly, careless where it may fall, to run the next moment after another. . . .

Many and various are the causes accounting for and explaining this peculiarity. The nervous irritability lying at the bottom, most probably is produced by the influences of a trying and changeable climate. This turn given to the character at an early epoch has become now hereditary. The uniformity of the ancient colonial life, the rigidity of the

Puritans and of their imitators, might have contributed to form it. Human imaginative nature revolts against uniformity, compression, against turning in one and the same circle. Single-track routine in life is repugnant, and any object or event is welcome which breaks such tiresome evenness. After contraction follows relaxation in some manner or other. So the imagination eagerly and indiscriminately seizes upon any provender with which to appease its cravings.

Even now, although new and more diversified elements are mingled in American life, a certain sameness still pervades it. The circle extends, the horizon enlarges, and nevertheless monotony dominates the whole. It becomes the more painfully sensible, as the multifariousness of the world from without, and the longings from within, excite, attract, and tickle the Americans. What therefore seems to offer a momentary interruption of monotony excites and carries away and often overpowers the better and cooler judgment. . . .

The great reproach made by Europeans to the Americans, and one which has become proverbial among themselves, is the excessive love of money, the fact that they are a money-making people. Undoubtedly money-making has eaten itself deep into the American character, but the love of money, although considered a moral disease by all the moralists of antiquity and of our times, has been and is now the most deeply rooted passion in human nature. Under one or another shape, in this or that manner, money has ruled the world at all times. Neither is the love of it less violent, less intense among the immense majority of Europeans than among the Americans. If among the latter money-making seems to form the main object of existence, it is the effect of various causes, intrinsic and normal, and explained as such by their history, by the concatenation of peculiar events and circumstances, which have surrounded them from the cradle.

Money and commerce were the only ties between the colonists and the mother or any other country. The colonies of modern Europe have been exclusively mercantile enterprises. Mercantile speculation sent out the first settlers, and even the Puritans looked to trade as the sole means of maintenance and of preserving the imperatively necessary intercourse with the old world. Mercantile relations therefore formed the pivot on which turned the existence of the colonists and of the colonies. Thrown upon their own scanty resources, the colonists could only obtain for money or money's worth, all the necessaries of life, the implements and requisites whose possession alone could preserve them from destruction when they first exhibited themselves on this soil. All this was to be paid for, in some way or other. Thus almost before the first immigrant took a firm root in the soil, money-making became the absorbing object of his activity, as upon money depended his domestic, his family, and his social existence. His entire social position and significance depended upon his commercial means. The colonist, his toilsome labors and sweat, must have been the object of greedy speculation in the mother country. Everything therefore powerfully urged and contributed to develop in him from the start the money-making propensity, and to make it paramount to all others. It was his defensive weapon and his salvation. So from infancy everything stimulated, nourished and developed this passion.

Since the Americans elevated themselves to the dignity of a nation, the character of the American community is even more industrial and commercial than it was of old. Their growth, their increase, their prosperity, are indissolubly connected with the extension of their mercantile or industrial operations. Thus money-making becomes more intense and all-absorbing, as the love of money is more inherent in commercial occupations than in any other, and in America every occupation runs out into a commercial one.

Only a prosperous nation can be considered as truly civilized, as enabled and prepared to enjoy democracy and self-government. The prosperity of such a nation consists in the prosperity of the whole population. It is the duty of every individual to devote all his faculties to securing this blessing to himself, and in this way to the community. Money-making, in its true sense, is the reward of intelligence, labor, and toil; it was and is the road to individual and to general prosperity. It is an inborn and noble pride to be the artisan of one's own position and independence. It is one of the noblest manifestations of the consciousness of human dignity. The possession of wealth has always been among the most powerful incentives to action; money-making by industry, enterprise, speculation is the only legitimate and honorable way to reach the goal. And of such a nature is money-making, which engrosses an immense majority of the Americans. It continually extends the area of culture. It conquers the rugged face of nature, transforms the wilderness into a habitable and cultivated soil. It is this which pushes the American to cross torrents, cut his path across primitive forests, disembowel the earth, people solitudes. He tries to make money out of the rough forces of nature. The sons of farmers, artisans, operatives, as soon as their faculties are developed, look forward to the means of securing their independence, of making money. They leave home, plunge into distant regions, and into hardships, privations and toils. They try to discount, to turn them into money, that is, into their own well-being and prosperity, and that of their families. Money-making has given the unparalleled expansion to American industry and commerce, covered the ocean with American bottoms, the land with prosperous cities, with nets of railroads, with mills and factories. In proportion as prosperity increases and expands, general civilization increases and expands. The genuine Yankee, that is, the man of the East and his kindred in other States, is considered the most sharp in this feverish pursuit. But they have the best and most numerous public schools and scientific establishments, buy the most books, and subscribe most generously for all public establishments and objects, as well as for alleviating private miseries and sufferings. True it is that this all-absorbing fever has likewise its morbid results. But when the good and the evil are summed up, good comes out victorious. . . .

The sneer at Americans for their money-making propensity does not become Europeans. As mentioned above, to this propensity the country owes the major part of its greatness. What is done by governments and sovereigns in Europe is done here either by private individuals or by communities rendered prosperous by their own exertions. European society had its origin in the absorption by one class of the labor of another, and this still continues to prevail. The European social organization contains various social parasitical existences, not less greedy to acquire and make money; only the greediness is overlaid by certain conventional definitions and encrusted prejudices. If the European aristocracy, if the world of leisure, the official world do not make money themselves, in the same way as the Americans, these European classes make money by oppressing millions, and living upon their labor, or upon the taxes. European society has various social inherited distinctions, to which it pays due, or oftener undue deference. American society, from the start a commercial one, very naturally paid and pays deference to the successful money-makers. . . .

With all the numerous and dark drawbacks of this propensity, it does not generate avarice in the Americans. If generally they are infuriated in the pursuit of money, they spend it as freely as they make it. If they are called men of the dollar, at any rate they are not hunters of cents. Parsimonious economy is not their characteristic, and in general the racing after dollars, the thirst for gain, does not make them contemptible misers, or callous to others. The celebrated axiom, "Help yourself," signifies that everyone ought to make his choice independently, and build up his position by personal exertions; but it is far from including any egotism, any cold indifference to his neighbor, to the efforts of anyone undertaking a difficult path in life. Americans are generally the most cautious persons in the world, in giving free advice, in going direct to the point. They shun the responsibility of deciding for another, of disillusioning him, or of interfering with a contrary advice or opinion. Thus when asked a question, they mostly answer in generalties. But if the choice is once made, the pursuit or object selected, then they stand by with counsel and action. The settler in a new and strange land, is heartily supported in his toils by his neighbors. A foreigner or native, starting in any honest undertaking finds support and credit, this mainspring and soul of a commercial society, and nowhere so largely and liberally conceived, or carried to such an extent, as in America. . . .

As almost every body is obliged to run the gauntlet, one that stops even for respite, is soon overwhelmed. The whirlwind seizes and carries them away. Money-making becomes an unquenchable thirst, an object of love, an attraction similar to that which art or study exercises over the artist or the scholar. It is a power and a distinction. Then money is made not merely for the sake of becoming independent and rich, of enjoying both, but from habit—on account of finding any other congenial occupation impossible. It becomes an intellectual drilling, and a test of skill. It becomes a game, deeply combined, complicated—a struggle with men and events, exciting, captivating, terrible, hand to hand, man to man, cunning to cunning. The socially passionate life in Europe, diversified, and full of various enjoyments, gives to a successful winner, new scopes, attractions and pleasures, such as society does not proffer, allow or create in this country. An American can with difficulty if at all turn in another direction, plunge in another passion, or activity, seek around for new and different drastic or soothing pastimes, to quench this ardor which for the greatest part of his life has been concentrated in money-making, and has been urging and directing his course. Thus where the European can stop or divert his attention to other objects, an American once in the middle of the torrent must go on, spurred by habits, by the force of events; as even to preserve an accumulated fortune becomes in itself another race, another almost deadly strife. Such is the exclusive money-maker, but he is not the type of the general character; he has no hold on the people at large, his dens are in large cities.

No nation is equally sensitive and impatient of criticism as the Americans. They often become irritated not only by the finding fault with their character, customs, manners, habits, institutions, or culture, but find it disagreeable when climate, soil, fauna, or flora is judged inferior to those of the old world. Various causes provoke this sensitiveness, and it can be accounted for in various ways. It results from both pride and diffidence. The Americans are well aware of their deficiencies, but they feel the sting of injustice done to them by those foreigners who obtrude themselves as unrelenting judges. Generally the faults are overrated, and the people are lashed by scorching and undeserved ridicule. The American, the last comer into the family of nations, is continually on the alert—not to be treated or considered as a parvenu, not to be slighted or disparaged. Youth is generally susceptible and irritable before it enters manhood. The more so, when occasional shortcomings are maliciously pointed out, when the intrinsic good is almost overlooked. The taunts of English travelers and writers, of the English press, have principally provoked this irritation, and made it nearly chronic. Such authors, taking a superficial glance at the country and at its inhabitants, have misunderstood, misrepresented what they saw. Without investigating the cause of certain effects, by which their genuine or assumed fastidiousness was offended, they deliberately calumniated by wholesale, for faults committed by some. The European standard, when forcibly applied here, must necessarily wound and be faulty, the two states of sociability differing wholly from each other.

Boasting is often carried by certain Americans to the extreme. Often however it is a reaction against slights, an

effort to veil deficiencies, an effort made by a people aware
of them, but on the other hand conscious of having accomplished in two or three generations what it took other nations
centuries to perform. Generally, human nature revolts at
taunts, at arrogant reproof, at undervaluation. Experience
and time alone teach a becoming equanimity. European nations bear scoffing more patiently because they have thrown
it occasionally for centuries at each other's head. Like old
war horses accustomed to the roar of battles, they remain
cool and self-possessed. There is on the American surface
much to be rubbed off and rounded. Rude angles are to be
softened, ease, flexibility instilled. Time must do the work.
Refinement is a fruit slowly ripened by ages. And in America
the whole people, not a class, is the tree on which the fruit
is to be borne. In the people at large reposes soft mold below
the apparently coarse crust, and in due time, the plastic virtue
of nature will cast it into congenial and sociable forms.

Gurowski, *America and Europe*.

16

YOUR CONSTITUTION IS ALL SAIL AND NO ANCHOR

THOMAS BABINGTON MACAULAY

STRICTLY speaking these famous letters of Lord Macaulay, predicting a dark future for American democracy, do not belong in this collection, for Macaulay neither visited the United States nor undertook, at any time, a systematic interpretation of American character or institutions. But this is one of those occasions when we may, perhaps, invoke Emerson's warnings against a "foolish consistency," for whatever the circumstances of their composition the letters are—as their frequent republication suggests—of permanent interest. The occasion for the letters was the presentation to Macaulay by Henry S. Randall of his great three-volume biography of Jefferson: characteristically Macaulay used Jefferson as a point of departure for strictures on the danger of Jeffersonian democracy. Macaulay himself needs no introduction. He was, when he penned these letters, at the height of his fame—and not far from death. He had already served brilliantly in Parliament, gone to India as member of the Supreme Council, published his *Lays of Ancient Rome*, his incomparable *Essays,* and four volumes of that *History* which was to enjoy a wider and more lasting fame than any other historical work in the English language, and had been elevated to the peerage as Baron Macaulay of Rothley. In politics, as in his history, Macaulay was an ardent Whig, but his liberalism was of the Manchester variety and did not predispose him to look favorably on the American experiment in democracy. "I wish I were as cocksure of any one thing as Macaulay is of everything," Lord Melbourne is reported to have said, and the observation applies to these letters on the future of democracy in America as it does to the *Essays* and the *History of England*. It is interesting that though these letters were included in an appendix to the original American edition of Trevelyan's life of Macaulay, they were omitted from all subsequent editions.

◇◇◇◇◇◇

HOLLY LODGE, KENSINGTON,
January 18, 1857.

SIR,—I beg you to accept my thanks for your letter inclosing the autograph of Washington, which reached me three weeks ago, and for the *History of the State of New York*, which I received the day before yesterday.

I shall look forward with curiosity to the appearance of your *Life of Jefferson*. I can not say that he is one of my heroes; but it is very probable that you may convince me that I have formed an erroneous estimate of his character.

I am a little surprised to learn from you that Americans generally consider him as a foil to Washington, as the Arimanes of the republic contending against the Oromasdes. There can, I apprehend, be no doubt that your institutions have, during the whole of the nineteenth century, been constantly becoming more Jeffersonian and less Washingtonian. It is surely strange that, while this process has been going on, Washington should have been exalted into a god, and Jefferson degraded into a demon.

If there were any chance of my living to write the history of your Revolution, I should eagerly and gratefully accept your kind offer of assistance. But I now look to the accession of the house of Hanover as my extreme goal. With repeated thanks, I have the honor to be, Sir, your faithful servant,

T. B. MACAULAY.

H. S. RANDALL, Esq., etc., etc., etc.

HOLLY LODGE, KENSINGTON,
LONDON, *May* 23, 1857.

DEAR SIR,—The four volumes of the *Colonial History of New York* reached me safely. I assure you that I shall value them highly. They contain much to interest an English as well as an American reader. Pray accept my thanks, and convey them to the Regents of the University.

You are surprised to learn that I have not a high opinion of Mr. Jefferson, and I am surprised at your surprise. I am certain that I never wrote a line, and that I never, in Parliament, in conversation, or even on the hustings—a place where it is the fashion to court the populace—uttered a word indicating an opinion that the supreme authority in a state ought to be intrusted to the majority of citizens told by the head; in other words, to the poorest and most ignorant part of society. I have long been convinced that institutions purely democratic must, sooner or later, destroy liberty or civilization, or both. In Europe, where the population is dense, the effect of such institutions would be almost instantaneous. What happened lately in France is an example. In 1848 a pure democracy was established there. During a short time there was reason to expect a general spoliation, a national bankruptcy, a new partition of the soil, a maximum of prices, a ruinous load of taxation laid on the rich for the purpose of supporting the poor in idleness. Such a system would, in twenty years, have made France as poor and barbarous as the France of the Carlovingians. Happily the danger was averted; and now there is a despotism, a silent tribune, an enslaved press. Liberty is gone, but civilization has been saved. I have not the smallest doubt that, if we had a purely democratic government here, the effect would be the same. Either the poor would plunder the rich, and civilization would perish, or order and prosperity would be saved by a strong military government, and liberty would perish. You may think that your country enjoys an exemption from these evils. I will frankly own to you that I am of a very different opinion. Your fate I believe to be certain, though it is deferred by a physical cause. As long as you have a boundless extent of fertile and unoccupied land, your laboring population will be far more at ease than the laboring population of the Old World, and, while that is the case, the Jefferson politics may continue to exist without causing any fatal calamity. But the time will come when New England will be as thickly peopled as old England. Wages will be as low, and will fluctuate as much with you as with us. You will have your Manchesters and Birminghams, and in those Manchesters and Birminghams hundreds of thousands of artisans will assuredly be sometimes out of work. Then your institutions will be fairly brought to the test. Distress every where makes the laborer mutinous and discontented, and inclines him to listen with eagerness to agitators who tell him that it is a monstrous iniquity that one man should have a million while another can not get a full meal. In bad years there is plenty of grumbling here, and sometimes a little rioting. But it matters little. For here the sufferers are not the rulers. The supreme power is in the hands of a class, numerous indeed, but select; of an educated class; of a class which is, and knows itself to be, deeply interested in the security of property and the maintenance of order. Accordingly, the malcontents are firmly yet gently restrained. The bad time is got over without robbing the wealthy to relieve the indigent. The springs of national prosperity soon begin to flow again: work is plentiful, wages rise, and all is tranquillity and cheerfulness. I have seen England pass three or four times through such critical seasons as I have described. Through such seasons the United States will have to pass in the course of the next century, if not of this. How will you pass through them? I heartily wish you a good deliverance. But my reason and my wishes are at war, and I can not help foreboding the worst. It is quite plain that your government will never be able to restrain a distressed and discontented

majority. For with you the majority is the government, and
has the rich, who are always a minority, absolutely at its
mercy. The day will come when in the State of New York
a multitude of people, none of whom has had more than half
a breakfast, or expects to have more than half a dinner, will
choose a Legislature. Is it possible to doubt what sort of a
Legislature will be chosen? On one side is a statesman preach-
ing patience, respect for vested rights, strict observance of
public faith. On the other is a demagogue ranting about the
tyranny of capitalists and usurers, and asking why any body
should be permitted to drink Champagne and to ride in a
carriage while thousands of honest folks are in want of necessaries. Which of the two candidates is likely to be preferred
by a working-man who hears his children cry for more
bread? I seriously apprehend that you will, in some such
season of adversity as I have described, do things which will
prevent prosperity from returning; that you will act like
people who should in a year of scarcity devour all the seed-
corn, and thus make the next a year not of scarcity, but of
absolute famine. There will be, I fear, spoliation. The spoliation will increase the distress. The distress will produce fresh
spoliation. There is nothing to stop you. <u>Your Constitution
is all sail and no anchor</u>. As I said before, when a society has
entered on this downward progress, either civilization or
liberty must perish. Either some Cæsar or Napoleon will
seize the reins of government with a strong hand, or your
republic will be as fearfully plundered and laid waste by
barbarians in the twentieth century as the Roman Empire
was in the fifth, with this difference, that the Huns and
Vandals who ravaged the Roman Empire came from without, and that your Huns and Vandals will have been engendered within your own country by your own institutions.

Thinking thus, of course I can not reckon Jefferson among
the benefactors of mankind. I readily admit that his intentions were good and his abilities considerable. Odious stories
have been circulated about his private life; but I do not know

on what evidence those stories rest, and I think it probable that they are false or monstrously exaggerated. I have no doubt that I shall derive both pleasure and information from your account of him.

I have the honor to be, dear Sir, your faithful servant,

T. B. MACAULAY.

H. S. RANDALL, Esq., etc., etc., etc.

HOLLY LODGE, KENSINGTON,
October 9, 1858.

SIR,—I beg you to accept my thanks for your volumes, which have just reached me, and which, as far as I can judge from the first hasty inspection, will prove both interesting and instructive.

Your book was preceded by a letter, for which I have also to thank you. In that letter you expressed, without the smallest discourtesy, a very decided dissent from some opinions which I have long held firmly, but which I should never have obtruded on you except at your own earnest request, and which I have no wish to defend against your objections. If you can derive any comfort as to the future destinies of your country from your conviction that a benevolent Creator will never suffer more human beings to be born than can live in plenty, it is a comfort of which I should be sorry to deprive you. By the same process of reasoning one may arrive at many very agreeable conclusions, such as that there is no cholera, no malaria, no yellow fever, no Negro slavery, in the world. Unfortunately for me, perhaps, I learned from Lord Bacon a method of investigating truth diametrically opposite to that which you appear to follow. I am perfectly aware of the immense progress which your country has made and is making in population and wealth. I know that the laborer with you has large wages, abundant food, and the means of giving some education to his children. But I see no reason for attributing these things to the policy of Jefferson. I see no reason to believe that your progress would have been less rapid, that your laboring people would have been worse fed or clothed or taught, if your government had been conducted on the principles of Washington and Hamilton. Nay, you will, I am sure, acknowledge that the progress which you are now making is only a continuation of the progress which you have been making ever since the middle of the seventeenth century, and that the blessings which you now enjoy were enjoyed by your forefathers who were loyal subjects of the kings of England. The contrast between the laborer of New York and the laborer of Europe is not stronger now than it was when New York was governed by noblemen and gentlemen commissioned under the English great seal. And there are at this moment dependencies of the English crown in which all the phenomena which you attribute to purely democratical institutions may be seen in the highest perfection. The colony of Victoria, in Australia, was planted only twenty years ago. The population is now, I suppose, near a million. The revenue is enormous, near five millions sterling, and raised without any murmuring. The wages of labor are higher than they are even with you. Immense sums are expended on education. And this is a province governed by the delegate of a hereditary sovereign. It therefore seems to me quite clear that the facts which you cite to prove the excellence of purely democratic institutions ought to be ascribed not to those institutions, but to causes which operated in America long before your Declaration of Independence, and which are still operating in many parts of the British Empire. You will perceive, therefore, that I do not propose, as you thought, to sacrifice the interests of the present generation to those of remote generations. It would, indeed, be absurd in a nation to part with institutions to which it is indebted for immense present prosperity from an apprehension that, after the lapse of a century, those institutions may be found to produce mischief. But I do not admit that the prosperity which your country enjoys arises from those parts of your polity which may be called, in an especial

178 THOMAS BABINGTON MACAULAY

manner, Jeffersonian. Those parts of your polity already produce bad effects, and will, unless I am greatly mistaken, produce fatal effects if they shall last till North America has two hundred inhabitants to the square mile.

With repeated thanks for your present, I have the honor to be, Sir, your faithful servant, MACAULAY.

17

GOD MADE AMERICA FOR THE POOR

EDWARD DICEY

FEW of the numerous Europeans who visited America during the Civil War were able to look at that conflict objectively, or to see it as a test of the American character. Edward Dicey, brother of the more famous Albert V. Dicey, was one of these few. Born in Leicestershire of a county family, and educated at Trinity College, Cambridge, he might have been forgiven had he adopted the typical upperclass British view of the American war. But his sympathies were not with the Confederacy. He came to the United States in 1862 and spent six months traveling through the length and breadth of the Union, visiting Lincoln at the White House, watching recruiting on Boston Common, seeing the soldiers in their encampments and on the march. His *Six Months in the Federal States* (1863), one of the few British reports which could be welcomed with pleasure by the people of the embattled North, was all the more welcome for its contrast with "Bull Run" Russell's acrimonious reports. After his return to England, Dicey divided his time between journalism, law, and literature. He was for almost twenty years editor of the London *Observer;* he was a bencher of Gray's Inn; and he wrote widely on American, Egyptian, and South African questions.

TO A STRANGER, there is something wonderfully pleasant about the first blush of American Society: the manners of your hosts appear to an Englishman so frank and cordial;

people seem so glad to see you, and so anxious to make you feel at home. And I believe that the appearance is not assumed. Life, hitherto, has flowed very easily for the American people. The country is so large that there is room for all and to spare: the battle of life is not an arduous one, compared to what it is in older countries. The morbid dread of poverty, which is the curse of English middle-class existence, is almost unknown in the New World. If the worst comes to the worst, and an American is ruined, the world lies open to him, and in a new State he can start afresh, with as fair prospects as when he set out in life. The desire to provide for one's children, and to secure them a similar position in life to that which the parent occupies himself, is almost unknown. Public opinion does not require the father of a family to do more than give his children a good education. As a rule, the daughters can always marry, and the sons can make their own way. Equal division of property amongst the children of a family is enforced by custom, though not by law. In the New England States, it has become very common for any wealthy citizen to leave a considerable sum toward some public object; and anyone who fails to comply with this custom is hardly considered to have acted correctly. The result of this state of things is that saving is very uncommon amongst the middle classes in America. Everybody, as a rule, spends the full amount of his income, and, in consequence, there is much greater luxury in Northern households than would be seen in English families of the same amount of wealth. Hospitality, therefore, is given very readily, and the wheels of life run more easily than they do with us. I was struck constantly with the extreme good-nature of the Americans in their private and social relations. I attribute it, not so much to the national character —which, owing to the climate, is a somewhat irritable one, but to the comparative absence of the sordid cares and petty considerations which the fierceness of our struggle for existence, and the exorbitant value attached by us to the respectability of wealth, give rise to perpetually in a densely peopled country like our own.

Paradoxical as the statement may seem, I think I have never known a country where money was less valued than in America. "The worship of the almighty dollar," which we are so apt to consider a characteristic of the Americans, cannot justly be charged to them in the sense in which we understand the phrase. The absence of all social distinctions, and the fact that there are no established positions to which birth and rank and station give an acknowledged entrance, render wealth the chief standard of distinction. In consequence, the natural ambition of every American is to acquire wealth, and thus distinguish himself in the only career which is practically open to the vast majority. Anybody who has known anything of Quakers will understand the working of the causes that I have attempted to describe. There is no body of men more liberal than the Society of Friends, and yet there is none more eager in the pursuit of money-making. So it is with the Yankee race. Money-making is the chief object of the nation; but they value the possession of the "almighty dollar" rather as a proof of success in life than as an end of existence. The mere ownership of wealth is less valued there than with us. The man who has made his own money is infinitely more respected than the man who has inherited it. Millionaires are rare in the second generation; and the bare accumulation of wealth gives a man fewer advantages in the North than in any Old World country.

I doubt, too, whether the accusation of extravagance, which is brought so frequently against the Northerners, is a just one. Money is spent freely, just as it is made; but, with the exception of New York, I was never in any American city where the style of living could compare for extravagance with that of the wealthy classes in the Old World. Americans in Europe are not, in this respect, fair specimens of their nation. They come over here for a holiday, and their expenditure is regulated on a holiday scale. But at home, the mode of living is in most respects remarkably simple. This is due, partly to the extreme difficulty of getting servants, and the impossibility of keeping a large household of domestics, but still more, I think, to a certain inherent simplicity of taste. Hours are much earlier than with us, equipages are few in number; and dwelling-houses, though eminently comfortable, very seldom possess any claim to splendor or magnificence. In the articles of dress, and also in the dainties of the table, Americans will go to an expense that English families of the same rank in life never think of indulging in. In New York, especially, the ladies must spend what we should consider an extravagant amount on Parisian toilettes. I hardly ever remember to have been present at a dinner party in America where champagne was not distributed almost as plentifully as malt liquor would be with us; but in other respects, there is but little ostentatious expense visible to a stranger.

In a moral as opposed to a material point of view, the most striking feature about American society is its uniformity. Everybody, as a rule, holds the same opinions about everything, and expresses his views, more or less, in the same language. These views are often correct, almost invariably intelligent and creditable to the holders. But still, even at the risk of hearing paradoxes defended, you cannot help wishing, at times, for a little more of originality. I believe that this monotony in the tone of American talk and opinion arises from the universal diffusion of education. Everybody is educated up to a certain point, and very few are educated above it. They have all learned the same lessons under the same teachers, and, in consequence, share the same sentiments to a degree which it is difficult for an Englishman to appreciate beforehand. This monotony is infinitely more striking in the men than in the women. Ninety-nine American lads in a hundred go through exactly the same system of training. Up to eighteen or nineteen, they are carefully, if not very deeply, grounded in all the branches of a good ordinary English education. Then they go into business, and from that time their intellectual self-culture ceases. Unless they happen to travel, they have very little time for reading anything except the newspapers. The women pursue their education even after marriage, and are in consequence better read and more intellectual in their tastes than English ladies. In the long run, however, the national tone of mind is always derived from the male sex, and therefore the prevalent tone of America is not that of a highly educated society. I do not mean to say, for one moment, that there are not hundreds and thousands of men of really first-class education in the Northern States. On the contrary, some of the most thoroughly educated men it has been my lot to meet with have been Americans. I am speaking of the mass, not of individuals. This opinion of mine, if it is correct, explains a fact which otherwise would seem discouraging: I mean the small share taken by educated men—in our sense of the word—in American politics. The truth is that if America were governed to any great extent by politicians of classical education, the country would not be fairly represented by its rulers. It is not the case that the fact of a gentleman having received a refined culture is any disqualification to him in the eyes of the constituencies. On the other hand, it is a very small recommendation. I do not deny that this is, in itself, an evil; but the true nature of the evil is not that men of education are disqualified from entering a political career in America, but that they form so small a class that they possess no political influence. Just in the same way, there is no doubt that, relatively to the period, there were more highly educated men in the Union half a century ago than there are now. The early settlers in any new country bring with them a higher degree of individual culture than they can impart to their children. In the same ratio, however, that the education of the individual decreases, the average education of the mass increases, and, on the whole, the general tone of the nation gains in consequence.

My friend, Mr. Holmes, once said to me: "We should find it very hard to match five thousand American gentlemen with five thousand English; but we could match five million ordinary Americans against the same number of your countrymen, without fear of the result." This explanation I believe to be the correct one with regard to the intellectual development of America.

The truth is the great mistake that we English make in judging of America is the assumption that the New World ought to be the reproduction of the Old Country. We expect our social system, our hierarchy of castes and rank, our forms of thought and feeling, to be repeated amongst a people growing up under conditions totally different from that in which we have been trained for hundreds of generations. Every departure from our own standard we consider to indicate moral degeneracy, while in reality it is only a symptom of development. No one who has lived in America can avoid coming to the conclusion that the Anglo-Saxon frame is gradually modifying itself to a form suited to the new conditions of climate and temperature under which it is called on to exist. What is true in the physical is true also in the moral world. By degrees the imported civilization and culture of the Old World are developing themselves into new forms and aspects. What will be the ultimate social system of America it is impossible to say. Never yet in history has a nation grown up under circumstances where all men have started equal, and where want and poverty have been practically unknown. That the product of these conditions will be a remarkable one, we are beginning to see already. I recollect a common Irishwoman I once traveled alongside of in the States, saying to me, when talking about her experience of her new home, "This is a blessed country, sir; I think God made it for the poor." And I have often fancied that this saying might be the clue to the future history of America.

I have been asked frequently, whether I should like to

live in America—and to this question my answer has always been that that depends entirely upon circumstances. Men of highly educated tastes, used to the social pleasures of the Old World, will not find their wants gratified as easily and as fully in a new state of society as in an old. In fact, in plain English, if your tastes and your habits are those of men whose income is counted by hundreds, you had better stop where you are. But the man who has his living to earn is better off, in almost every respect, in America than he is in England. The very circumstances that render the United States unattractive as a residence for the man of wealth and refinement are a positive boon to those who possess neither of the attributes; and I am afraid that in this world the latter class is larger and more important than the former.

These reflections on American society would be imperfect if I said nothing as to the great charm which surrounds all family relations in the North. Compared with Europe, domestic scandals are unknown; and between parents, and their grown-up children, there exists a degree of familiarity and intimacy which one seldom witnesses in this country. If family life is the foundation of all permanent good in the social system, then, in spite of its present defects and shortcomings, the outlook for the American society of the future is a very bright one.

Dicey, *Six Months in the Federal States.*

18

AN ENGLISH WORKINGMAN TAKES A DIM VIEW OF AMERICAN WOMEN

JAMES D. BURN

WHEN James Burn came to write his autobiography he entitled it *The Beggar Boy.* The title was accurate as a description of his boyhood, but somewhat unfair to his later career. Burn was born in Dumfries, Scotland, about the year 1800, grew up in dire poverty, begged, was an itinerant peddler, worked spasmodically as an engraver, book agent, shipyard laborer, and hat-maker. He learned to read and write after he was married, and gradually achieved respectability, becoming eventually president of the Burns Club in Edinburgh. In 1862 he came to America to better his fortunes, but without success. In his *Autobiography* he wrote: "My journey to America was an unlooked-for failure, but though my sufferings while in that country were greater than I can describe, I do not regret having taken it." Although he admitted that the United States was the best country for the laborer, he felt that Britain was the country of greatest freedom. His failure in America undoubtedly contributed to the sour view that he took of American society and politics. After his return to England, in 1865, Burn worked for the Fisheries Office and the Great Eastern Railway, finding time to write a *History of Mercantile Enterprise* and a *History of Strikes,* as well as numerous articles for newspapers and journals.

❖❖❖❖❖❖❖

IN ALL civilized society, if we except America, women, from the very nature of their weakness, look up to a man as a power above them, but they esteem that power with feelings of love rather than fear. In America, female notions of equality and personal independence have to a great extent reversed the old order of things in the relation of the sexes to each other. Among the class of married people who keep house it is a common thing for the man to do a considerable part of the slip-slop work. In the morning he lights the stove-fire, empties the slops, makes ready his own breakfast, and if his work lies at a distance he packs up his midday meal, and leaving his wife in bed, he packs himself off to work. Even among the trading classes who have private dwellings, it is quite common to see the men bringing parcels from the market, the grocer's, fishmonger's, or butcher's, for the morning meal. It may be supposed from this bending of masculine dignity in the dishclout-service of their wives, the men are examples of kind and affectionate husbands, and that the ladies are so many connubial doves! But this would be a hasty conclusion. Since the opening of the Divorce Court in England strange disclosures have been made of the mystery of married life, and civilized humanity has often been startled by the savage conduct of its members. But through selfishness, incompatibility of temper, and even brutality of disposition have caused much suffering, the bond of matrimony as it exists in the old country is esteemed not the less a holy tie and a safeguard of public morality. In America, notwithstanding the ready performance of the domestic duties mentioned above, the matrimonial tie is comparatively loose. The woman who has made up her mind not to be bossed by her husband, which means that she will do as she likes irrespective of his will, is not likely to run smoothly in hymeneal harness, and this is the case with a large number of wives in the lower stratum of society. But here again a distinction must be drawn between the natives and the immigrants. I have reason to believe that the real

American women make by far the best wives and mothers.

To be a mother of a family by which the branches of the matrimonial tree may be extended is the ambition of nearly all married women in the old country. This feeling is dictated by the law of nature; but in America, the natural law is frequently made to bend to circumstances opposed to nature. Instead of children being accepted as a blessing, and a cause of rejoicing, the thread of life is too frequently cut before they have drawn breath by their inhuman mothers. Nor is the practice of abortion confined to any one grade of society. The wife of the mechanic, and the fashionable partner of the independent gentleman, have recourse to the same means for relieving themselves of a duty against which their selfishness revolts. . . .

Numbers of men holding diplomas live and grow rich by this unholy calling, and scores of advertising ladies follow in their wake. It is a common practice with parents who look upon their children as an incumbrance to advertise them in their infancy for adoption; these affectionate fathers and mothers either dispose of their little ones for a consideration, or, in their generosity, give them away under the condition, in either case, that they "never see their darlings any more!" An old acquaintance of mine, who has been in the country about twelve years, has two married daughters, both of whom have imbibed American notions of conjugal duty and motherly affection—each has given away an infant, and each has left her husband. I have reason to believe that both these girls were ruined as wives by the habit of living in boarding-houses, when left there without domestic occupation, and, like all idle people, exposed to the temptations of the worst kind.

It appears to me that the natural affections of the sexes in this country are perverted, and that passion or self-interest are the only attractions which draw them together. If the wives and mothers of a nation are not in a healthy moral condition, their offspring are not likely to enjoy the blessings of domestic happiness. In the towns many of the young women are ruined by vanity and false notions of personal independence. Pride of dress is rampant in all ranks, a masterly self-will sets them above advice, and there are few who will bend to parental authority. Fashion is a tyrant among the women of all grades. Four times a year this great despot, like an inexorable magician, waves his wand of change, and all of womankind appear in new costumes. Think of a workingman's partner being obliged to decorate her head with four different styles of bonnets in the course of twelve months! In the country, young women are instructed in all the household duties; but in the towns it is difficult to find a girl who can darn a pair of stockings, much less do the duties of a domestic establishment.

As a general rule the young women who come to this country as domestic servants, particularly the Irish and the Dutch, have many difficulties to encounter during the time of their probation. In either case these girls come from a country where the manners and habits of the people are of a very primitive character, and as a necessary consequence the social and domestic appliances are both simple and few in number. Life among the middle and upper ranks of society is decidedly more artificial than it is in the aristocratic circles in Great Britain. The simple and homely habits of the early settlers have long ago been superseded by a luxurious mode of living, and the refined tastes and manners of Old World gentility are burlesqued by being overdone. Of course this description of social life applies to town-society, but even in the country there is a good deal of walking upon the stilts of modern fashion.

The relation of domestic servants to their bosses is often of a very unsatisfactory character; both parties hold themselves to be free agents, and thoroughly independent of each other. The master of a private establishment might just as well ask one of his female help to sweep his chimney, if such a thing were required, as to clean his boots or shoes. I was in the country a considerable time before I could learn how it was that so many respectable-looking men were seen leaving their homes in the morning with every part of their dress, except their boots, clean and neat; I learned ultimately that unless they did the shoe-black business themselves, neither their servants nor their wives would condescend to perform such vile drudgery. For my part I really cannot see the difference, in point of principle or duty, between cooking a man's food, washing dishes and linen, and cleaning his shoes. Yet there is a conventional difference, and this distinction is so much a matter of servant-girl etiquette, that were a domestic girl to disobey its requirements she would infallibly lose caste. . . .

I have frequently had occasion to observe servant-girls leave their situations with the idea of bettering their condition, and going into establishments where large numbers of females are engaged in sedentary occupations. This change in nine cases out of every ten turns out to be a serious mistake. Nearly all the females employed in these places of business lodge in boarding-houses. If the morals of a young woman are not destroyed by her associates in the workshop, she stands an excellent chance of being stripped of them in the place she has made her temporary home. The great majority of females in the warehouses have little or no certainty of permanent employment, and even with steady employment their wages would leave them but little after paying their board and washing. Both from personal observation, and what I have been able to learn, I find that very few of these girls make fortunate marriages. I do not see how it could be otherwise; they are neither fitted for wives by a due regard for the feelings and wishes of their husbands, nor a knowledge of even the simple rudiments of housekeeping. One of the worst traits in the character of this class of females is that they will not be instructed by their husbands, and as a proof of their obstinacy, one of their common remarks to each other when speaking of their husbands is that they "would like to see a man who would boss them."

The gallantry of the American men, the purity of sentiment, the refinement of manners and the amiable politeness of her women, have long been held up to the rest of the civilized world as moral and social traits of character to be admired rather than imitated. So long as women are in a decided minority, it is only natural that men should pet and flatter them, and it is not wonderful that the deference then paid should be claimed by the darlings themselves as a prescriptive right. How far this constrained gallantry of the men, and the purity and politeness of the women, are really in advance of Old World morality, is another question, and becomes extremely doubtful when the rudeness with which women are treated in private is considered. If the gentlemen's gallantry were the result of good breeding, they would certainly avoid the use of profane language, expectorating regardless of time or place, and elevating their understandings in the presence of the ladies. These masculine habits, however, may be matters which foreigners do not understand in the everyday life of a people whose civilization is based upon human equality and social freedom. . . .

Generally speaking, the male and female members of the human family are mutually drawn to each other; but as the greater attraction is vested in the female, the men, like so many Sinbads, in their tiny barques, are constantly being drawn to their rocky charms by an irresistible force. This law of human magnetism seems in some measure to be reversed in America; the active power of attraction is changed, and instead of the lovely dears containing their vestal souls in patience, they frequently find themselves impelled to rush into the arms of their other halves. . . .

Go-aheadism is as common among many of the women in the United States as it is in the ranks of the men. When at home it is quite a common practice to come and go without asking leave or taking counsel. Matrimony in the old country is looked upon as a bond of union effected by mutual affection; but from what I have witnessed, a goodly number of both sexes here possess very different ideas upon the subject. The philosophy of "adaptability" regulates the conduct of not a few married people who have promised to love, honor, and obey. In the first blush of married life many of the young men and women mistake passion for that deep-seated feeling which should unite two sympathies in one; and when they find that they do not run smoothly together in matrimonial traces, one or the other flies off. These *halves* of disappointed beings are to be met in every direction, and if one of these ladies should have the misfortune to become a mother, ten to one but she will relieve herself of the responsibility by transfering her child to a stranger for adoption. Women do not wear the charms of youth long under the changing temperature of America; they are aware of the melancholy fact, and as a consequence the fast ladies make up their minds to enjoy life as best they may, and so long as their feelings are warmed by the fire of youth.

Within the range of my own experience, I have known several second-hand wives who were sailing under the black flags of widowhood, and fishing for other experimental partners. The peculiar notions of personal independence indulged in by the women's rights' ladies in America has been the means of placing a great portion of the fabric of female society in a false position. Woman was evidently assigned to be the companion of man, and as he is stronger, both mentally and physically, it follows as a necessary consequence that he is a power above her; this power, however, when properly exercised, is directed to shield her from harm as well as be a means for her support. The class of ladies I refer to take a different view of the matter; they are not content to hold the position Providence has placed them in as handmaidens to the men, but they too must be rulers beyond the regions of the kitchen and nursery. In thus speaking of the American ladies, I allude to that large class whose notions of equality lead them to be more than the equals of their husbands. If a man marries a woman who has been employed at any of the sedentary avocations, and cannot place her in a house of his own fitted up to her taste, she will prefer to take up her residence in a boarding establishment, where she can have a good table and enjoy the luxury of idleness, and have both time and opportunity for flirtation. I was in the company of a woman a short time ago who had left her husband because, among other things, he did not allow her more than thirteen dollars a week, out of which she had to provide food for themselves and a baby; the husband paying rent, coals, and clothing. This model wife was the partner of a sober, hard-working man. The father has the child, and she is performing in the character of a young widow in a boarding-house in another State, two hundred miles from all her woman's heart should hold dear. . . .

The old-fashioned notions which exercised so much influence over the hopes and fears of great numbers of the people in my boyish days, when fays and fairies controlled the actions of men unseen, have given place to a new order of things. Like the garments we wear, there may be, and no doubt is, a fashion even in our faiths, to which we become wedded for the time being. As the Americans are the smartest, and by far the best-educated people in the world, it may be taken for granted that they know how to regulate all their everyday affairs without the aid of seers, star-gazing philosophers, or people upon familiar terms with undistilled spirits! This, however, is not the case, and I question very much if there is any class in the civilized world who rely so much for information relative to the concerns of everyday life on the truly reliable class of fortune-tellers as the American ladies. There is not a town in the United States in which numbers of modest astrologers, clairvoyants, and spirit consulters may not be found reveling in the luxury and idleness procured for them by the money of a credulous people. I have known women of social standing who had recourse to these second-sighted public benefactors whenever they wished to obtain information, either about their own concerns, or the affairs of other people in which they may have had a friendly interest. The newspaper advertising columns are continually embellished with statements in which the wonderful occult power of these people is set forth. The lady professors among them are not only in the habit of relieving the minds of their confiding patients by foretelling the good things the gods have in store for them, but in many instances they persuade their credulous dupes to purchase magic powders with which to charm the men they would wish for husbands or occasional lovers. If these human vampires were only consulted by the uneducated classes, I should have passed the subject without a remark; but the fact that many of them support splendid establishments in fashionable localities furnishes a good proof that the education of the people has not raised them above the groveling superstition of the most ignorant members of Old World communities.

Burn, *Three Years Among the Working Classes in the United States.*

19

AMERICA IS NOT INTERESTING

MATTHEW ARNOLD

FAMOUS on two continents for his poetry and essays, and as the son of the great Arnold of Rugby, Matthew Arnold came to the United States in 1883 to satisfy his curiosity about this country and to make money by lecturing. In a way he did both: his visit to the United States provided him with material for a number of essays, and he went home with some money. Yet his lectures were not a success, and his curiosity about the United States was easily satisfied. Arnold meant to be fair, but he was incapable of appreciating American democracy and his attitude toward almost everything in America was a supercilious one. The essay on Civilization in the United States—part of which is reproduced here—illuminates the inadequacies of Arnold rather than of his subject. For a citizen of a country which boasted such village names as Upper Puddle and Nether Slaughter to gag at Jacksonville was amusing, and it was William James who remarked the absurdity of using the word "interesting" as an objective and substantive term. Yet it must be added that Arnold's view was representative of the views of many upper-class Britons and Europeans, for no observation about the United States was more hackneyed than that America was dull.

◇◇◇◇◇◇◇

Bᴜᴛ we must get nearer still to the heart of the question raised as to the character and worth of American civilization. I have said how much the word civilization really means—the humanization of man in society; his making progress there toward his true and full humanity. Partial and material achievement is always being put forward as civilization. We hear a nation called highly civilized by reason of its industry, commerce, and wealth, or by reason of its liberty or equality, or by reason of its numerous churches, schools, libraries, and newspapers. But there is something in human nature, some instinct of growth, some law of perfection, which rebels against this narrow account of the matter. And perhaps what human nature demands in civilization, over and above all those obvious things which first occur to our thoughts—what human nature, I say, demands in civilization, if it is to stand as a high and satisfying civilization, is best described by the word *interesting*. Here is the extraordinary charm of the old Greek civilization; that it is so *interesting*. Do not tell me only, says human nature, of the magnitude of your industry and commerce; of the beneficence of your institutions, your freedom, your equality; of the great and growing number of your churches and schools, libraries and newspapers; tell me also if your civilization—which is the grand name you give to all this development—tell me if your civilization is *interesting*.

An American friend of mine, Professor Norton, has lately published the early letters of Carlyle. If any one wants a good antidote to the unpleasant effect left by Mr. Froude's *Life of Carlyle*, let him read those letters. . . .

Thomas Carlyle, the eldest son, a young man in wretched health and worse spirits, was fighting his way in Edinburgh. One of his younger brothers talked of emigrating. "The very best thing he could do!" we should all say. Carlyle dissuades him. "You shall never," he writes, "you shall never seriously meditate crossing the great Salt Pool to plant yourself in the Yankee-land. That is a miserable fate for anyone, at best; never dream of it. Could you banish yourself from all that is interesting to your mind, forget the history, the glorious institutions, the noble principles of old Scotland—that you might eat a better dinner, perhaps?"

There is our word launched—the word *interesting*. I am not saying that Carlyle's advice was good, or that young men should not emigrate. I do but take note, in the word *interesting*, of a requirement, a cry of aspiration, a cry not sounding in the imaginative Carlyle's own breast only, but sure of a response in his brother's breast also, and in human nature. . . .

Now the great sources of the *interesting* are distinction and beauty; that which is elevated, and that which is beautiful. Let us take the beautiful first, and consider how far it is present in American civilization. Evidently, that is the civilization's weak side. There is little to nourish and delight the sense of beauty there. In the long-settled states east of the Alleghanies the landscape in general is not interesting, the climate harsh and in extremes. The Americans are restless, eager to better themselves and to make fortunes; the inhabitant does not strike his roots lovingly down into the soil, as in rural England. In the valley of the Connecticut you will find farm after farm which the Yankee settler has abandoned in order to go West, leaving the farm to some new Irish immigrant. The charm of beauty which comes from ancientness and permanence of rural life the country could not yet have in a high degree, but it has it in an even less degree than might be expected. Then the Americans come originally, for the most part, from that great class in English society amongst whom the sense for conduct and business is much more strongly developed than the sense for beauty. If we in England were without the cathedrals, parish churches, and castles of the Catholic and Feudal Age, and without the houses of the Elizabethan Age, but had only the towns and buildings which the rise of our middle class has created in the modern age, we should be in much the same case as the Americans. We should be living with much the same absence of training for the sense of beauty through the eye, from the aspect of outward things. The American cities have hardly anything to please a trained or a natural sense for beauty. They have buildings which cost a great deal of money and produce a certain effect—buildings, shall I say, such as our Midland Station at St. Pancras; but nothing such as Somerset House or Whitehall. One architect of genius they had—Richardson. I had the pleasure to know him; he is dead, alas! Much of his work was injured by the conditions under which he was obliged to execute it; I can recall but one building, and that of no great importance, where he seems to have had his own way, to be fully himself; but that is indeed excellent. In general, where the Americans succeed best in their architecture—in that art so indicative and educative of a people's sense for beauty—is in the fashion of their villa-cottages in wood. These are often original and at the same time very pleasing, but they are pretty and coquettish, not beautiful. Of the really beautiful in the other arts, and in literature, very little has been produced there as yet. I asked a German portrait painter, whom I found painting and prospering in America, how he liked the country. "How *can* an artist like it?" was his answer. The American artists live chiefly in Europe; all Americans of cultivation and wealth visit Europe more and more constantly. The mere nomenclature of the country acts upon a cultivated person like the incessant pricking of pins. What people in whom the sense for beauty and fitness was quick could have invented, or could tolerate, the hideous names ending in *ville*, the Briggsvilles, Higginsvilles, Jacksonvilles, rife from Maine to Florida; the jumble of unnatural and inappropriate names everywhere? On the line from Albany to Buffalo, you have, in one part, half the names in the classical dictionary to designate the stations; it is said that the folly is due to a surveyor who, when the country was laid out, happened to possess a classical dictionary; but a people with any artist-sense would have put down that surveyor. The Americans meekly retain his names; and, indeed, his strange Marcellus or Syracuse is perhaps not much worse than their congenital Briggsville.

So much as to beauty, and as to the provision, in the United States, for the sense of beauty. As to distinction, and the interest which human nature seeks from enjoying the effect made upon it by what is elevated, the case is much the same. There is very little to create such an effect, very much to thwart it. Goethe says somewhere that "the thrill of awe is the best thing humanity has." But, if there be a discipline in which the Americans are wanting, it is the discipline of awe and respect. An austere and intense religion imposed on their Puritan founders the discipline of respect, and so provided for them the thrill of awe; but this religion is dying out. The Americans have produced plenty of men strong, shrewd, upright, able, effective; very few who are highly distinguished. Alexander Hamilton is indeed a man of rare distinction; Washington, though he has not the high mental distinction of Pericles or Cæsar, has true distinction of style and character. But these men belong to the pre-American age. Lincoln's recent American biographers declare that Washington is but an Englishman, an English officer; the typical American, they say, is Abraham Lincoln. Now Lincoln is shrewd, sagacious, humorous, honest, courageous, firm; he is a man with qualities deserving the most sincere esteem and praise, but he has not distinction.

In truth, everything is against distinction in America, and against the sense of elevation to be gained through admiring and respecting it. The glorification of the "average man," who is quite a religion with statesmen and publicists there, is against it. The addiction to the "funny man," who is the national misfortune there, is against it. Above all, the newspapers are against it.

It is often said that every nation has the government it deserves. What is much more certain is that every nation has the newspapers it deserves. The newspaper is the direct product of the want felt; the supply answers closely and inevitably to the demand. I suppose no one knows what the American newspapers are, who has not been obliged, for some length of time, to read either those newspapers or none at all. Powerful and valuable contributions occur scattered about in them. But on the whole, and taking the total impression and effect made by them, I should say that if one were searching for the best means to efface and kill in a whole nation the discipline of respect, the feeling for what is elevated, one could not do better than take the American newspapers. The absence of truth and soberness in them, the poverty in serious interest, the personality and sensation-mongering, are beyond relief. There are a few newspapers which are in whole, or in part, exceptions. The *New York Nation*, a weekly paper, may be paralleled with the *Saturday Review* as it was in its old and good days; but the *New York Nation* is conducted by a foreigner, and has an extremely small sale. In general, the daily papers are such that when one returns home one is moved to admiration and thankfulness not only at the great London papers, like the *Times* or the *Standard*, but quite as much at the great provincial newspapers, too— papers like the *Leeds Mercury* and the *Yorkshire Post* in the north of England, like the *Scotsman* and the *Glasgow Herald* in Scotland. . . .

I once declared that in England the born lover of ideas and of light could not but feel that the sky over his head is of brass and iron. And so I say that, in America, he who craves for the *interesting* in civilization, he who requires from what surrounds him satisfaction for his sense of beauty, his sense for elevation, will feel the sky over his head to be of brass and iron. The human problem, then, is as yet solved in the United States most imperfectly; a great void exists in the civilization over there; a want of what is elevated and beautiful, of what is interesting.

The want is grave; it was probably, though he does not exactly bring it out, influencing Sir Lepel Griffin's feelings when he said that America is one of the last countries in which one would like to live. The want is such as to make any educated man feel that many countries, much less free and prosperous than the United States, are yet more truly civilized; have more which is interesting, have more to say to the soul; are countries, therefore, in which one would rather live.

The want is graver because it is so little recognized by the mass of Americans; nay, so loudly denied by them. If the community over there perceived the want and regretted it, sought for the right way of remedying it, and resolved that remedied it should be; if they said, or even if a number of leading spirits amongst them said: "Yes, we see what is wanting to our civilization, we see that the average man is a danger, we see that our newspapers are a scandal, that bondage to the common and ignoble is our snare; but under the circumstances our civilization could not well have been expected to begin differently. What you see are *beginnings,* they are crude, they are too predominantly material, they omit much, leave much to be desired—but they could not have been otherwise, they have been inevitable, and we will rise above them"; if the American frankly said this, one would not have a word to bring against it. One would *then* insist on no shortcoming, one would accept their admission that the human problem is at present quite insufficiently solved by them, and would press the matter no further. One would congratulate them on having solved the political problem and the social problem so successfully, and only remark, as I have said already, that in seeing clear and thinking straight on *our* political and social questions, we have great need to follow the example they set on theirs.

But now the Americans seem, in certain matters, to have agreed, as a people, to deceive themselves that they have what they have not, to cover the defects in their civilization by boasting, to fancy that they well and truly solve, not only the political and social problem, but the human problem too. One would say that they really do hope to find in tall talk and inflated sentiment a substitute for that real sense of elevation which human nature, as I have said, instinctively craves—and a substitute which may do as well as the genuine article. The thrill of awe, which Goethe pronounces to be the best thing humanity has, they would fain create by proclaiming themselves at the top of their voices to be "the greatest nation upon earth," by assuring one another, in the language of their national historian, that "American democracy proceeds in its ascent as uniformly and majestically as the laws of being, and is as certain as the decrees of eternity."

Or, again, far from admitting that their newspapers are a scandal, they assure one another that their newspaper press is one of their most signal distinctions. Far from admitting that in literature they have as yet produced little that is important, they play at treating American literature as if it were a great independent power; they reform the spelling of the English language by the insight of their average man. For every English writer they have an American writer to match; and him good Americans read. The Western States are at this moment being nourished and formed, we hear, on the novels of a native author called Roe, instead of those of Scott and Dickens. Far from admitting that their average man is a danger, and that his predominance has brought about a plentiful lack of refinement, distinction, and beauty, they declare in the words of my friend Colonel Higginson, a prominent critic at Boston, that "Nature said, some years since: 'Thus far the English is my best race, but we have had Englishmen enough; put in one drop more of nervous fluid and make the American.'" And with that drop a new range of promise opened on the human race, and a lighter, finer, more highly organized type of mankind was born. Far from admitting that the American accent, as the pressure of their climate and of their average man has made it, is a thing to be striven against, they assure one another that it is the right accent, the standard English speech of the future. It reminds me of a thing in Smollet's dinner-party of authors. Seated by "the philosopher who is writing a most orthodox refutation of Bolingbroke, but in the meantime has just been presented to the Grand Jury as a public nuisance for having blasphemed in an alehouse on the Lord's day"—seated by this philosopher is "the Scotchman who is giving lectures on the pronunciation of the English language."

The worst of it is that all this tall talk and self-glorification meets with hardly any rebuke from sane criticism over there. . . .

The new West promises to beat in the game of brag even the stout champions I have been quoting. Those belong to the old Eastern States; and the other day there was sent to me a Californian newspaper which calls all the Easterners "the unhappy denizens of a forbidding clime," and adds: "The time will surely come when all roads will lead to California. Here will be the home of art, science, literature, and profound knowledge."

Common-sense criticism, I repeat, of all this hollow stuff there is in America next to none. There are plenty of cultivated, judicious, delightful individuals there. They are our hope and America's hope; it is through their means that improvement must come. They know perfectly well how false and hollow the boastful stuff talked is; but they let the storm of self-laudation rage, and say nothing. For political opponents and their doings there are in America hard words to be heard in abundance; for the real faults in American civilization, and for the foolish boasting which prolongs them, there is hardly a word of regret or blame, at least in public. Even in private, many of the most cultivated Americans shrink from the subject, are irritable and thin-skinned when it is canvassed. Public treatment of it, in a cool and sane spirit of criticism, there is none. In vain I might plead that I had set a good example of frankness, in confessing over here, that, so far from solving our problems successfully, we in England find ourselves with an upper class materialized, a middle class vulgarized, and a lower class brutalized. But it seems that nothing will embolden an American critic to say firmly and aloud to his countrymen and to his newspapers, that in America they do not solve the human problem successfully, and that with their present methods they never can. Consequently, the masses of the American people do really come to believe all they hear about their finer nervous organization, and the rightness of the American accent, and the importance of American literature; that is to say, they see things not as they are, but as they would like to see them be; they deceive themselves totally. And by such self-deception they shut against themselves the door to improvement, and do their best to make the reign of *das Gemeine* eternal. In what concerns the solving of the political and social problem they see clear and think straight; in what concerns the higher civilization they live in a fool's paradise. That it is which makes a famous French critic speak of "the hard unintelligence of the people of the United States"—of the very people who in general pass for being specially intelligent; and so, within certain limits, they are. But they have been so plied with nonsense and boasting that outside those limits, and where it is a question of things in which their civilization is weak, they seem, very many of them, as if in such things they had no power of perception whatever, no idea of a proper scale, no sense of the difference between good and bad. And at this rate they can never, after solving the political and social problem with success, go on to solve happily the human problem too, and thus at last make their civilization full and interesting.

To sum up, then. What really dissatisfies in American civilization is the want of the *interesting*, a want due chiefly to the want of those two great elements of the interesting, which are elevation and beauty. And the want of these elements is increased and prolonged by the Americans being assured that they have them when they have them not. And it seems to me that what the Americans now most urgently require is not so much a vast additional development of orthodox Protestantism, but rather a steady exhibition of cool and sane criticism by their men of light and leading over there.

Arnold, *Civilization in the United States, First and Last Impressions of America.*

20

THE FAULTS AND STRENGTH
OF AMERICAN DEMOCRACY

JAMES BRYCE

NO foreigner ever wrote more comprehensively, more un-
derstandingly, or more sympathetically about America than
the beloved British Ambassador, James Bryce, and *The
American Commonwealth* (1888), from which these chapters are taken, has justly become a classic. Born in Belfast in
1838, educated at the universities of Glasgow, Oxford, and
Heidelberg, Bryce achieved fame at the age of twenty-four
with his remarkable book on the *Holy Roman Empire*, and
thereafter devoted his long life to scholarship and public
service. Admitted to the bar in 1867, Bryce became Regius
Professor of Law at Oxford in 1870, and began those studies
in jurisprudence and politics which won him international
fame. His political career began with election to Parliament in 1880; he rapidly became one of the most influential
figures in the counsels of the Liberal party, serving in many
important secretarial and cabinet offices. An indefatigable
traveler, Bryce visited the United States frequently, and
The American Commonwealth was based on an intimate
personal acquaintance as well as on thorough scholarly investigation. On its publication it was greeted with almost
unqualified praise, and for over half a century it has
held its position as the most thorough, discriminating, and
penetrating analysis of American politics and society in
literature. In 1907 Bryce was appointed Ambassador to the
United States, a position which he filled with distinction.
Of his numerous other writings, his two-volume work on
Modern Democracies is the most important.

❖❖❖❖❖❖❖

THE TRUE FAULTS OF AMERICAN DEMOCRACY

WE HAVE seen that the defects commonly attributed to democratic government are not specially characteristic of the United States. It remains to inquire what are the peculiar blemishes which the country does show. So far as regards the constitutional machinery of the Federal and of the State government this question has been answered in earlier chapters. It is now rather the tendency of the institutions generally, the disposition and habits of the governing people, that we have to consider. The word Democracy is often used to mean a spirit or tendency, sometimes the spirit of revolution, sometimes the spirit of equality. For our present purpose it is better to take it as denoting simply a form of government, that in which the numerical majority rules, deciding questions of state by the votes, whether directly, as in the ancient republics, or mediately, as in modern representative government, of the body of citizens, the citizens being if not the whole, at least a very large proportion of the adult males. We may properly begin by asking, What are the evils to which we may expect such a form of government to be exposed? and may then go on to see whether any others are discoverable in the United States which, though traceable to democracy, are not of its essence, but due to the particular form which it has there taken.

It is an old maxim that republics live by Virtue—that is, by the maintenance of a high level of public spirit and justice among the citizens. If the republic be one in which power is confined to, or practically exercised by, a small educated class, the maintenance of this high level is helped by the sense of personal dignity which their position engenders. If the republic itself be small, and bear rule over others, patriotism may be intense, and the sense of the collective dignity of the state may ennoble the minds of the citizens, make them willing to accept sacrifices for its sake, to forego private interests

and suppress private resentments, in order to be strong
against the outer world. But if the state be very large, and the
rights of all citizens equal, we must not expect them to rise
above the average level of human nature. Rousseau and Jefferson will tell us that this level is high, that the faults which
governments have hitherto shown are due to the selfishness
of privileged persons and classes, that the ordinary unsophis-
ticated man will love justice, desire the good of others, need
no constraint to keep him in the right path. Experience will
contradict them, and whether it talks of Original Sin or
adopts some less scholastic phrase, will recognize that the
tendencies to evil in human nature are not perhaps as strong,
but as various and abiding even in the most civilized societies,
as its impulses to good. Hence the rule of numbers means the
rule of ordinary mankind without those artificial helps which
their privileged position has given to limited governing
classes, though also, no doubt, without those special temptations which follow in the wake of power and privilege.

Every question that arises in the conduct of government
is either a question of ends or a question of means; and errors
may be committed by the ruling power either in fixing on
wrong ends or in choosing wrong means to secure those ends.
It is now, after long resistance by those who maintained that
they knew better what was good for the people than the people knew themselves, at last agreed that as the masses are better judges of what will conduce to their own happiness than
are the classes placed above them, they must be allowed to
determine ends. This is in fact the essence of free or popular
government, and the justification for vesting power in numbers. But assuming the end to be given, who is best qualified
to select the means for its accomplishment? To do so needs in
many cases a knowledge of the facts, a skill in interpreting
them, a power of forecasting the results of measures, unattainable by the mass of mankind. Such knowledge is too high
for them. It is attainable only by trained economists, legists,
statesmen. If the masses attempt it they will commit mis-

takes not less serious than those which befall a litigant who
insists on conducting a complicated case instead of leaving it
to his attorney and counsel. But in popular governments this
distinction between ends and means is apt to be forgotten.
Often it is one which cannot be sharply drawn, because some
ends are means to larger ends, and some means are desired
not only for the sake of larger ends, but for their own sakes
also. And the habit of trusting its own wisdom and enjoying
its own power, in which the multitude is encouraged by its
leaders and servants, disposes it to ignore the distinction even
where the distinction is clear, and makes it refer to the direct
arbitrament of the people matters which the people are unfit
to decide, and which they might safely leave to their trained
ministers or representatives. Thus we find that the direct
government of the multitude may become dangerous not
only because the multitude shares the faults and follies of
ordinary human nature, but also because it is intellectually
incompetent for the delicate business of conducting the daily
work of government, *i.e.* of choosing and carrying out with
vigour and promptitude the requisite executive means. The
fact that it is called by a singular name has made many forget
that the people means nothing more than so many millions
of individual men. There is a sense in which it is true that
the people are wiser than the wisest man. But what is true
of their ultimate judgment after the lapse of time sufficient
for full discussion, is not equally true of decisions that have
to be promptly taken.

What are the consequences which we may expect to follow from these characteristics of democracy and these conditions under which it is forced to work?

Firstly, a certain commonness of mind and tone, a want of
dignity and elevation in and about the conduct of public affairs, an insensibility to the nobler aspects and finer responsibilities of national life.

Secondly, a certain apathy among the luxurious classes and
fastidious minds, who find themselves of no more account

than the ordinary voter, and are disgusted by the superficial vulgarities of public life.

Thirdly, a want of knowledge, tact, and judgment in the details of legislation, as well as in administration, with an inadequate recognition of the difficulty of these kinds of work, and of the worth of special experience and skill in dealing with them. Because it is incompetent, the multitude will not feel its incompetence, and will not seek or defer to the counsels of those who possess the requisite capacity.

Fourthly, laxity in the management of public business. The persons entrusted with such business being only average men, thinking themselves and thought of by others as average men, with a deficient sense of their high responsibilities, may succumb to the temptations which the control of legislation and the public funds present, in cases where persons of a more enlarged view and with more of a social reputation to support would remain incorruptible. To repress such derelictions of duty is every citizen's duty, but for that reason it is in large communities apt to be neglected. Thus the very causes which implant the mischief favour its growth.

The above-mentioned tendencies are all more or less observable in the United States. As each of them has been described already in its proper place, a summary reference may here be sufficient to indicate their relation to the democratic form of government and to the immanent spirit or theory which lies behind that form.

The tone of public life is lower than one expects to find it in so great a nation. Just as we assume that an individual man will at any supreme moment in his own life rise to a higher level than that on which he usually moves, so we look to find those who conduct the affairs of a great state inspired by a sense of the magnitude of the interests entrusted to them. Their horizon ought to be expanded, their feeling of duty quickened, their dignity of attitude enhanced. Human nature with all its weaknesses does show itself capable of being thus roused on its imaginative side; and in Europe, where the traditions of aristocracy survive, everybody condemns as mean or unworthy acts done or language held by a great official which would pass unnoticed in a private citizen. It is the principle of *noblesse oblige* with the sense of duty and trust substituted for that of mere hereditary rank.

Such a sentiment is comparatively weak in America. A cabinet minister, or senator, or governor of a State, sometimes even a President, hardly feels himself more bound by it than the director of a railway company or the mayor of a town does in Europe. Not assuming himself to be individually wiser, stronger, or better than his fellow-citizens, he acts and speaks as though he were still simply one of them, and so far from magnifying his office and making it honourable, seems anxious to show that he is the mere creature of the popular vote, so filled by the sense that it is the people and not he who governs as to fear that he should be deemed to have forgotten his personal insignificance. There is in the United States abundance of patriotism, that is to say, of a passion for the greatness and happiness of the Republic, and a readiness to make sacrifices for it. The history of the Civil War showed that this passion is at least as strong as in England or France. There is no want of an appreciation of the collective majesty of the nation, for this is the theme of incessant speeches, nor even of the past and future glories of each particular State in the Union. But these sentiments do not bear their appropriate fruit in raising the conception of public office, of its worth and its dignity. The newspapers assume public men to be selfish and cynical. Disinterested virtue is not looked for, is perhaps turned into ridicule where it exists. The hard commercial spirit which pervades the meetings of a joint-stock company is the spirit in which most politicians speak of public business, and are not blamed for speaking. Something, especially in the case of newspapers, must be allowed for the humorous tendencies of the American mind, which likes to put forward the absurd and even vulgar side of things for the sake of getting fun out of them.

But after making such allowances, the fact remains that, although no people is more emotional, and even in a sense more poetical, in no country is the ideal side of public life, what one may venture to call the heroic element in a public career, so ignored by the mass and repudiated by the leaders. This affects not only the elevation but the independence and courage of public men; and the country suffers from the want of what we call distinction in its conspicuous figures.

I have discussed in a previous chapter the difficulties which surround the rule of public opinion where it allows little discretion to its agents, relying upon its own competence to supervise administration and secure the legislation which a progressive country needs. The American masses have been obliged, both by democratic theory and by the structure of their government, to proceed upon the assumption of their own competence. They have succeeded better than could have been expected. No people except the choicest children of England, long trained by the practice of local self-government at home and in the colonies before their revolt, could have succeeded half so well. Still the masses of the United States as one finds them to-day are no exception to the rule that some problems are beyond the competence of the average man. They can deal with broad and simple issues, especially with issues into which a moral element enters. They spoke out with a clear strong voice upon slavery, when at last it had become plain that slavery must either spread or vanish, and threw themselves with enthusiasm into the struggle for the Union. Their instinctive dislike for foreign annexation foiled President Grant's plan for acquiring San Domingo. Their sense of national and commercial honour has defeated more than one mischievous scheme for tampering with the public debt. But when a question of intricacy presents itself, requiring either keen foresight, exact reasoning, or wide knowledge, they are at fault. Questions relating to currency and coinage, free trade and protection, improvements in the machinery of constitutions or of municipal governments, the control of corporations by the law, the method of securing purity of elections, these are problems which have continued to baffle them, just as the Free Soil question did before the war or the reconstruction of the revolted Southern States for a long time after it. In those two instances a solution came about, but in the former it was not so much effected by the policy of the people or their statesmen as forced on them by events, in the latter it has left serious evils behind.

Is this a defect incidental to all popular governments, or is there anything in the American system specially calculated to produce it?

A state must of course take the people as it finds them, with such elements of ignorance and passion as exists in masses of men everywhere. Nevertheless a representative or parliamentary system provides the means of mitigating the evils to be feared from ignorance or haste, for it vests the actual conduct of affairs in a body of specially chosen and presumably specially qualified men, who may themselves entrust such of their functions as need peculiar knowledge or skill to a smaller governing body or bodies selected in respect of their more eminent fitness. By this method the defects of democracy are remedied, while its strength is retained. The masses give their impulse to the representatives: the representatives, directed by the people to secure certain ends, bring their skill and experience to bear on the choice and application of the best means. The Americans, however, have not so constructed or composed their representative bodies as to secure a large measure of these benefits. The legislatures are disjoined from the administrative offices. The members of legislatures are not chosen for their ability or experience, but are, five-sixths of them, little above the average citizen. They are not much respected or trusted, and finding nothing exceptional expected from them, they behave as ordinary men. The separation of the executive from the legislature is a part of the constitutional arrangements of the country, and has no doubt some advantages. The character of the legislatures is due to a mistaken view of human equality and an exaggerated devotion to popular sovereignty. It is a result of democratic theory pushed to extremes, but is not necessarily incident to a democratic government. The government of England, for instance, has now become substantially a democracy, but there is no reason why it should imitate America in either of the points just mentioned, nor does democratic France, apt enough to make a bold use of theory, seem to have pushed theory to excess in these particular directions. I do not, however, deny that a democratic system makes the people self-confident, and that self-confidence may easily pass into a jealousy of delegated power, an undervaluing of skill and knowledge, a belief that any citizen is good enough for any political work. This is perhaps more likely to happen with a people who have really reached a high level of political competence: and so one may say that the reason why the American democracy is not better is because it is so good. Were it less educated, less shrewd, less actively interested in public affairs, less independent in spirit, it might be more disposed, like the masses in Europe, to look up to the classes which have hitherto done the work of governing. So perhaps the excellence of rural local self-government has lowered the conception of national government. The ordinary American farmer or shopkeeper or artisan bears a part in the local government of his township or village, or county, or small municipality. He is quite competent to discuss the questions that arise there. He knows his fellow-citizens, and can, if he takes the trouble, select the fittest of them for local office. No high standard of fitness is needed, for the work of local administration can be adequately despatched by any sensible man of business habits. Taking his ideas from this local government, he images Congress to himself as nothing more than a larger town council or board of county commissioners, the President and his Cabinet as a sort of bigger mayor and city treasurer and education superintendent; he is therefore content to choose for high Federal posts such persons as he would elect for these local offices. They are such as he is himself; and it would seem to him a disparagement of his own civic worth were he to deem his neighbours, honest, hard-working, keen-witted men, unfit for any places in the service of the Republic.

The comparative indifference to political life of the educated and wealthy classes which is so much preached at by American reformers and dwelt on by European critics is partly due to this attitude of the multitude. These classes find no smooth and easy path lying before them. Since the masses do not look to them for guidance, they do not come forward to give it. If they wish for office they must struggle for it, avoiding the least appearance of presuming on their social position. I think, however, that the abstention of the upper class is largely ascribable to causes, set forth in a previous chapter, that have little to do with democracy; and while believing that the United States have suffered from this abstention—it seems to be now passing away—do not regard it as an inseparable incident of their government. Accidental causes, such as the Spoils System, which is a comparatively recent and evidently curable distemper, have largely contributed to it.

The Spoils System reminds us of the Machine and the whole organization of Rings and Bosses. This is the ugliest feature in the current politics of the country. Must it be set down to democracy? To some extent, yes. It could not have grown up save in a popular government; and some of the arrangements which have aided its growth, such as the number and frequency of elections, have been dictated by what may be called the narrow doctrinarism of democracy. But these arrangements are not essential to the safety of the government; and the other causes which have brought about the machine politics of cities seem to be preventible causes. The city masses may improve if immigration declines, offices may

cease to be the reward of party victory, the better citizens
may throw themselves more actively into political work.

That corruption should exist under a democracy is no
doubt a reproach to a government which holds up, and needs
for its safe working, a higher standard of virtue than any
other. Remembering, however, that it was rife in the English
Parliament a century and a half ago, in English constituencies
thirty years ago, and that it prevails under the despotism of
Russia to-day, while not uncommon in some other European
monarchies, we shall be in no danger of connecting it with
the form of the American government. There are diseases
which attack the body politic, like the natural body, at certain stages of growth, but disappear when a nation has passed
into another stage, or when sedulous experimentation has
discovered the appropriate remedy. The corruption of Parliament in Sir Robert Walpole's days characterized a period
of transition when power had passed to the House of Com-
mons, but the control of the people over the House had not
yet been fully established, and when, through a variety of
moral causes, the tone of the nation was comparatively low.
The corruption of the electorate in English boroughs appeared when a seat had become an object of desire to rich
men, while yet the interest of the voters in public affairs was
so feeble that they were willing to sell their votes, and their
number often so small that each vote fetched a high price.
The growth of intelligence and independence among the
people, as well as the introduction of severe penalties for
bribery, and the extinction of small constituencies, have now
almost extinguished electoral corruption. So in America it
may be expected that the more active conscience of the people and the reform of the civil service will cut down, if they
do not wholly eradicate, such corruption as now infests the
legislative bodies, while better ballot and election laws may
do the same for the constituencies.

A European critic may remark that this way of presenting

the case ignores the evils and losses which defective government involves. "If," he will say, "the mass of mankind possess neither the knowledge nor the leisure nor the skill to determine the legislation and policy of a great state, will not the vigour of the commonwealth decline and its resources be squandered? Will not a nation ruled by its average men in reliance on their own average wisdom be overtaken in the race of prosperity or overpowered in a warlike struggle by a nation of equal resources which is guided by its most capable minds?" The answer to this criticism is that America has hitherto been able to afford to squander her resources, and that no other state threatens her. With her wealth and in her position she can with impunity commit errors which might be fatal to the nations of Western Europe.

Of the deficiencies summarized in this chapter, those which might seem to go deepest, because they have least to do with the particular constitutional arrangements of the country, and are most directly the offspring of its temper and habits, are the prominence of inferior men in politics and the absence of distinguished figures. The people are good, but not good enough to be able to dispense with efficient service by capable representatives and officials, wise guidance by strong and enlightened leaders. But they are neither well served nor well led. If it were clear that these are the fruits of liberty and equality, the prospects of the world would be darker than we have been wont to think them. They are the fruits not of liberty and equality, but of an optimism which has underrated the inherent difficulties of politics and failings of human nature, of a theory which has confused equality of civil rights and duties with equality of capacity, and of a thoughtlessness which has forgotten that the problems of the world and the dangers which beset society are always putting on new faces and appearing in new directions. The Americans started their Republic with a determination to prevent abuses of power such as they had suffered from the British Crown. Freedom seemed the one thing necessary; and freedom was thought to consist in cutting down the powers of legislatures and officials. Freedom was the national boast during the years that followed down till the Civil War, and in the delight of proclaiming themselves superior in this regard to the rest of the world they omitted to provide themselves with the other requisites for good government, and forgot that power may be abused in other ways than by monarchic tyranny or legislative usurpation. They continued to beat the drum along the old ramparts erected in 1776 and 1789 against George III., or those who might try to imitate him, when the enemy had moved quite away from that side of the position, and was beginning to threaten their rear. No maxim was more popular among them than that which declares eternal vigilance to be the price of freedom. Unfortunately their vigilance took account only of the old dangers, and did not note the development of new ones, as if the captain of a man-of-war were to think only of his guns and armour-plating, and neglect to protect himself against torpedoes. Thus abuses were suffered to grow up, which seemed trivial in the midst of so general a prosperity; and good citizens who were occupied in other and more engrossing ways, allowed politics to fall into the hands of mean men. The efforts which these citizens are now making to recover the control of public business would have encountered fewer obstacles had they been made sooner. But the obstacles will be overcome. No one, I think, who has studied either the history of the American people, or their present mind and habits, will conclude that there is among them any jealousy of merit, any positive aversion to culture or knowledge. Neither the political arrangements nor the social and economical conditions of the country tend at this moment to draw its best intellects and loftiest characters into public life. But the democratic temper of the people does not stand in the way.

The commonest of the old charges against democracy was that it passed into ochlocracy. I have sought to show that this has not happened, and is not likely to happen in America.

The features of mob-rule do not appear in her system, whose most characteristic faults are the existence of a class of persons using government as a means of private gain and the menacing power of wealth. Plutocracy, which the ancients contrasted with democracy, has shown in America an inauspicious affinity for certain professedly democratic institutions.

Perhaps no form of government needs great leaders so much as democracy. The fatalistic habit of mind perceptible among the Americans needs to be corrected by the spectacle of courage and independence taking their own path, and not looking to see whither the mass are moving. Those whose material prosperity tends to lap them in self-complacency and dull the edge of aspiration, need to be thrilled by the emotions which great men can excite, stimulated by the ideals they present, stirred to a loftier sense of what national life may attain. In some countries men of brilliant gifts may be dangerous to freedom; but the ambition of American statesmen has been schooled to flow in constitutional channels, and the Republic is strong enough to stand any strain to which the rise of heroes may expose her.

THE STRENGTH OF AMERICAN DEMOCRACY

Those merits of American government which belong to its Federal Constitution have been already discussed: we have now to consider such as flow from the rule of public opinion, from the temper, habits, and ideas of the people.

I. The first is that of Stability.—As one test of a human body's soundness is its capacity for reaching a great age, so it is high praise for a political system that it has stood no more changed than any institution must change in a changing world, and that it now gives every promise of durability. The people are profoundly attached to the form which their national life has taken. The Federal Constitution is, to their eyes, an almost sacred thing, an Ark of the Covenant, whereon no man may lay rash hands. Everywhere in Europe one hears schemes of radical change freely discussed. There is a strong monarchical party in France, a republican party in Italy and Spain. There are anarchists in Germany and Russia. Even in England, it is impossible to feel confident that any one of the existing institutions of the country will be standing fifty years hence. But in the United States the discussion of political problems busies itself with details and assumes that the main lines must remain as they are for ever. This conservative spirit, jealously watchful even in small matters, sometimes prevents reforms, but it assures to the people an easy mind, and a trust in their future which they feel to be not only a present satisfaction but a reservoir of strength.

The best proof of the well-braced solidity of the system is that it survived the Civil War, changed only in a few points which have not greatly affected the balance of National and State powers. Another must have struck every European traveller who questions American publicists about the institutions of their country. When I first travelled in the United States, I used to ask thoughtful men, superior to the prejudices of custom, whether they did not think the States' system defective in such and such points, whether the legislative authority of Congress might not profitably be extended, whether the suffrage ought not to be restricted as regards negroes or immigrants, and so forth. Whether assenting or dissenting, the persons questioned invariably treated such matters as purely speculative, saying that the present arrangements were far too deeply rooted for their alteration to come within the horizon of practical politics. So when a serious trouble arises, a trouble which in Europe would threaten revolution, the people face it quietly, and assume that a tolerable solution will be found. At the disputed election of 1876, when each of the two great parties, heated with conflict, claimed that its candidate had been chosen President, and the Constitution supplied no way out of the difficulty, public tranquillity was scarcely disturbed, and the public funds fell but little. A method was invented of settling the question which both sides acquiesced in, and although the decision was a boundless disappointment to the party which had cast the majority of the popular vote, that party quietly submitted to lose those spoils of office whereon its eyes had been feasting.

II. Feeling the law to be its own work, the people is disposed to obey the law.—In a preceding chapter I have examined occasional instances of the disregard of the law, and the supersession of its tardy methods by the action of the crowd. Such instances scarcely affect the credit which the Americans are specially eager to claim of being a law-abiding community. It is the best result that can be ascribed to the direct participation of the people in their government that they have the love of the maker for his work, that every citizen looks upon a statute as a regulation made by himself for his own guidance no less than for that of others, every official as a person he has himself chosen, and whom it is therefore his interest, with no disparagement to his personal independence, to obey. Plato thought that those who felt their own sovereignty would be impatient of all control: nor is it to be denied that the principle of equality may result in lowering the status and dignity of a magistrate. But as regards law and order the gain much exceeds the loss, for every one feels that there is no appeal from the law, behind which there stands the force of the nation. Such a temper can exist and bear these fruits only where minorities, however large, have learned to submit patiently to majorities, however small. But that is the one lesson which the American government through every grade and in every department daily teaches, and which it has woven into the texture of every citizen's mind. The habit of living under a rigid constitution superior to ordinary statutes—indeed two rigid constitutions, since the State Constitution is a fundamental law within its own sphere no less than is the Federal—intensifies this legality of view, since it may turn all sorts of questions which have not been determined by a direct vote of the people into questions of legal construction. It even accustoms people to submit to see their direct vote given in the enactment of a State Constitution nullified by the decision of a court holding that the Federal Constitution has been contravened. Every page of American history illustrates the wholesome results. The events of the last few years present an instance of the constraint which the people put on themselves in order to respect every form of law. The Mormons, a community not exceeding 140,000 persons, persistently defied all the efforts of Congress to root out polygamy, a practice eminently repulsive to American notions. If they inhabited a State, Congress could not have interfered at all, but as Utah is only a Territory, Congress has a power of legislating for it which overrides Territorial ordinances passed by the local legislature. Thus they were really at the mercy of Congress, had it chosen to employ violent methods. But by entrenching themselves behind the letter of the Constitution, they continued for many years to maintain their "peculiar institution" by evading the statutes passed against it and challenging a proof which under the common law rules of evidence it has been usually found impossible to give. Vehement declaimers hounded on Congress to take arbitrary means for the suppression of the practice, but Congress and the executive submitted to be outwitted rather than exceed their proper province, and succeeded at last (if indeed they have completely succeeded) only by a statute whose searching but moderate and strictly constitutional provisions the recalcitrants failed to evade. The same spirit of legality shows itself in misgoverned cities. Even where it is notorious that officials have been chosen by the grossest fraud and that they are robbing the city, the body of the people, however indignant, recognize the authority, and go on paying the taxes which a Ring levies, because strict legal proof of the frauds and robberies is not forthcoming. Wrong-doing supplies a field for the display of virtue.

III. There is a broad simplicity about the political ideas of the people, and a courageous consistency in carrying them out in practice. When they have accepted a principle, they do not shrink from applying it "right through," however disagreeable in particular cases some of the results may be. I am far from meaning that they are logical in the French sense of the word. They have little taste either for assuming abstract propositions or for syllogistically deducing practical conclusions therefrom. But when they have adopted a general maxim of policy or rule of action they show more faith in it than the English for instance would do, they adhere to it where the English would make exceptions, they prefer certainty and uniformity to the advantages which might occasionally be gained by deviation. If this tendency is partly the result of obedience to a rigid constitution, it is no less due to the democratic dislike of exceptions and complexities, which the multitude finds not only difficult of comprehension but disquieting to the individual who may not know how they will affect him. Take for instance the boundless freedom of the press. There are abuses obviously incident to such freedom, and these abuses have not failed to appear. But the Americans deliberately hold that in view of the benefits which such freedom on the whole promises, abuses must be borne with and left to the sentiment of the people and the private law of libel to deal with. When the Ku Klux outrages disgraced several of the Southern States after the military occupation of those States had ceased, there was much to be said for sending back the troops to protect the negroes and northern immigrants. But the general judgment that things ought to be allowed to take their natural course prevailed; and the result justified this policy, for the outrages after a while died out, when ordinary self-government had been restored. When recently a gigantic organization of unions of working men, purporting to unite the whole of American labour, attempted to enforce its sentences against particular firms or corporations by a boycott in which all labourers were urged to join, there was displeasure, but no panic, no call for violent remedies. The prevailing faith in liberty and in the good sense of the mass was unshaken; and the result is already justifying this tranquil faith. This tendency is not an unmixed blessing, for it sometimes allows evils to go too long unchecked. But on the whole it works for good. In giving equability to the system of government it gives steadiness and strength. It teaches the people patience, accustoming them to expect relief only by constitutional means. It confirms their faith in their institutions, as friends value one another more when their friendship has stood the test of a journey full of hardships.

IV. It is a great merit of American government that it relies very little on officials, and arms them with little power of arbitrary interference. The reader who has followed the description of Federal authorities, State authorities, county and city or township authorities, may think there is a great deal of administration; but the reason why these descriptions are necessarily so minute is because the powers of each authority are so carefully and closely restricted. It is natural to fancy that a government of the people and by the people will be led to undertake many and various functions for the people, and in the confidence of its strength will constitute itself a general philanthropic agency for their social and economic benefit. There has doubtless been of late years a tendency in this direction, a tendency to which I shall advert in a later chapter. But it has taken the direction of acting through the law rather than through the officials. That is to say, when it prescribes to the citizen a particular course of action it has relied upon the ordinary legal sanctions, instead of investing the administrative officers with inquisitorial duties or powers that might prove oppressive, and when it has devolved active functions upon officials, they have been functions serving to aid the individual and the community rather than to interfere with or supersede the action of private enterprise. As I have dwelt on the evils which may flow from the undue application of the doctrine of direct popular sovereignty, so one must place to the credit of that doctrine and the arrangements it has dictated, the intelligence which the average native American shows in his political judgments, the strong sense he entertains of the duty of giving a vote, the spirit of alertness and enterprise, which has made him self-helpful above all other men.

V. There are no struggles between privileged and unprivileged orders, not even that perpetual strife of rich and poor which is the oldest disease of civilized states. One must not pronounce broadly that there are no classes, for in parts of the country social distinctions have begun to grow up. But for political purposes classes scarcely exist. No one of the questions which now agitate the nation is a question between rich and poor. Instead of suspicion, jealousy, and arrogance embittering the relations of classes, good feeling and kindliness reign. Everything that government, as the Americans have hitherto understood the term, can give them, the poor have already, political power, equal civil rights, a career open to all citizens alike, not to speak of that gratuitous higher as well as elementary education which on their own economic principles the United States might have abstained from giving, but which political reasons have led them to provide with so unstinting a hand. Hence the poor have had nothing to fight for, no grounds for disliking the well-to-do, no complaints to make against them. The agitation of the last few years has been directed, not against the richer classes generally, but against incorporated companies and a few individual capitalists, who have not unfrequently abused the powers which the privilege of incorporation conferred upon them, or employed their wealth to procure legislation opposed to the public interests. Where language has been used like that with which France and Germany are familiar, it has been used, not by native Americans, but by new-comers, who bring their Old World passions with them. Property is safe, because those who hold it are far more numerous than those who do not: the usual motives for revolution vanish; universal suffrage, even when vested in ignorant new-comers, can do comparatively little harm, because the masses have obtained everything which they could hope to attain except by a general pillage. And the native Americans, though the same cannot be said of some of the recent immigrants, are shrewd enough to see that the poor would suffer from such pillage no less than the rich.

A European censor may make two reflections on the way in which I have presented this part of the case. He will observe that, after all, it is no more than saying that when you have got to the bottom you can fall no farther. You may be wounded and bleeding for all that. And he will ask whether, if property is safe and contentment reigns, these advantages are not due to the economical conditions of a new and resourceful country, with an abundance of unoccupied land and mineral wealth, rather than to the democratic structure of the government. The answer to the first objection is, that the descent towards equality and democracy has involved no injury to the richer or better educated classes: to the second, that although much must doubtless be ascribed to the bounty of nature, her favours have been so used by the people as to bring about a prosperity, a general diffusion of property, an abundance of freedom, of equality, and of good feeling which furnish the best security against the recurrence in America of chronic Old World evils, even when her economic state shall have become less auspicious than it now is. Wealthy and powerful such a country must have been under any form of government, but the speed with which she has advanced, and the employment of the sources of wealth to diffuse comfort among millions of families, may be placed to the credit of stimulative freedom. Wholesome habits have been established among the people whose value will be found when the times of pressure approach, and though the troubles that have arisen between labour and capital may not soon pass away, the sense of human equality, the absence of offensive privileges distinguishing class from class, will make those troubles less severe than in Europe, where they are complicated by the recollection of old wrongs, by arrogance on the one side and envy on the other.

VI. The government of the Republic, limited and languid in ordinary times, is capable of developing immense vigour. It can pull itself together at moments of danger, can put forth unexpected efforts, can venture on stretches of authority transcending not only ordinary practice but even ordinary law. This is the result of the unity of the nation. A divided people is a weak people, even if it obeys a monarch; a united people is doubly strong when it is democratic, for then the force of each individual will swells the collective force of the government, encourages it, relieves it from internal embarrassments. Now the American people is united at moments of national concern from two causes. One is that absence of class divisions and jealousies which has been already described. The people are homogeneous: a feeling which stirs them stirs alike rich and poor, farmers and traders, Eastern men and Western men—one may now add, Southern men also. Their patriotism has ceased to be defiant, and is conceived as the duty of promoting the greatness and happiness of their country, a greatness which, as it does not look to war or aggression, does not redound specially, as it might in Europe, to the glory or benefit of the ruling caste or the military profession, but to that of all the citizens. The other source of unity is the tendency in democracies for the sentiment of the majority to tell upon the sentiment of a minority. That faith in the popular voice whereof I have already spoken strengthens every feeling which has once become strong, and makes it rush like a wave over the country, sweeping everything before it. I do not mean that the people become wild with excitement, for beneath their noisy demonstrations they retain their composure and shrewd view of facts. I mean only that the pervading sympathy stirs them to unwonted efforts. The steam is superheated, but the effect is seen only in the greater expansive force which it exerts. Hence a spirited executive can in critical times go forward with a courage and confidence possible only to those who know that they have a whole nation behind them. The people fall into rank at once. With that surprising gift for organization which they possess, they concentrate themselves on the immediate object; they dispense with the ordinary constitutional restrictions; they make personal sacrifices which remind one of the self-devotion of Roman citizens in the earlier and better days of Rome.

Speaking thus, I am thinking chiefly of the spirit evolved by the Civil War both in the North and South. But the sort of strength which a democratic government derives from its direct dependence on the people is seen in many smaller instances. In 1863, when on the making of a draft of men for the war, the Irish mob rose in New York City, excited by the advance of General Robert E. Lee into Pennsylvania, the State governor called out the troops, and by them restored order with a stern vigour which would have done credit to Redetzsky or Cavaignac. More than a thousand rioters were shot down, and public opinion entirely approved the slaughter. Years after the war, when the Orangemen of New York purposed to have a 12th of July procession through the streets, the Irish Catholics threatened to prevent it. The feeling of the native Americans was aroused at once; young men of wealth came back from their mountain and seaside resorts to fill the militia regiments which were called out to guard the procession, and the display of force was so overwhelming that no disturbance followed. These Americans had no sympathy with the childish and mischievous partisanship which leads the Orangemen to perpetuate Old World feuds on New World soil. But processions were legal, and they were resolved that the law should be respected, and the spirit of disorder repressed. They would have been equally ready to protect a Roman Catholic procession.

Given an adequate occasion, executive authority is more

energetic in America, more willing to take strong measures, more sure of support from the body of the people than it is in England. I may further illustrate what I mean by referring to the view which I found ordinary Americans take some eight years ago—for as to their present views I express no opinion—of the troubles of the English government and parliament in their efforts to govern Ireland. They thought that England was erring in her refusal of the demand for trenchant land legislation, and for enlarged self-government; that she would never succeed in doing everything by the imperial parliament, and through officials taken from a particular class. They held that she ought to adopt a more broadly consistent and courageous policy, ought, in fact, to grant all such self-government as might be compatible with the maintenance of ultimate imperial control and imperial unity, and ought to take the results, be they pleasant or the reverse. But they also thought that she was erring by executive leniency, that the laws ought while they stood to be more unsparingly carried out, that parliamentary obstruction ought to be more severely repressed, that any attempts at disobedience ought to be met by lead and steel. "Make good laws," they said, "but see that whatever laws you make, you enforce. At present you are doing harm both ways. You are honouring neither liberty nor authority."

VII. Democracy has not only taught the Americans how to use liberty without abusing it, and how to secure equality: it has also taught them fraternity. That word has gone out of fashion in the Old World, and no wonder, considering what was done in its name in 1793, considering also that it still figures in the programme of assassins. Nevertheless there is in the United States a sort of kindliness, a sense of human fellowship, a recognition of the duty of mutual help owed by man to man, stronger than anywhere in the Old World, and certainly stronger than in the upper or middle classes of England, France, or Germany. The natural impulse of every citizen in America is to respect every other citizen, and to feel that citizenship constitutes a certain ground of respect. The idea of each man's equal rights is so fully realized that the rich or powerful man feels it no indignity to take his turn among the crowd, and does not expect any deference from the poorest. An employer of labour has, I think, a keener sense of his duty to those whom he employs than employers have in Europe. He has certainly a greater sense of responsibility for the use of his wealth. The number of gifts for benevolent and other public purposes, the number of educational, artistic, literary, and scientific foundations, is larger than even in England, the wealthiest and most liberal of European countries. Wealth is generally felt to be a trust, and exclusiveness condemned not merely as indicative of selfishness, but as a sort of offence against the public. No one, for instance, thinks of shutting up his pleasure-grounds; he seldom even builds a wall round them, but puts up low railings or a palisade, so that the sight of his trees and shrubs is enjoyed by passers-by. That any one should be permitted either by opinion or by law to seal up many square miles of beautiful mountain country against tourists or artists is to the ordinary American almost incredible. Such things are to him the marks of a land still groaning under feudal tyranny.

It may seem strange to those who know how difficult European states have generally found it to conduct negotiations with the government of the United States, and who are accustomed to read in European newspapers the defiant utterances which American politicians address from Congress to the effete monarchies of the Old World, to be told that this spirit of fraternity has its influence on international relations also. Nevertheless if we look not at the irresponsible orators, who play to the lower feelings of a section of the people, but at the general sentiment of the whole people, we shall recognize that democracy makes both for peace and for justice as between nations. Despite the admiration for military exploits which the Americans have sometimes shown, no country is at bottom more pervaded by a hatred of war,

and a sense that national honour stands rooted in national
fair dealing. The nation is often misrepresented by its statesmen, but although it allows them to say irritating things and
advance unreasonable claims, it has not for more than forty
years permitted them to abuse its enormous strength, as most
European nations possessed of similar strength have in time
past abused theirs.

The characteristics of the nation which I have passed in
review are not due solely to democratic government, but
they have been strengthened by it, and they contribute to its
solidity and to the smoothness of its working. As one sometimes sees an individual man who fails in life because the different parts of his nature seem unfitted to each other, so that
his action, swayed by contending influences, results in nothing definite or effective, so one sees nations whose political
institutions are either in advance of or lag behind their social
conditions, so that the unity of the body politic suffers, and
the harmony of its movements is disturbed. America is not
such a nation. It is made all of a piece; its institutions are the
product of its economic and social conditions and the expression of its character. The new wine has been poured into
new bottles: or to adopt a metaphor more appropriate to the
country, the vehicle has been built with a lightness, strength,
and elasticity which fit it for the roads it has to traverse.

THE PLEASANTNESS OF AMERICAN LIFE

I have never met a European of the upper or middle classes
who did not express astonishment when told that America
was a more agreeable place than Europe to live in. "For
working men," he would answer, "yes; but for men of education or property, how can a new rough country, where
nothing but business is talked and the refinements of life are
only just beginning to appear, how can such a country be
compared with England, or France, or Italy?"

It is nevertheless true that there are elements in the life of the United States which may well make a European of any class prefer to dwell there rather than in the land of his birth. Let us see what they are.

In the first place there is the general prosperity and material well-being of the mass of the inhabitants. In Europe, if an observer takes his eye off his own class and considers the whole population of any one of the greater countries (for I except Switzerland and parts of Scandinavia and Portugal), he will perceive that by far the greater number lead very laborious lives, and are, if not actually in want of the necessaries of existence, yet liable to fall into want, the agriculturists when nature is harsh, the wage-earners when work is scarce. In England the lot of the labourer has been hitherto a hard one, incessant field toil, with rheumatism at fifty and the workhouse at the end of the vista; while the misery massed in such cities as London, Liverpool, and Glasgow is only too well known. In France there is less pauperism, but nothing can be more pinched and sordid than the life of the bulk of the peasantry. In the great towns of Germany there is constant distress and increasing discontent. The riots of 1886 in Belgium told an even more painful tale of the wretchedness of the miners and artisans there. In Italy the condition of the rural population of Lombardy and Venetia as well as of the southern provinces seems to grow worse, and fills her statesmen with alarm. Of Russia, with her eighty millions of ignorant peasants living in half-barbarism, there is no need to speak. Contrast any one of these countries with the United States, where the working classes are as well fed, clothed, and lodged as the lower middle-class in Europe, and the farmers who till their own land (as nearly all do) much better, where a good education is within the reach of the poorest, where the opportunities for getting on in one way or another are so abundant that no one need fear any physical ill but disease or the results of his own intemperance. Pauperism already exists and increases in some of the larger cities, where drink breeds misery, and where recent immigrants, with the shiftlessness of Europe still clinging round them, are huddled together in squalor. But outside these few cities one sees nothing but comfort. In Connecticut and Massachusetts the operatives in many a manufacturing town lead a life far easier, far more brightened by intellectual culture and by amusements, than that of the clerks and shopkeepers of England or France. In cities like Cleveland or Chicago one finds miles on miles of suburb, filled with neat wooden houses, each with its tiny garden plot, owned by the shop assistants and handicraftsmen who return on the horse cars in the evening from their work. All over the wide West, from Lake Ontario to the Upper Missouri, one travels past farms of two to three hundred acres, in every one of which there is a spacious farmhouse among orchards and meadows, where the farmer's children grow up strong and hearty on abundant food, the boys full of intelligence and enterprise, ready to push their way on farms of their own or enter business in the nearest town, the girls familiar with the current literature of England as well as of America. The life of the new emigrant in the further West has its privations in the first years, but it is brightened by hope, and has a singular charm of freedom and simplicity. The impression which this comfort and plenty makes is heightened by the brilliance and keenness of the air, by the look of freshness and cleanness which even the cities wear, all of them except the poorest parts of those few I have referred to above. The fog and soot-flakes of an English town, as well as its squalor, are wanting; you are in a new world, and a world which knows the sun. It is impossible not to feel warmed, cheered, invigorated by the sense of such material well-being all around one, impossible not to be infected by the buoyancy and hopefulness of the people. The wretchedness of Europe lies far behind; the weight of its problems seems lifted from the mind. As a man suffering from depression feels the clouds roll away from his spirit when he meets a friend whose good humour and energy present the better side of things and point the way through difficulties, so the sanguine temper of the Americans, and the sight of the ardour with which they pursue their aims, stimulates a European, and makes him think the world a better place than it had seemed amid the entanglements and sufferings of his own hemisphere.

To some Europeans this may seem fanciful. I doubt if any European can realize till he has been in America how much difference it makes to the happiness of any one not wholly devoid of sympathy with his fellow-beings, to feel that all round him, in all classes of society and all parts of the country, there exist in such ample measure so many of the external conditions of happiness: abundance of the necessaries of life, easy command of education and books, amusements and leisure to enjoy them, comparatively few temptations to intemperance and vice.

The second charm of American life is one which some Europeans will smile at. It is social equality. To many Europeans—to Germans, let us say, or Englishmen—the word has an odious sound. It suggests a dirty fellow in a blouse elbowing his betters in a crowd, or an ill-conditioned villager shaking his fist at the parson and the squire; or, at any rate, it suggests obtrusiveness and bad manners. The exact contrary is the truth. Equality improves manners, for it strengthens the basis of all good manners, respect for other men and women simply as men and women, irrespective of their station in life. Probably the assertion of social equality was one of the causes which injured American manners forty years ago, for that they were then bad among townsfolk can hardly be doubted in face of the testimony, not merely of sharp tongues like Mrs. Trollope's, but of calm observers like Sir Charles Lyell and sympathetic observers like Richard Cobden. In those days there was an obtrusive self-assertiveness among the less refined classes, especially towards those who, coming from the Old World, were assumed to come in a patronizing spirit. Now, however, social equality has grown so naturally out of the circumstances of the country, has been so long established, and is so ungrudgingly admitted, that all excuse for obtrusiveness has disappeared. People meet on a simple and natural footing, with more frankness and ease than is possible in countries where every one is either looking up or looking down. There is no servility on the part of the humbler, and if now and then a little of the "I am as good as you" rudeness be perceptible, it is almost sure to proceed from a recent immigrant, to whom the attitude of simple equality has not yet become familiar as the evidently proper attitude of one man to another. There is no condescension on the part of the more highly placed, nor is there even that sort of scrupulously polite coldness which one might think they would adopt in order to protect their dignity. They have no cause to fear for their dignity, so long as they do not themselves forget it. And the fact that your shoemaker or your factory hand addresses you as an equal does not prevent him from respecting, and showing his respect for, all such superiority as your birth or education or eminence in any line of life may entitle you to receive.

This naturalness of intercourse is a distinct addition to the pleasure of social life. It enlarges the circle of possible friendship, by removing the *gêne* which in most parts of Europe persons of different ranks feel in exchanging their thoughts on any matters save those of business. It raises the humbler classes without lowering the upper; indeed, it improves the upper no less than the lower by expunging that latent insolence which deforms the manners of so many of the European rich or great. It relieves women in particular, who in Europe are specially apt to think of class distinctions, from that sense of constraint and uneasiness which is produced by the knowledge that other women with whom they come in contact are either looking down on them, or at any rate trying to gauge and determine their social position. It expands the range of a man's sympathies, and makes it easier for him to enter into the sentiments of other classes than his own. It gives a sense of solidarity to the whole nation, cutting away the ground for all sorts of jealousies and grudges which distract people, so long as the social pretensions of past centuries linger on to be resisted and resented by the levelling spirit of a revolutionary age. And I have never heard native Americans speak of any drawbacks corresponding to and qualifying these benefits.

There are, moreover, other rancours besides those of social inequality whose absence from America brightens it to a European eye. There are no quarrels of churches and sects. Judah does not vex Ephraim, nor Ephraim envy Judah. No Established Church looks down scornfully upon Dissenters from the height of its titles and endowments, and talks of them as hindrances in the way of its work. No Dissenters pursue an Established Church in a spirit of watchful jealousy, nor agitate for its overthrow. One is not offended by the contrast between the theory and the practice of a religion of peace, between professions of universal affection in pulpit addresses and forms of prayer, and the acrimony of clerical controversialists. Still less, of course, is there that sharp opposition and antagonism of Christians and anti-Christians which lacerates the private as well as public life of France. Rivalry between sects appears only in the innocent form of the planting of new churches and raising of funds for missionary objects, while most of the Protestant denominations, including the four most numerous, constantly fraternize in charitable work. Between Roman Catholics and Protestants there is little hostility, and sometimes co-operation for a philanthropic purpose. The sceptic is no longer under a social ban, and discussions on the essentials of Christianity and of theism are conducted with good temper. There is not a country in the world where Frederick the Great's principle, that every one should be allowed to go to heaven his own way, is so fully applied. This sense of religious peace as well as religious freedom all around one is soothing to the weary European, and contributes not a little to sweeten the lives of ordinary people.

I come last to the character and ways of the Americans themselves, in which there is a certain charm, hard to convey by description, but felt almost as soon as one sets foot on their shore, and felt constantly thereafter. They are a kindly people. Good nature, heartiness, a readiness to render small services to one another, an assumption that neighbours in the country, or persons thrown together in travel, or even in a crowd, were meant to be friendly rather than hostile to one another, seem to be everywhere in the air, and in those who breathe it. Sociability is the rule, isolation and moroseness the rare exception. It is not merely that people are more vivacious or talkative than an Englishman expects to find them, for the Western man is often taciturn and seldom wreathes his long face into a smile. It is rather that you feel that the man next you, whether silent or talkative, does not mean to repel intercourse, or convey by his manner his low opinion of his fellow-creatures. Everybody seems disposed to think well of the world and its inhabitants, well enough at least to wish to be on easy terms with them and serve them in those little things whose trouble to the doer is small in proportion to the pleasure they give to the receiver. To help others is better recognized as a duty than in Europe. Nowhere is money so readily given for any public purpose; nowhere, I suspect, are there so many acts of private kindness done, such, for instance, as paying the college expenses of a promising boy, or aiding a widow to carry on her husband's farm; and these are not done with ostentation. People seem to take their own troubles more lightly than they do in Europe, and to be more indulgent to the faults by which troubles are caused. It is a land of hope, and a land of hope is a land of good humour. And they have also, though this is a quality more perceptible in women than in men, a remarkable faculty for enjoyment, a power of drawing more happiness from obvious pleasures, simple and innocent pleasures, than one often finds in overburdened Europe.

As generalizations like this are necessarily comparative, I

may be asked with whom I am comparing the Americans. With the English, or with some attempted average of European nations? Primarily I am comparing them with the English, because they are the nearest relatives of the English. But there are other European countries, such as France, Belgium, Spain, in which the sort of cheerful friendliness I have sought to describe is less common than it is in America. Even in Germany and German Austria, simple and kindly as are the masses of the people, the upper classes have that *roideur* which belongs to countries dominated by an old aristocracy, or by a plutocracy trying to imitate aristocratic ways. The upper class in America (if one may use such an expression) has not in this respect differentiated itself from the character of the nation at large.

If the view here presented be a true one, to what causes are we to ascribe this agreeable development of the original English type, a development in whose course the sadness of Puritanism seems to have been shed off?

Perhaps one of them is the humorous turn of the American character. Humour is a sweetener of temper, a copious spring of charity, for it makes the good side of bad things even more visible than the weak side of good things: but humour in Americans may be as much a result of an easy and kindly turn as their kindliness is of their humour. Another is the perpetuation of a habit of mutual help formed in colonial days. Colonists need one another's aid more constantly than the dwellers in an old country, are thrown more upon one another, even when they live scattered in woods or prairies, are more interested in one another's welfare. When you have only three neighbours within five miles, each of them covers a large part of your horizon. You want to borrow a plough from one; you get another to help you to roll your logs; your children's delight is to go over for an evening's merrymaking to the lads and lasses of the third. It is much pleasanter to be on good terms with these few neighbours, and when others come one by one, they fall into the same habits of intimacy. Any one who has read those stories of rustic New England or New York life which delighted the English children of thirty years ago—I do not know whether they delight children still, or have been thrown aside for more highly-spiced food—will remember the warm-hearted simplicity and atmosphere of genial goodwill which softened the roughness of peasant manners and tempered the sternness of a Calvinistic creed. It is natural that the freedom of inter-course and sense of interdependence which existed among the early settlers, and which have always existed since among the pioneers of colonization in the West as they moved from the Connecticut to the Mohawk, from the Mohawk to the Ohio, from the Ohio to the Mississippi, should have left on the national character traces not effaced even in the more artificial civilization of our own time. Something may be set down to the feeling of social equality, creating that respect for a man as a man, whether he be rich or poor, which was described a few pages back; and something to a regard for the sentiment of the multitude, a sentiment which forbids any man to stand aloof in the conceit of self-importance, and holds up geniality and good fellowship as almost the first of social virtues. I do not mean that a man consciously suppresses his impulses to selfishness or gruffness because he knows that his faults will be ill regarded; but that, having grown up in a society which is infinitely powerful as com-pared with the most powerful person in it, he has learnt to realize his individual insignificance, as members of the upper class in Europe never do, and has become permeated by the feeling which this society entertains—that each one's duty is not only to accept equality, but also to relish equality, and to make himself pleasant to his equals. Thus the habit is formed even in natures of no special sweetness, and men become kindly by doing kindly acts.

Whether, however, these suggestions be right or wrong, there is, I think, no doubt as to the fact which they attempt to explain. I do not, of course, give it merely as the casual

impression of European visitors, whom a singularly frank
and ready hospitality welcomes and makes much of. I base
it on the reports of European friends who have lived for
years in the United States, and whose criticism of the ways
and notions of the people is keen enough to show that they
are no partial witnesses.

Bryce, *The American Commonwealth.*

HIGH SOCIETY AT NEWPORT

PAUL BOURGET

NOVELIST, poet, and critic, Paul Bourget is perhaps best known in America for his travel sketches, and especially for *Outre-Mer* (1894), from which this picture of Newport society is taken. Born at Amiens, in 1852, the son of a civil engineer, Bourget studied at the École des Hautes Études, specializing in Greek philology. His easy fluency, however, and his lively interest in society, deflected him from scholarship to journalism, and before he was thirty he was earning his living by writing travel sketches and critical reviews for the French journals. Enormously prolific, Bourget wrote a long series of novels, several volumes of criticism—including *Sociology and Literature* and the *Physiology of Modern Love*, and a half dozen volumes of poems. *Outre-Mer* was a vivacious description of American society as Bourget saw it during the depths of the depression of the early nineties. His observations, if superficial, were on the whole sympathetic, and he concluded that "the consciousness that humanity has yonder so colossal a field of experiment in which to continue its work, fills me with a sort of mysterious exaltation, as though an act of faith in human will had declared itself in me, and I opened my heart quite fully to this great breath of courage and hope that has come to me from *outre-mer*."

The picture of Newport painted here might well be compared with that drawn by Henry James in *An International Episode* and *The Ivory Tower*.

❖❖❖❖❖❖

I CAME to Newport for a few days. I have remained here a whole month, taking my part in this life which has indeed no counterpart, at least, not to my knowledge. Neither Deauville nor Brighton nor Biarritz resembles it, nor Cannes, although the last approaches it in the splendor of its villas and the almost total absence of the lower middle class. But Cannes is a *Cosmopolis* like Rome or Florence, perhaps more so, while Newport is exclusively, absolutely American. A few European visitors have passed through it this summer, on their way to Chicago and the World's Fair. Usually they may be counted by six or seven. The French know nothing of Newport. The English—a very few of them—come here for the yachting; but they prefer the Isle of Wight, with Cannes and the convenient Solent. . . .

Between old Newport, where the quiet homely life keeps on all through the winter, and the other, the summer Newport, fashionable and transient, there is no intermediate. Nothing suggests the rough draught of a watering-place; first efforts corrected, worked over and over, a gradual encroachment of fashion. The same outbreak of individuality which reared the palaces of Fifth Avenue in New York, almost as by Aladdin's lamp, created in a flash of miracle this town of cottages. The only difference is in the complicated architecture where the rich have vied with the rich as to who shall excel the others. The "go-ahead" American spirit is seen here in a costliness of construction very significant, when one reflects that these dwellings do duty for six weeks, perhaps for two months, in the year, and that each one takes for granted such accessories as a four-in-hand, a yacht, or perhaps two, for cruising along the coast, a private car for railway journeys, a New York house and another country house!

One of these men has spent some time in England, and it has pleased him to build for himself on one of these Rhode Island lawns an English abbey of the style of Queen Elizabeth. It rises up, gray and stern, so like, so perfect, that it

might, without changing a single stone, be transported to
Oxford on the shores of Isis, to make a pendant to the delicious cloister of Magdalen or the façade of Oriel. Another
man loves France, and he has seen fit to possess in sight of
the Atlantic a château in the style of the French Renascence.
Here is the château; it reminds you of Azay, Chenonceaux,
and the Loire, with its transparent ribbon of water winding
idly in and out amid the yellow sand of the islands. A third
has built a marble palace precisely like the Trianon, with
Corinthian pillars as large as those of the Temple of the Sun
at Baalbek. And these are not weak imitations, pretentious
and futile attempts, such as in every country bring ridicule
upon braggarts and upstarts. No. In detail and finish they
reveal conscientious study, technical care. Evidently the best
artist has been chosen and he has had both freedom and
money.

Especially money! Caprices like these take for granted
such quantities of it that after a walk from cottage to cottage,
from château to abbey, you half fancy that you have been
visiting some isle consecrated to the god Plutus, whose most
modern incarnation is the god Dollar. But this is a Plutus
who yesterday sat at the hearthstone of Penia, the untamed
goddess of poverty; a Plutus whom neither wealth nor luxury has enervated or enfeebled; a Plutus who, being no
longer obliged to work, wills that his gold shall work, that it
shall make itself manifest, spread itself, "show off," to use
the real Yankee word. And this gold makes itself so manifest,
it shows off with such violent intensity, that it impresses you
like the deploying of an army. Flaubert wrote to one of his
pupils: "If you cannot construct the Parthenon, build a
pyramid." All America seems to be instinctively repeating to
itself in other words this stern but stimulating counsel. As in
the harbor and streets of New York you are dismayed at so
much activity, so in these Newport avenues you are amazed
at so much wealth. It either revolts or charms you, according
as you lean toward socialism or snobbery. The psychologist

who looks upon a city as a naturalist looks upon an ant-hill, will recognize in it the fact which I observed at the very first, —something indescribably extravagant, unbridled. The American spirit seems not to understand moderation. Their high business buildings are too high. Their pleasure-houses are too elegant. Their fast trains go too fast. Their newspapers have too many pages; too much news. And when they set themselves to spend money, they are obliged to spend too much in order to have the feeling of spending enough.

How do they furnish their houses?

I have in mind, as I write these words, the interior of some fifty of these villas, perhaps more. From the week of my arrival, upon the presentation of my letters of introduction, I was caught up in the whirlwind of luncheons, coaching-parties, yachtings, dinners, and balls, which for several weeks sweeps over Newport like a simoon. "Be in the rush," says an advertisement in the electric car which runs between the beach and the lower town. A recommendation of a special brand of yeast accompanies this eloquent appeal, this "all aboard" which the Americans speedily force you to act upon.

Their energy extends even to their hospitality, which bestirs itself in your behalf, multiplying its "five-o'clock teas" and its "to meets." It is a warm spontaneity of welcome of which we have no notion in Latin countries. With us the foreigner may get into society if he settles down and does us the honor of preferring our country to his own. As for him who is simply passing through not to return, it takes us some time to overcome a certain distrust; we do not, without a thorough acquaintance, pass over from formal courtesy to intimacy. The American throws his house wide open to you as soon as you are duly presented. He wants you to know his friends; he wants all his friends to treat you as he does.

Slanderers say that there is no merit in this; that their large way of living prevails in all Anglo-Saxon countries where

children are many, needs complicated, incomes proportionately large, and economy unknown. One more guest hardly
counts in such a home. This is true. Still I think I perceive
here a feeling more complex than that opulent and indifferent hospitality which is still that of wealthy Orientals.

The American, who lives so fast, carries to the highest
pitch a fondness for seeing himself live. It seems as if he
looked upon himself and his surroundings in the light of a
singular experiment in social life, and as if he hardly knew
what he ought to think of it. He makes it a point that you,
a European, shall be correctly informed before judging of
this experiment, and he helps to inform you. "You see such
or such a one," he will say to you. "He is an American of
this or that type. Read such a book—you will find there a
true picture of the American of that State." If he knows that
you are travelling for the purpose of taking notes, he is disturbed, and yet he finds pleasure in it as an act of homage.
He wants your notes to be taken from life. If he sees in you
a simple tourist, he wants your reports when you return
home to be something other than the erroneous legends of
which, to his exasperation, he finds traces in our newspapers.
There is a curious mixture of doubt and pride in the pleasure
which he feels in escorting you from one end of his house to
the other, showing you in a breath the picture gallery and
the linen closet, the drawing-rooms and the bed-chambers.
One of their best novelists, Howells, has sagaciously noted
this peculiar trait of character, this facility of offering oneself as a lesson of things.

"We men of the modern world," says March, in *A Hazard
of New Fortunes*, "are inclined to take ourselves too objectively, to consider ourselves more representative than is
necessary."

Meanwhile, to the professional observer this turn of mind
lightens half his task. It is so difficult in Italy, Spain, Germany, in France itself, to picture to oneself the "home" of
those we know the best, and yet the witness that tells the most

is the objects which we gather around us according to our own whims. A drawing-room, a bed-chamber, a dining-room, have a physiognomy, almost a countenance, in the likeness of our tastes, our needs, the things in ourselves which often we ourselves do not suspect.

A first impression emerges from the homes of Newport. It ought to be correct, so much does it accord with the rest of American life, even outside of villas like these. This is a new evidence of excess, abuse, absence of moderation. On the floors of halls which are too high there are too many precious Persian and Oriental rugs. There are too many tapestries, too many paintings on the walls of the drawing-rooms. The guest-chambers have too many *bibelots*, too much rare furniture, and on the lunch or dinner table there are too many flowers, too many plants, too much crystal, too much silver.

At this moment I can see in the centre of one of these tables a vase of solid silver, large and deep as the pot of a huge plant, too small, however, for a bunch of grapes, a prodigal bunch with grapes as large as small cannon balls. I see again a screen made of an Italian painting of the school of the Carracci, cut into four parts. The canvas has not been much injured and the work was well done, but what a symbol of this perpetual extravagance of luxury and refinement!

This excess has its prototype in the rose so justly called the "American beauty," enormous bunches of which crown these tables. It has so long a stem, it is so intensely red, so wide open, and so strongly perfumed, that it does not seem like a natural flower. It requires the greenhouse, the exposition, a public display. Splendid as it is, it makes one long for the frail wild eglantine with its rosy petals which a breath of wind will crumple. For the eglantine is a bit of nature, and also of aristocracy, at least in the sense in which we Europeans understand the word, for with us it is inseparable from an idea of soft coloring and absence of pretension. It is certain that this excess reveals in this people an energy much more like that of the Renascence, for example, under divers forms, than that meagreness of individuality which we moderns disguise under the name of distinction. That vigor of blood and nerves which has enabled the men of the United States to conquer fortune, persists in him through all his fortunes and manifests itself by splendor within the house as it was first manifested by splendor outside of it. You find vigor everywhere, even in the senseless prodigalities of high life.

Yet, these millionaires do not entirely accept themselves. This is the second impression forced upon you by a more attentive observation of these "halls" and drawing-rooms. They do not admit that they are thus different from the Old World, or if they admit it, it is to insist that if they chose they could equal the Old World, or, at least, could enjoy it. "We have made money enough to be artists now," said an architect to me, "and we have no time to wait. So I am studying the French eighteenth century; I intend to build houses of that type, with every modern improvement,—water, light, electricity."

His patriotism is perfectly sincere, very intense, and he makes it consist in the conquest or at least the loan of a foreign style! The furnishings of the Newport houses betray a similar effort,—a constant, tireless endeavor to absorb European ideas. One might count in these villas all the articles made in America. It is in Europe that the silk of these stuffed chairs and these curtains was woven; in Europe that these chairs and tables were turned. This silverware came from Europe, and this dress was woven, cut, sewn in Europe; these shoes, stockings, gloves came from there. "When I was in Paris;" "Then we go to Paris;" "We want to go to Paris to buy our gowns."

These expressions continually recur in conversation, and it was certainly a Parisian salon which served as model of the one in which you find yourself. These toilettes are surely modelled on the same pattern as those of the elegant Parisian women. Only, drawing-room and dresses alike have, like everything else, that indescribable something too much. The fashion of these gowns is not of to-day but of to-morrow. The dressmakers have a very expressive way of noting this almost indescribable shade of difference. They say, "We will try the new designs first on the foreigners—then we shall weed them out for the Parisian women."

Thus is explained this characteristic of the excessive; this art of being on dress parade, which these women—often so beautiful—still further heighten by a profusion of jewels worn in daylight. At noon they will have at their waists turquoises as big as almonds, pearls as large as filberts at their throats, rubies and diamonds as large as their finger-nails. Yes, it is indeed Europe, but overgrown, exaggerated; and this inordinate imitation only accentuates the difference between the Old World and the New.

Among the freaks of decoration thus borrowed from our country, one has become singularly changed during its passage of the Atlantic. I speak of the taste for old things—the fancy for bric-à-brac and *bibelots* so characteristic of our age. It has become hateful to us, because universal competition has so raised the prices that very few European fortunes are large enough to permit it. Counterfeiting has followed, and second-rate articles are especially abundant.

The Americans have come to market with their full purses. With us a millionaire is a man who has a million francs. Here a millionaire is one who has a million dollars; that is, five million francs. They have brought to market that universal knowledge which comes from the constant habit of having seriously undertaken collecting and looked at it in the light of a true lesson in things. For the last thirty or forty years, thanks to their full purses, they have laid hands upon the finest pictures, tapestries, carvings, medals, not only of

France, England, Holland, Italy, but also of Greece, Egypt,
India, Japan. Hence they have in their town and country
houses a wealth of masterpieces worthy of a museum. In
some Newport villas which I could name, is an entire private
gallery, which has been transported thither bodily; its original owner having spent years in collecting it from among
the rarest works of the early German school. And they keep
on in this way! The other day I heard an amateur say sadly,
alluding to the financial crisis which happens to bear heavily
upon Italy and the United States at once:—

"The Italians are rather low down just now, and there are
things to be had *sub rosa*. But at present nobody can profit
by it."

One asks oneself where they would put these Italian things,
so completely covered by paintings is the Cordovan leather
which covers the walls of their houses. And then there are
the glass cases under which treasures of cut stones await the
magnifying-glass, with enamels, engraved armor, ancient
books, medals, especially portraits. In two adjacent villas, a
quarter of an hour apart, I thus saw the portrait of a great
Genoese seigneur, a Venetian admiral, an English lord of the
last century, that of Louis XV. by Vanloo, with the inscription "Given by the King," that of Louis XIV. by
Mignard, with the same inscription, that of Henry IV. by
Porbus. F——, who does not like the Americans, said to me
with irony:—

"Yes; they have the portrait of the great King, but where
is their grandfather's portrait?"

And he attributes this love of old pictures to a vague and
awkward attempt to make a false gallery of ancestors. In my
opinion he does not recognize the sincerity, almost the pathos,
of this love of Americans for surrounding themselves with
things around which there is an idea of time and of stability.
This sensation, so difficult for us to conceive, and which my
companion of the Players artlessly expressed to me in New
York, is intelligible to me, and after these few weeks of the

United States I feel it myself. It is almost a physical satisfaction of the eyes to meet here the faded colors of an ancient painting, the blurred stamp of an antique coin, the softened shades of a tapestry of the Middle Ages. In this country, where everything is of yesterday, they hunger and thirst for the long ago. We must believe that the soul of man is possessed by an indestructible desire to be surrounded with things of the past, since these extravagances of luxury subserve such a desire. They do not discern it in themselves, but they feel it all the same. Last week one of these men ordered his carriage to turn back that he might show me the statue of a Newporter who was a friend of his grandfather.

"One likes to think of a time so far away," he said.

This desire for a deeply prepared soil is just what a tree would feel on being transplanted to a new place with its roots too near the surface. This unconscious effort to surround themselves with the past, to ennoble themselves by it, is what saves these homes of millionaires from being coarse, so formed by sheer force of money, and for the purpose of showing that they were so formed. It is an unexpected bit of poetry in what but for that would be merely "the apotheosis of the check and the *chic*," to repeat a low pleasantry of a very low song of a former day. It consoles one for seeing strewed about among these magnificences a few inexpressibly vulgar and childish ornaments such as an outrageous toy,—a moon-faced doll with an eyeglass and a tall hat, smoking a lighted cigarette, while a music box hidden in its body plays a vulgar air. Written below it, to the shame of those writers who first made use of the expression, are the words, "*Fin de siècle.*" What a mosaic is the taste of this race which takes everything pell-mell from our civilization, the excellent and the bad, our finest works of art and our most deplorable caricatures!

How do they recruit their numbers? By a single method and from a single class. In this respect, when we compare this summer Newport with our Deauville, or with Brighton on the other side of the Channel, there is a never-to-be-forgotten difference. There is here no upper class, as in England, no aristocratic Olympus whose customs are followed by all "tuft-hunters"—the picturesque word with which Oxford students banter those of their comrades who are trying to get into the smart set, hypnotized by the golden tassel that dangles from the caps of the students who belong to the nobility. There is not here as in France that irrational but potent survival of an ancient order in the very midst of a vigorous democracy, whose most expressive sign is without doubt our notion of the "club." With us the "circle" has ceased to be the natural, almost the necessary, sphere of those who keep up a certain style. It has come to be a sort of brevet, almost a rank, in an undetermined social regiment, the staff of which lives at the Union, the Jockey, or the Rue Royale.

In America all men in society have been and still are business men. They were not born to social station; they have achieved it. They did not find it ready made and handed over to them. They made it themselves, because it suited them to add such a refinement to their wealth, by way of coping to their edifice. The result is a profound equality among them, a singular uniformity of habits, thought, tastes, which speak their absolute similarity of origin. The attempt has indeed been made, of late years, to break up this uniformity, to establish an artificial Olympus, that of the "four hundred," which are drawn from the families of oldest traditions and most wealth. This whim could not be carried out, because the true foundations of all these great fortunes are too recent, too well known; and besides, they could not be kept up without a continuance of the toil which produced them. Such a one became rich through the discovery of a gold mine twenty-five years ago. A railroad built in 1860 made such a one a millionaire. Behind each of the names which appear in the newspaper reports of social functions, any American can see this or that factory, commercial house, bank, land speculation, and generally the factory is at full blast, the wickets of the commercial house and the bank are always open, the speculation is still going on. Democrats may say that such titles to a place in society are worth quite as much as a coat of arms crossed by bastardy or doubtful marriages, or a historic celebrity which has no counterpart in those that inherit it. Certain it is that the foundations of American society are frankly evident. Their immediate results are no less so.

First among them is the almost total absence of adventurers and adventuresses in a watering-place like Newport. It is easy to deceive a composite society, but not a society of business men. A family whose revenues are doubtful may make a figure in a circle where the authentic nobility must needs resort to expedients for its support, in which reigns that spirit of shiftiness in money matters which is habitual with those who earn nothing. In America, every one knows what his neighbor is "worth," and besides, society life is here a luxury, while the minor daily expenses are so great as to be unsupportable by an ill-balanced budget.

French novelists since Balzac have often painted the type of the ambitious poor young man who keeps himself in the full current of high life by the superior management of very modest resources. Here a presentable evening suit costs a hundred and fifty dollars,—seven hundred and fifty francs, —a carriage to go to dinner costs three dollars, and five if you also return by carriage. A woman pays fifty per cent duty on the evening dress she brought from Paris. The New York dressmakers' and milliners' bills come up to about the same figure. It is hardly an economy to have a seamstress in the house to copy the models of the great dressmakers,—that resource of the prudent Parisian woman,—in a place where a clever maid has forty dollars a month and a good dress-

maker three dollars a day. This sort of abuse of wealth, not
peculiar to Newport but found all over America, is at once
a folly and a purifying process. We may rail at the frivolity
of this existence, condemn its extravagance. It may deserve
many satires. It is at least very upright and very sound.

(It is all that, in this summer sojourn; witness the total
suppression of the element which in Europe adorns and cor-
rupts so many watering-places—I refer to the *demi-monde*.)
As American society is principally drawn from business
circles, the men have but little leisure. They are all absent
several days in the week, occupied in making the money
which it is the function of their wives to display. It follows
that if they have relations outside of their own homes, they
are not to be found here. Those who remain in Newport the
whole week round are few in number, and for the most part
old, since they are "out of business," or very young and not
yet in it. A few diplomatists on their vacation and a few flying visitors complete the masculine part of society, the small-
ness of whose number would compel them to good conduct
if, indeed, their inherited puritan morality, always present
in a country of Anglo-Saxon traditions,—at least under the
form of hypocrisy,—did not make all scandal impossible.

For that matter, by what diplomatic processes would the
most adroit member of the *demi-monde* succeed in brushing
up against the real society, in offering a facile imitation of it,
as with us, in a circle where all forms of pleasure are organized into a club and one must have an admission, a presentation, patronage, in order to take a cup of tea here, to play
a game of tennis there? More than this, the race is not old
enough for the courtesan to have become the petted but refined creature, scoffing and witty, who amuses a man and
little by little makes her way into his daily intimacy. Simply
to recognize how entirely she is absent from a city which
elsewhere would be her favorite field of operation is to see
that she is here reduced to the condition of a mere instrument

of pleasure. Theo, who has lived ten years in the United States, said to me,—

"Women are not necessary to Americans as they are to us. A man only goes with them here when he is slightly drunk and wants to keep it up."

Bourget, *Outre-Mer*.

22

THE AMERICAN IS AN ELECTRIC ANGLO-SAXON

GEORGE WARRINGTON STEEVENS

BORN at Sydenham, England, in 1869, and educated at Balliol College, Oxford, George Steevens turned to journalism at the age of twenty-four and rose rapidly to be one of the most brilliant of English journalists. After working briefly for the *National Observer* and the *Pall Mall* Gazette, Steevens joined the staff of the *Daily Mail* and was sent by that paper to cover the exciting election of 1896 in the United States. His description of that election, and particularly of the Bryan campaign—*The Land of the Dollar* (1898)—is one of the liveliest in our literature. On his return to London he was sent out as a roving reporter to Greece, Turkey, Egypt, India and South Africa. His reports on the second Dreyfus trial were published as *The Tragedy of Dreyfus*, and his articles on the Boer War as *With Kitchener to Khartum*. Steevens died of enteric fever at Ladysmith at the age of thirty-one.

✧✧✧✧✧✧✧

THE proudest moment of my fifteen thousand miles of wandering came upon me in a bank in Chicago. As I was waiting there the policeman on duty approached me stealthily, as one about to confide a secret of deep importance.

"Are ye not an Englishman, sorr?" he whispered.

"Yes," I said.

"I knew ut," he responded with enthusiasm. "I knew ut

the minute ye came through the dure. There is nothing like ut in the worrld."

Howbeit, there is something very strangely like it, and at the same time most strangely unlike. That is the American. He does not look like an Englishman, yet it is manifest at sight that he cannot be of any other known breed of man. He talks English . . . often with a clarity of pronunciation that put me again and again to shame. When I was dictating to a typewriter and she could not understand what I said, when at last she caught the word and repeated it, I wondered why I could not make a vowel sound with the same distinctness and purity. Yet that typewriter could not spell; for the Americans, as I have hinted, are a nation of but superficial education.

But the essential difference which new environment has grafted into the English stock strikes deeper than appearance and language. If I am asked to give it a name, it is hard to find one. The American is a highly electric Anglo-Saxon. His temperament is of quicksilver. There is as much difference in vivacity and emotion between him and an Englishman as there is between an Englishman and an Italian. Yet curiously there is just as much difference between him and the Italian. His emotion is not the least like that of the Southern European. For behind the flash of his passion there shines always the steady light of dry, hard, practical reason. Shrewd yet excitable, hot-hearted and cool-headed, he combines the northern and the southern temperaments, and yet is utterly distinct from either. He has developed into a new sort of Anglo-Saxon, a new national character, a new race.

The keynote of this character is its irresistible impulse to impress all its sentiments externally by the crudest and most obvious medium. The Americans are the most demonstrative of all the peoples of the earth. Everything must be brought to the surface, embodied in a visible, palpable form. For a fact to make any effect on the American mind it must be put in a shape where it can be seen, heard, handled. If you want to impress your fellows you must do it not through their reasoning powers, but through the five senses of their bodies.

I noticed it first in connection with their way of conducting an election. A hundred thousand men are going to vote for M'Kinley; that is nothing. Put your hundred thousand men down in Broadway, so that we can see them marching, hear them shouting; then we will begin to appreciate the fact. And the more you give us to see and hear in the way of banners and bands, the more we shall appreciate it. The demonstrative nature of the race, once discovered in this respect, soon appeared a master-key which would unlock most of the puzzles in the American. The most patriotic of men, his patriotism seems always to centre rather on his flag than on his country: he can see the flag, but he can't see the country. Why does he cover his person with childish buttons and badges? Because you can see them, and you can't see the sentiments in his mind. Why does he cling all his life to the title of some rank or office he held twenty years ago? You can hear the title pronounced, but you can't see the history of his life. A man's self is no good unless he can put a big legible label on it. Thus, again, they will not intrust their goods to anybody without receiving a check—something you can see and jingle in your pocket. They do not read Shakespeare, but would think it almost a sin to visit England without seeing Shakespeare's house. In business they are the most unwearied and ingenious advertisers in the world. In dress they appear vain, out of just the same reverence for the concrete and indifference to the abstract. No nation in the world is in such bondage to fashion as democratic America. Her men and women, young and old, wear boots that narrow to a sharp point, like skates, two inches beyond the toes; they tinker at their faces with complexion-washes and nose-machines as zealously as some people in England tinker at their souls. But the extremest case I met of the appeal to the concrete was a lawsuit in which parents claimed damages for an assault on their child. A kick had brought on necrosis of the bone, and the necrosised bone was duly produced in court and handed round among the jury. That settled it. There was plenty of medical evidence as to the cause of death, but all this weighed as nothing to the sight and feel of the accusing bone.

It is in this sense that the Americans may fairly be called the most materialistic people of the world. Materialistic in the sense of being avaricious, I do not think they are: they make money, as I have said, because they must make something, and there is nothing else to make. But materialistic, in the sense that they must have all their ideas put in material form, they unquestionably are.

Another characteristic which may perhaps be partly explained on the same theory, is the American want of thoroughness. Whether in building a railway or in tilling a field, in enforcing a law or in keeping an appointment, they are less thorough than we. Everything is left, to the English mind, half finished. Perhaps one reason is that a certain amount has been done; there is something to show; the instinct of display is gratified. Without waiting to perfect the details that make no show, the American turns to attain palpable and striking results elsewhere. This may not be the whole explanation. There is also the roving temperament innate in the emigrant's children. Still more to the point is the very wise and practical turn which forbids wasting further effort on what will serve its purpose as it is. This virtue they have most eminently: except for little foibles born of the desire for outward effect, they are most free from pedantry. If the American is less doggedly resolute and persevering than the Englishman, he is proportionately more irresistible and ingenious in devising possible means to attain any impossible end.

To pass from the manufactory, and the farm, and the mine, into the home, it is believed by people in this country that the American still preserves the private life of the Puritan, from whom, in some not unexaggerated measure, he descends. But there is a good deal of misapprehension about this. As to the home, the Americans talks about it a great deal. A man never builds himself a house: he builds himself a home. But you cannot call a people who will never be happy ten years in the same place, who build themselves houses with the view of shortly moving them bodily somewhere else, who often voluntarily live in public and comfortless hotels—you cannot call them home-loving in the English sense. As to Puritanism, people point to their irreproachable novels. Yes, but look at their disreputable newspapers. They will refuse to call legs anything but limbs, yet they will readily produce generous pictures of those limbs in tights. There is no need to go into the evidence, but I am satisfied that in point of morality the Americans are neither more nor less puritanical than ourselves. And the facts that they are the hardiest of gamblers and the most ingenious of blasphemers, though far from utterly damning, are hardly evidence of direct spiritual descent from the Puritans. Still less is the more important fact that, while often hide-bound by convention, America is magnificently free from intolerance.

In one virtue these men furnish a shining example to all the world—in their devoted chivalry towards their women. They toil and slave, they kill themselves at forty, that their women may live in luxury and become socially and intellectually superior to themselves. They do it without even an idea that there is any self-sacrifice in it. Whether it is good for the women might be doubted, but it is unspeakably noble and honouring to the men. The age of chivalry is not gone; until America it never came.

On the other side of the picture is the American attitude to children and to the old. With children they are merely foolishly indulgent, thus producing an undisciplined, conceited, and ignorant youth. No American is fit to talk to until he is thirty, and he retains all his life a want of discipline, an incapacity for ordered and corporate effort. The individual may be the fresher and the stronger for it, but it is not productive of good government. With the old the accusation is graver; they are shouldered unmercifully out of existence. It would be impossible in America to find a newspaper correspondence like one which appeared in the "Daily Mail" upon "reasonable correction" of wives. But I found in New York a correspondence on the open question whether the old have any right to respect. Many of the public thought, quite seriously, they had no right even to existence. Why, it was asked, should those who had spent their lives in self-indulgence (that is, who had not saved money) presume to stand in the way of the self-denying (or money-making)? Away with them! Now that would be impossible in England.

One explanation is that virtually there are no old in America at all. The strenuous fever of life kills the American at fifty or so. An American woman is old at thirty. And certainly the climate helps. It is not yet certain that North America is not the deadliest white man's grave in the world. For the old families die out; the native-born population at the last census had not increased, but had heavily decreased. Maybe the climate is a man-killing one; the French-Canadians breed prodigiously, but it appears from remains that the country never carried a population comparable to many areas of the Old World. Partly it may be that the nervous unrest of life in the States is antagonistic to the begetting of children; partly it is the deliberate refusal of pampered women to assume the responsibilities of motherhood. Both these dangers are real ones. From whatever cause, the old element, the English element, the natural leaders of the country, are dying out, and the vacancies are filled by contributions from every nation of the earth. Will they blend? Will these tributaries of new blood turn the stream of national character into another channel? It is too early to say.

It is entirely to be hoped not, for the character of the present American is not one to be lightly lost from the world.

His worst fault is that he dislikes us. But that—though it sound a paradox—is because he respects us. Entirely free from personal self-consciousness, the Americans are nationally most self-conscious; they resent the existence of a nation they are bound to respect. But that will go with time. Meanwhile the American may make his mind easy about his country. It is a credit to him, and he is a credit to it. You may differ from him, you may laugh at him; but neither of these is the predominant emotion he inspires. Even while you differ or laugh, he is essentially the man with whom you are always wanting to shake hands.

Steevens, *The Land of the Dollar.*

23

A PHILOSOPHER EXPLAINS
THE AMERICAN PASSION
FOR MONEY

HUGO MUNSTERBERG

MUNSTERBERG came to America as Professor of Psychology at Harvard University in 1892, and thereafter he belonged to American scholarship. Yet acclimated as he was to the United States, his views of American society were those of a sympathetic outsider. Born in Danzig in 1863, Munsterberg studied at Leipzig and Heidelberg and taught at the University of Freiburg before coming to the United States. At Harvard he was associated with James, Royce, and Palmer in making that institution the center of philosophical studies in the United States. An indefatigable worker and prolific writer he set himself the task of interpreting America to Americans—and to Germans—and his *American Traits* and *The Americans* (1904), from which we have taken this selection, constitute on the whole the fairest and most sympathetic analysis of the American character by any German interpreter. He is, with the possible exception of his compatriot Müller-Freienfels, the only professional philosopher represented in our collection, and his observations on such matters as education, or the role of women in American life, or American materialism, are distinguished by objectivity and understanding.

✧✧✧✧✧✧✧

ONE who wishes to understand the most fabulous economic development of the United States must, indeed, not simply consider its ore deposits and gold mines, its coal and oil fields, its wheat lands and cotton districts, its great forests and the supplies of water. The South Americans live no less in a country prospered by nature, and so also do the Chinese. South Africa offers entirely similar conditions to those of the North American continent, and yet its development has been a very different one; and, finally, a consideration of the peculiar forms of American industrial organization, as, for instance, the trusts, reveals merely symptoms and not the real causes which have been at work.

The colossal industrial successes, along with the great evils and dangers which have come with them, must be understood from the make-up of the American character. Just as we have traced the political life of America back to a powerful instinct for free self-determination, the free self-guidance of the undivided, so we shall here find that it is the instinct for free self-initiative which has set in motion this tremendous economic fly-wheel. The pressure to be up and doing has opened the earth, tilled the fields, created industries, and developed such technical skill as today may even dream of dominating the world.

But to grant that the essentials of such movements are not to be found in casual external circumstances, but must lie in the mental make-up of the nation, might lead in this case to ascribing the chief influence to quite a different mental trait. The average European, permeated as he is with Old World culture, is, in fact, convinced that this intense economic activity is the simple result of unbounded greed. The search for gold and the pursuit of the dollar, we often hear, have destroyed in the American soul every finer ambition; and since the American has no higher desire for culture, he is free to chase his Mammon with undisguised and shameless greed. The barbarity of his soul, it is said, gives him a considerable economic advantage over others who have some heart as well as a pocketbook, and whose feelings incline to the humane. . . .

In the first place, we might look into the American's greed

for gold. A German observes immediately that the American does not prize his possessions much unless he has worked for them himself; of this there are innumerable proofs, in spite of the opposite appearances on the surface. One of the most interesting of these is the absence of the bridal dower. In Germany or France, the man looks on a wealthy marriage as one of the most reliable means of getting an income; there are whole professions which depend on a man's eking out his entirely inadequate salary from property which he inherits or gets by marriage; and the eager search for a handsome dowry—in fact, the general commercial character of marriage in reputable European society everywhere—always surprises Americans. They know nothing of such a thing at home. Even when the parents of the bride are prosperous, it is unusual for a young couple to live beyond the means of the husband. Everywhere one sees the daughters of wealthy families stepping into the modest homes of their husbands, and these husbands would feel it to be a disgrace to depend on their prosperous fathers-in-law. An actual dowry received from the bride's parents during their lifetime is virtually unknown. Another instance of American contempt for unearned wealth, which especially contrasts with European customs, is the disapproval which the American always has for lotteries. If he were really bent on getting money, he would find the dower and the lottery a ready means; whereas, in fact, the lottery is not only in all its forms forbidden by law, but public opinion wholly disapproves of games of chance. The President of Harvard University, in a public address given a short time since, in which he spoke before a large audience of the change in moral attitude, was able to give a striking illustration of the transformation in the fact that two generations ago the city of Boston conducted a lottery, in order to raise money for rebuilding a university structure which had been destroyed by fire. He showed vividly how such a transaction would be entirely unthinkable today, and how all American feelings would revolt at

raising money for so good a cause as an educational institution by so immoral a means as a public lottery. The entire
audience received this as a matter of course, apparently
without a suspicion as to how many cathedrals are being
built in Europe today from tickets at half a dollar. It was
amusing to observe how Carnegie's friend, Schwab, who
had been the greatly admired manager of the steel works,
fell in public esteem when news came from the Riviera that
he was to be seen at the gaming-tables of Monaco. The true
American despises anyone who gets money without working for it. Money is not the thing which is considered, but
the manner of getting it. This is what the American cares
for, and he prizes the gold he gets primarily as an indication
of his ability.

At first sight it looks as if this disinclination to gambling
were not to be taken seriously. It would signify nothing that
the police discover here and there a company of gamblers
who have barricaded the door; but a European might say
that there is another sort of speculative fever which is prevalent. Even Americans on the stock exchange often say, with
a smile: We are a gambling nation; and from the point of
view of the broker it would be so. He sees how all classes
of people invest in speculative securities, and how the public
interests itself in shares which are subject to the greatest
fluctuations; how the cab-driver and the hotel waiter pore
nervously over the quotations, and how new mining stocks
and industrial shares are greedily bought by schoolteachers
and commercial clerks. The broker sees in this the people's
desire for gambling, because he is himself thoroughly aware
of the great risks which are taken, and knows that the in-
vestors can see only a few of the factors which determine
prices.

But in the public mind all this buying and selling looks
very different. The small man, investing a few dollars in such
doubtful certificates, never thinks of himself as a gambler;
he thinks that he understands the market; he is not trusting

to luck, but follows the quotations day by day for a long time, and asks his friends for "tips," until he is convinced that his own discretion and cunning will give him an advantage. If he were to think of his gain as matter of chance, as the broker thinks it is, he would not only not invest his money, but would be no longer attracted by the transactions. And whenever he loses, he still goes on, believing that he will be able the next time to figure out the turn of the market more accurately.

The same is true of the wagers which the Anglo-Saxon is always making, because he loves excitement. For him a wager is not a true wager when it is merely a question of chance. Both sides make calculations, and have their special considerations which they believe will determine the outcome, and the winner feels his gain to be earned by his shrewdness. An ordinary game of chance does not attract the American—a fact which may be seen even in the grotesque game of poker. In a certain sense, the American's aversion to tipping servants reveals, perhaps, the same trait. The social inferiority which he feels to be implied in the acceptance of a fee goes against the self-respect of the individual; but there is the additional disinclination here to receiving money which is not strictly earned.

There are positive traits corresponding to these negative ones; and especially among them may be noticed the use to which money is put after it is gotten. If the American were really miserly, he would not distribute his property with such a free hand. Getting money excites him, but keeping it is less interesting, and one sees not seldom the richest men taking elaborate precautions that only a small part of their money shall fall to their children, because they think that the possession of money which is not self-earned is not a blessing. From these motives one may understand at once the magnificent generosity shown toward public enterprises.

One sees clearly, again, that the real attraction which the American feels for money-making does not lie in the having but only in the getting, from the perfect equanimity, positively amazing to the European, with which he bears his losses. To be sure, his irrepressible optimism stands him in good stead; he never loses hope, but is confident that what he has lost will soon be made up. But this would be no comfort to him if he did not care much less for the possession than for the getting of it. The American chases after money with all his might, exactly as on the tennis-court he tries to hit the ball, and it is the game he likes and not the prize. If he loses he does not feel as if he had lost a part of himself, but only as if he had lost the last set in a tournament. When, a short time ago, there was a terrific crash in the New York stock market and hundreds of millions were lost, a leading Parisian paper said: "If such a financial crisis had happened here in France, we should have had panics, catastrophes, a slump in *rentes*, suicides, street riots, a ministerial crisis, all in one day: while America is perfectly quiet, and the victims of the battle are sitting down to collect their wits. France and the United States are obviously two entirely different worlds in their civilization and in their way of thinking."

As to the estimation of money and its acquirement, France and the United States are indeed as far apart as possible, while Germany stands in between. The Frenchman prizes money as such; if he can get it without labor, by inheritance or dowry, or by gambling, so much the better. If he loses it he loses a part of himself, and when he has earned enough to be sure of a livelihood, he retires from money-making pursuits as soon as possible. It is well known that the ambition of the average Frenchman is to be a rentier. The American has exactly the opposite idea. Not only does he endure loss with indifference and despise gain which is not earned, but he would not for any price give up the occupation of making money. Whether he has much or little, he keeps patiently at work; and, as no scholar or artist would ever think of saying that he had done enough work, and would from now on become a scientific or literary rentier and live on his reputation, so no American, as long as he keeps his health, thinks of giving up his regular business.

The profession of living from the income of investments is virtually unknown among men, and the young men who take up no money-making profession because they "don't need to" are able to retain the social respect of their fellows only by undertaking some sort of work for the common-wealth. A man who does not work at anything, no matter how rich he is, can neither get nor keep a social status.

This also indicates, then, that the American does not want his money merely as a means for material comfort. Of course, wealthy Americans are becoming more and more accus-tomed to provide every thinkable luxury for their wives and daughters. Nowhere is so much expended for dresses, jew-elry, equipages and services for country houses and yachts, works of art and private libraries; and many men have to keep pretty steadily at work year in and year out in order to meet their heavy expenditures. And the same thing is re-peated all down the social scale. According to European standards, even the working-man lives luxuriously. But, in spite of this, no person who has really come into the country will deny that material pleasures are less sought after for themselves in the New World than in the Old. It always strikes the European as remarkable how very industrious American society is, and how relatively little bent on pleas-ure. It has often been said that the American has not yet learned how to enjoy life; that he knows very well how to make money, but not how to enjoy it. And that is quite true; except that it leaves out of account the main point— which is, that the American takes the keenest delight in the employment of all his faculties in his work, and in the exer-cise of his own initiative. This gives him more pleasure than the spending of money could bring him.

It is, therefore, fundamentally false to stigmatize the American as a materialist, and to deny his idealism. . . . The economic life means to the American a realizing of efforts which are in themselves precious. It is not the means to an end, but is its own end. If two blades of grass grow where one grew before, or two railroad tracks where there was but one; if production, exchange, and commerce increase and undertaking thrives, then life is created, and this is, in itself, a precious thing. The European of the Continent esteems the industrial life as honest, but not as noble; economic activities seem to him good for supporting himself and his family, but his duty is merely to supply economic needs which are now existing.

The merchant in Europe does not feel himself to be a free creator like the artist or scholar: his is no discoverer, no maker; and the mental energy which he expends he feels to be spent in serving an inferior purpose, which he serves only because he has to live. That creating economic values can itself be the very highest sort of accomplishment, and in itself alone desirable, whether or not it is useful for the person who creates, and that it is great in itself to spread and increase the life of the national economic organization, has been, indeed, felt by many great merchants in the history of Europe, and many a Hanseatic leader realizes it today. But the whole body of people in Europe does not know this, while America is thoroughly filled with the idea. . . . Every individual feels himself exalted by being a part of such a mighty whole, and the general intellectual effects of this temper show themselves in the entire national life.

A nation can never do its best in any direction unless it believes thoroughly in the intrinsic value of its work; whatever is done merely through necessity is never of great national significance, and second-rate men never achieve the highest things. If the first minds of a nation look down with contempt on economic life, if there is no real belief in the ideal value of industry, and if creative minds hold aloof from it, that nation will necessarily be outdone by others in the economic field. But where the ablest strength engages with idealistic enthusiasm in the service of the national economic problems, the nation rewards what the people do as done in the name of civilization, and the love of fame and work together spur them on more than the material gain which they will get. Indeed, this gain is itself only their measure of success in the service of civilization.

The American merchant works for money in exactly the sense that a great painter works for money; the high price which is paid for his picture is a very welcome indication of the general appreciation of his art: but he would never get this appreciation if he were working for the money instead of his artistic ideals. Economically to open up this gigantic country, to bring the fields and forests, rivers and mountains into the service of economic progress, to incite the millions of inhabitants to have new needs and to satisfy these by their own resourcefulness, to increase the wealth of the nation, and finally economically to rule the world and within the nation itself to raise the economic power of the individual to undreamt-of importance, has been the work which has fascinated the American. And every individual has felt his co-operation to be ennobled by his firm belief in the value of such an aim for the culture of the world.

Munsterberg, *The Americans*.

24

IS AMERICA A YOUNG OR
A DYING NATION?

GILBERT KEITH CHESTERTON

CHESTERTON is best known in the United States for
his Father Brown stories; he will be remembered for his
poetry. Born in 1874, Chesterton attended St. Paul's School,
then turned to art, and for some years was art critic for
the London *Bookman*. In 1905 he began to write for the
Illustrated London News, contributing a weekly essay to
that journal for a quarter of a century. Very early in his
career he began to indulge that passion for paradox which
is associated with his literary reputation; the early volume,
Heretics (1905), from which this essay on America is taken,
illustrates this trick. His conclusion on the basis of the art
of two expatriates, Henry James and Whistler, that America
is decadent and that "out of America has come a sweet and
startling cry as unmistakable as the cry of a dying man" can
only be regarded as precious. *What I Saw in America*
(1922) elaborates and embroiders this early point of view.
Here again Chesterton indulges his passion for paradox,
arguing that America is in fact an old nation, that the gulf
between the Old World and the New is steadily broadening,
and that democracy is on the decline.

In 1922 Chesterton became converted to Catholicism, and
thereafter, until his death in 1936, he wrote widely on philosophical and religious subjects. Among his best known books
are studies of Browning, Dickens, Stevenson, and the Vic-
torian Age in Literature.

❖❖❖❖❖❖❖

WHEN we come actually to examine the main stock notions of our modern practical politicians, we find that those main stock notions are mainly delusions. A great many instances might be given of the fact. We might take, for example, the case of that strange class of notions which underlie the word "union" and all the eulogies heaped upon it. . . .

This example of union, however, is not the example which I propose to take of the ingrained futility and deception underlying all the assumptions of the modern practical politician. I wish to speak especially of another and much more general delusion. It pervades the minds and speeches of all the practical men of all parties; and it is a childish blunder built upon a single false metaphor. I refer to the universal modern talk about young nations and new nations; about America being young, about New Zealand being new. The whole thing is a trick of words. America is not young, New Zealand is not new. It is a very discussable question whether they are not both much older than England or Ireland.

Of course we may use the metaphor of youth about America or the colonies, if we use it strictly as implying only a recent origin. But if we use it (as we do use it) as implying vigor, or vivacity, or crudity, or inexperience, or hope, or a long life before them, or any of the romantic attributes of youth, then it is surely as clear as daylight that we are duped by a stale figure of speech. . . .

Anyone who adopted the young-community delusion with regard to a bank or a butcher's shop would be sent to an asylum. But the whole modern political notion that America and the colonies must be very vigorous because they are very new rests upon no better foundation. That America was founded long after England does not make it even in the faintest degree more probable that America will not perish a long time before England. That England existed before her colonies does not make it any the less likely that she will exist after her colonies. And when we look at the

actual history of the world, we find that great European
nations almost invariably have survived the vitality of their
colonies. When we look at the actual history of the world,
we find that if there is a thing that is born old and dies young,
it is a colony. The Greek colonies went to pieces long before
the Greek civilization. The Spanish colonies have gone to
pieces long before the nation of Spain—nor does there seem
to be any reason to doubt the possibility or even the probability of the conclusion that the colonial civilization, which
owes its origin to England, will be much briefer and much
less vigorous than the civilization of England itself. The
English nation will still be going the way of all European
nations when the Anglo-Saxon race has gone the way of all
fads. Now, of course, the interesting question is, have we,
in the case of America and the colonies, any real evidence of
a moral and intellectual youth as opposed to the indisputable
triviality of a merely chronological youth? Consciously or
unconsciously, we know that we have no such evidence, and
consciously or unconsciously, therefore, we proceed to make
it up. . . .

Touching these English colonies, I do not wish to be misunderstood. I do not say of them or of America that they
have not a future, or that they will not be great nations. I
merely deny the whole established modern expression about
them. I deny that they are "destined" to a future. I deny that
they are "destined" to be great nations. I deny (of course)
that any human thing is destined to be anything. All the absurd physical metaphors, such as youth and age, living and
dying, are, when applied to nations, but pseudo-scientific attempts to conceal from men the awful liberty of their lonely
souls.

In the case of America, indeed, a warning to this effect is
instant and essential. America, of course, like every other
human thing, can in a spiritual sense live or die as much as it
chooses. But at the present moment the matter which America has very seriously to consider is not how near it is to its

birth and beginning, but how near it may be to its end. It is only a verbal question whether the American civilization is young; it may become a very practical and urgent question whether it is dying. When once we cast aside, as we inevitably have after a moment's thought, the fanciful physical metaphor involved in the word "youth," what serious evidence have we that America is a fresh force and not a stale one? It has a great many people, like China; it has a great deal of money, like defeated Carthage or dying Venice. It is full of bustle and excitability, like Athens after its ruin, and all the Greek cities in their decline. It is fond of new things; but the old are always fond of new things. Young men read chronicles, but old men read newspapers. It admires strength and good looks; it admires a big and barbaric beauty in its women, for instance; but so did Rome when the Goth was at the gates. All these are things quite compatible with fundamental tedium and decay. There are three main shapes or symbols in which a nation can show itself essentially glad and great: by the heroic in government, by the heroic in arms, and by the heroic in art. Beyond government, which is, as it were, the very shape and body of a nation, the most significant thing about any citizen is his artistic attitude toward a holiday and his moral attitude toward a fight—that is, his way of accepting life and his way of accepting death.

Subjected to these eternal tests, America does not appear by any means as particularly fresh or untouched. She appears with all the weakness and weariness of modern England or of any other Western power. In her politics she has broken up, exactly as England has broken up, into a bewildering opportunism and insincerity. In the matter of war and the national attitude toward war, her resemblance to England is even more manifest and melancholy. It may be said with rough accuracy that there are three stages in the life of a strong people. First, it is a small power, and fights small powers. Then it is a great power and fights great powers. Then it is a great power, and fights small powers, but pretends that they are great powers, in order to rekindle the ashes of its ancient emotion and vanity. After that, the next step is to become a small power itself. England exhibited this symptom of decadence very badly in the war with the Transvaal; but America exhibited it worse in the war with Spain. There was exhibited more sharply and absurdly than anywhere else the ironic contrast between the very careless choice of a strong line and the very careful choice of a weak enemy. America added to all her other late Roman or Byzantine elements the element of the Caracallan triumph, the triumph over nobody.

But when we come to the last test of nationality, the test of arts and letters, the case is almost terrible. The English colonies have produced no great artists; and that fact may prove that they are still full of silent possibilities and reserve force. But America has produced great artists. And that fact most certainly proves that she is full of a fine futility and the end of all things. Whatever the American men of genius are, they are not young gods making a young world. Is the art of Whistler a brave, barbaric art, happy and headlong? Does Mr. Henry James infect us with the spirit of a schoolboy? No; the colonies have not spoken, and they are safe. Their silence may be the silence of the unborn. But out of America has come a sweet and startling cry, as unmistakable as the cry of a dying man.

Chesterton, *Heretics.*

25

AMERICA COMBINES THE BEST TRAITS OF OLD-WORLD NATIONS

COUNT VAY DE VAYA

A DISTINGUISHED churchman and aristocrat, Count Peter Vay de Vaya found the United States very much to his liking. Born in Austria in 1865, son of Count Ladislas, Vay de Vaya entered the diplomatic service at the age of twenty-three, but turned, after a few years, to the church. In 1895 he became Privy Chamberlain to Pope Leo XIII, and four years later, as Protonotary Apostolic, traveled in the Far East and throughout the Americas. In 1906 he published *Empires and Emperors of Russia, China, Korea, and Japan*, and the following year *Ethics and Aesthetics of the East*. *The Inner Life of the United States* shows none of that superciliousness which marred so much of the writing of European aristocrats about this country. What impressed Count de Vaya most was the success of America as a melting pot. "His industry is German," he wrote of the American, "his endurance is British, but his acuteness is almost that of the Latin races," and he concluded handsomely that the American spirit filled him with "surprise and admiration." In 1908 Vay de Vaya was named Lord Abbot of St. Martin's in Hungary, and ten years later he retired to the Carmel at Leopoldan, where he died.

✦✦✦✦✦✦

W HAT was it in America that surprised you most?" This was the question which everywhere greeted me on my return from the United States. . . .

The will-power of the Americans astonished me, and the manifestations of this will-power impressed my mind more than anything else. The determination that has transformed a handful of emigrants into a powerful nation; the industry which has made it great and wealthy; and the wisdom which is leading it onward to a glorious and assured future—these were the subjects of my profoundest attention.

Whether we are to attribute this wonderful energy of America to individuals, as a quality peculiar to a few; to society, as a united force; or to the nation as a political creed, is a question which, in spite of all my studies, I do not feel competent to decide.

How is it possible for a day-laborer to become a millionaire, an ambassador, or President of the Republic? How can a society as classically cultured as that of Boston or Baltimore be formed? How has a collection of emigrants come to constitute a flourishing state?

In the course of one century North America has shown a development the like of which the whole history of mankind has never known. What, then, have been the most important factors in this marvelous growth, those which have formed, maintained and inspired it?

On the whole it is safe to say that too much has been attributed to America's geographical position. . . . The mixture of races has had a far more powerful influence than that of climate or geographical position. When it is remembered that people of every latitude have emigrated to the New World, and that the children of the North have intermarried with those of the tropics, it will be admitted that this intermingling has undoubtedly made for the rejuvenation of all the races concerned.

The principles of natural selection have had an even wider influence. The poor wanderers who, in the seventeenth century, landed on the coast of Massachusetts, were not in any way men of an everyday type. . . . In this struggle for existence only the strong could triumph; the weak went under at once. In a new life under new conditions which admitted of no privileges or protection, a man was valued for himself alone and for the worth that was in him. The difficulties and unending struggles of this existence fostered such natural qualities. Industry, endurance, strength of purpose, and frugality, developed as natural virtues, and were handed down from generation to generation.

During this time the North American type developed into an enduring one, which to this day remains distinct. Physically, it has much of the Anglo-Saxon in strength and form, but it is not so slender nor so refined. The facial peculiarities are more Dutch than English, although the broad cheeks, the dark-hued skin, and the shape of the head are sometimes reminiscent of the Indian type. The character shows many contrasts: serious and unsympathetic in public, by contrast the friendliness and kindness of the family circle are all the more remarkable. The American husband and father dispenses generously in the home what he has so hardly earned abroad, and is not concerned to keep even a small share for himself.

His industry is German, his endurance is British, but his acuteness is almost that of the Latin races. It is scarcely credible that abstruse matters engross public attention in this practical and commercial country: originated in the daily papers or reviews, a great part of the press is engaged in the discussion of abstract questions. The occult sciences have nowhere so many or such ardent devotees, and there is no teacher of any doctrine, however childish or absurd, who has not his disciples.

The American temperament is remarkably youthful, spontaneous in society, naive in its diversions, and with a taste for the brilliant and the eccentric. Americans are gregarious in disposition and make friends quickly, for they are a talkative and open-hearted nation. Their hospitality is sincere, and when they are entertaining a friend, or one whom they wish to honor, this hospitality is almost unbounded.

Rich and poor vie with each other in befriending the traveler. The dollar-king will open the gates of his palace with no greater readiness than will the poor cottager the door of his humble home. Millionaires and miners are one as delighted as the other to explain their work and its ways, and to give all information as to their respective callings. They have a very clear idea of their own position and importance, which gives them an ease of manner; they talk with pleasure, for each man speaks of that which he thoroughly understands, and when it is all explained, they will invite the stranger home with them to share a meal with the same easy naturalness of manner that they have displayed all through.

Hospitality is certainly a leading trait in the American character. It is in their blood, just as it is in that of us Hungarians. The American is delighted when old, or unknown, friends seek him out, and he loves to dilate to such on the progress made by his country, its power and its greatness. With almost childish vanity he will retail the story of its successes, and with unbounded contentment comment on its past history. . . .

Those who earn the dollars are of more interest, as types, than those who spend them. There is a wonderful potentiality about the millions, but it is even more important to observe how the first cents of such fortunes are accumulated.

In spite of great social contrasts, the two groups of worker and employer are much nearer each other than one would suppose. Those whose labors are crowned with success can, at one stride, from the lowest ascend to the highest rung of the social ladder, for there are no prejudices and traditions to bar their progress. Both parties are equally proud of their freedom and rights of citizenship. They are convinced that on the whole the conditions of life, laws, and form of government of their country are those which are best suited to present-day requirements. They never tire of expounding their principles and opinions to the stranger, and they do everything in their power to make him grasp all the good points and advantages of their ideas. . . .

Everything in this country is gigantic. The rivers are as broad as lakes, while the lakes are inland seas. The monotony of the great prairies is unending, and as the express train rushes across them, hour after hour, and day after day, it is difficult to believe that one has not been standing still the whole time, so unchanged is the landscape. The standard of natural beauty is quite different in America, and "beautiful" is a word seldom used with appropriateness; exclamations, such as "extraordinary," "magnificent," "grand" come more aptly to the tongue. The inhabitants of these landscapes, and the life they lead, offer, however, even more material for observation and wonder.

How is it possible for new towns to spring up in the wilderness in the course of a few months? How do they become inhabited? How do they so quickly grow populous and wealthy? Truly the strength of a young nation and its powers of production and absorption are incalculable!

From whatever point of view we study America, and taking its unique features into consideration, we shall always find animating it that national spirit which carries all before it, whether in the crowded cities or the lonely forest, in the workshop or under the dome of the Capitol, and which is ceaselessly at work urging the nation forward. This spirit fills me with surprise and admiration, for it inspires alike, and in equal degree, the Commerce, the Literature, the Art, the Government, and the policy of the country.

Count Vay De Vaya and Luskod, *The Inner Life of the United States.*

26

THE AMERICAN AT HOME AND
IN HIS CLUB

GEORGE BIRMINGHAM

CANON JAMES HANNAY, who writes under the pen-name of George Birmingham, is one of the most delightful of contemporary humorists. Born in Belfast in 1865 and educated at Trinity College, Dublin, Canon Hannay was for twenty years rector in County Mayo, the scene of many of his stories, then Canon of St. Patrick's Cathedral, chaplain in the British Army, University preacher at Oxford, and Vicar of Holy Trinity in London. Besides a number of theological works and travel books, he has written over forty novels, some of them—*Spanish Gold, General John Reagan, Up the Rebels*—likely to have an enduring fame, and in "J. J." Meldon, curate of the Church of Ireland, he has created a character as sure to live as Bertie Wooster or Jeeves. *From Dublin to Chicago* (1914), from which this selection is taken, gives a cheerful but none the less thoughtful view of American society on the eve of the First World War.

IN THE American house there are no "dens." The American likes to feel that he is in direct personal contact with the members of his family and with his guest. It does not annoy him, even if he happens to be reading a book on economics, to feel that his wife may sit down beside him or his daughter walk past the back of his chair humming a tune without his having had any warning that either of them was at hand.

The noise made by a servant collecting knives and plates after dinner, reaching him through a drawn curtain, does not disturb his enjoyment of a cigar. The servant is to him a fellow human being, and the sound of her activities is a pleasant reminder of the comradeship of man. He too has had his moments of activity during the day. A guest in an American house is for the time being a member of the family, not a stranger who, however welcome he may be, does not presume to intrude upon his host's privacy.

The "porch," as it is called, a striking feature of the American house, is another evidence of the spirit of sociability. A "porch" is a glorified and perfected veranda. In summer it is a large open-air sitting room. In winter it can, by a common arrangement, be made into a kind of sun parlor. It has its roof, supported by wooden posts. When the cold weather comes, frames, like very large window sashes, are fitted between the posts and a glass-sided room is made. It is evident that the life in these porches is of a very public kind. The passer-by, the casual wanderer along the road outside, sees the American family in its porch, can, if he cares to, note what each member of the family is doing. The American has no objection to this publicity. He is not doing anything of which he is the least ashamed. If other people can see him, he can see them in return. The arrangement gratifies his instinct for sociability. The Englishman, on the other hand, hates to be seen. Nothing would induce him to make a habit of sitting in a veranda. Even in the depths of the country, when his house is a long way from the road, he fits thin muslin curtains across the lower part of his windows. These keep out a good deal of light and in that way are annoying to him, but he puts up with gloom rather than run any risk, however small, that a stranger, glancing through the window, might actually see him. Yet the Englishman commonly leads a blameless life in his own home. He seldom employs his leisure in any shameful practices. His casement curtains are simply evidences of an almost morbid love of privacy.

The first thing an Englishman does when he builds a house is to surround it with a high wall. This, indeed, is not an English peculiarity. It prevails all over Western Europe. It is a most anti-social custom and ought to be suppressed by law, because it robs many people of a great deal of innocent pleasure. The suburbs of Dublin, to take an example, ought to be very beautiful. There are mountains to the south and hills to the west and north of the city, all of them lovely in outline and coloring. There is a wide and beautiful bay on the east. But the casual wayfarer cannot see either the mountains or the bay. He must walk between high yellow walls, walls built, I suppose, round houses; but we can only know this by hearsay. For the walls hide the houses as well as the view. In Sorrento, which is even more exquisitely situated than Dublin, you walk for miles and miles between high walls, white in this case. The only difference between the view you see at Dublin and that which you see at Sorrento is that the patch of sky you see in Dublin is gray, at Sorrento generally blue. At Cintra, one of the world's most famous beauty spots, the walls are gray, and there you cannot even see the sky, because the owners of the houses inside the walls have planted trees and the branches of the trees meet over the road. The Americans do not build walls round their houses. The humblest pedestrian, going afoot through the suburbs of Philadelphia, Indianapolis or any other city, sees not only the houses but anything in the way of a view which lies beyond them.

This is not because America is a republic and therefore democratic in spirit. Portugal is a republic too, having very vigorously got rid of its king, but the walls of Cintra are as high as ever. No one in the world is more democratic than an English Liberal, but the most uncompromising Liberals build walls round their houses as high as those of any Tory. The absence of walls in America is simply another evidence of the wonderful sociability of the people. Walls outside houses are like doors inside. The European likes both because the desire of privacy is in his blood. The American likes neither.

The "Country Club" is an institution which could flourish only among a very sociable people. There are of course clubs of many sorts in England. There is the club proper, the club without qualification, which is found at its very best in London. In books like Whitaker's *Almanac*, which classify clubs, it is described as "social," but this is only intended to distinguish it from political or sporting clubs. There is no suggestion that it is sociable, and in fact it is not. It is possible to belong to a club in London for years without knowing a dozen of your fellow members. It often seems as if the members of these clubs went to them mainly for the purpose of not getting to know each other; a misfortune which might happen to them anywhere else, but from which they are secure in their clubs. There are also all over England clubs especially devoted to particular objects, golf clubs, yacht clubs and so forth. In these the members are drawn together by their interest in a common pursuit, and are forced into some sort of acquaintanceship. But these are very different in spirit and intention from the American Country Club. It exists as a kind of center of the social life of the neighborhood. There may be and often are golf links connected with it. There are tennis courts, sometimes swimming baths. There is always a ball-room. There are luncheon rooms, tea rooms, reading rooms. In connection with one such club which I saw there are sailing matches for a one-design class of boats. But neither golf nor tennis, dancing nor sailing, is the object of the club's existence. Sport is encouraged by these clubs for the sake of general sociability. In England sociability is a by-product of an interest in sport.

The Country Club at Tuxedo is not perhaps the oldest, but it is one of the oldest institutions of the kind in America. In connection with it a man can enjoy almost any kind of recreation from a Turkish bath to a game of tennis, either the lawn or the far rarer original kind. At the proper time of year there are dances, and a debutante acquires, I believe, a certain prestige by "coming out" at one of them. But the club exists primarily as the social center of Tuxedo. It is in one way the ideal, the perfect country club. It not only fosters, it regulates and governs the social life of the place.

Tuxedo has been spoken of as a millionaire's colony. It is a settlement, if not of millionaires, at all events of wealthy people. The park, an immense tract of land, is owned by the club. Ground for building can be obtained only by those who are elected members of the club and who are prepared to spend a certain sum as a minimum on the building of their houses. In theory the place is reserved for people who either do or will know each other socially, who are approximately on the same level as regards wealth and who all want to meet each other frequently, for one purpose or another, in the club. In practice, certain difficulties necessarily arise. A man may be elected a member of the club and build a house. He may be a thoroughly desirable person, but in course of time he dies. His son may be very undesirable, or his son may sell the house to some one whom the club is not willing to admit to membership. But Tuxedo society, instead of becoming, as might have been expected, a very narrow clique, seems to be singularly broad-minded and tolerant. The difficulty of preserving the character of the place and keeping a large society together as, in all its essentials, a club, is very much less than might be expected. The place is extremely interesting to any observer of American social life. The club regulates everything. It runs a private police force for the park. It keeps up roads. It supplies electric light and, what is hardly less necessary in America, ice to all the houses. It levies, though I suppose without any actual legal warrant, regular rates. The fact that the experiment was not wrecked long ago on the rocks of snobbery goes to show that society in America is singularly fluid compared to that of any European country. That a considerable number of people should want to live together in such a way is a witness to the sociability of America. No other country club has realized its ideal as the club at Tuxedo has, but every country-club—and you find them all over America—has something of the spirit of Tuxedo.

Birmingham, *From Connaught to Chicago.*

27

THE SENTIMENTALITY, KIND-
NESS AND INNOCENCE
OF THE AMERICANS

WALTER LIONEL GEORGE

AMERICA has had no kindlier interpreter than the distinguished novelist, W. L. George. Born in Paris in 1882, of English parents, George studied at the Sorbonne and in Germany, dabbled in chemistry, engineering and law, before turning finally to the profession of letters. With the publication of *A Bed of Roses* in 1911, he emerged as one of the most promising of the younger Georgian novelists, but it was a promise that was never wholly fulfilled, though *Blind Alley, Caliban,* and *The Confession of Ursula Trent* were well received and widely read, and the semi-autobiographical volume, *The Making of an Englishman,* has lasting merits. *Hail Columbia* (1921), from which we have taken this friendly chapter, he called the "random impressions of a conservative English radical." George was an ardent feminist, and his curious theory that Americans do not appreciate their women attracted a good deal of attention because it was so sharply in conflict with the usual foreign view of the place of women in American life. He was immensely impressed, however, with American vitality, energy, and spontaneity, with business, and with the Middle West. His death, in 1926, at the age of forty-four, was a serious loss to English letters.

✦✦✦✦✦✦✦

HERE is a favored land which, owing to its area and to its wealth, can give a chance to every young man, and, if it chooses, even to every young woman. All benefits have been poured out upon America and America is using them as a cheerful prodigal; America is conscious of her good fortune, and that is why she can afford the manifestation of pride which is called democracy. Democracy is the most arrogant of all forms; it is the converse of snobbery, for the snob conceives only superiors and inferiors. The snob is a man who thinks he has no equals, while the democrat is the man who thinks he has only equals. He is often mistaken in his view.

And so a European thinks it picturesque and delightful to go to a bathing hut on a lake, ask for his bathing things, and hear a youth call out to his boss, "Say, where's *this man's* bathing suit?" To have a colored chambermaid stop him on the stairs and bluntly ask, "Where's your wife?" It is amusing, after the bent backs of the English servant class, though I should add that these backs are bending less and less now. It is pleasing because, like most things American, the democratic notion is cut out in sharp lines and painted in bright colors. The American fantasia, if I may so call it, is scarlet and gold. The scarlet of American excess creeps even into the pale blue of American sentimentality. Let not the reader conclude that I claim for England freedom from sentimentality; we, too, suffer greatly from what I may call emotion gone moldy. But England feels a little ashamed of her sentimentality, while America tends to account it as righteousness. The sentimental attitude toward women, noblest and purest, I will say something of a little farther on. It sometimes takes a strange lyrical form, particularly in the newspapers. And the newspapers matter, for the newspaper exhibition of the national character is the national character seen under a magnifying glass. The newspaper character is the national character—more so. For instance, I read in a newspaper that a certain lady has extraordinary courage, a keen sense of intuition, and a sublime faith in God. A very sagacious diagnosis inside a single interview.

But sentimentality, which so naturally envelops the young bride, the good mother, the little child, takes in America some forms that interest me more. One of them is the sweet and simple life of millionaires. I am continually reading descriptions showing that the financial superman does not live on caviar off diamond-studded plates; that his subtle mind subsists upon the rudest fare and the highest thought; that he likes to set aside the nurture of his millions for a peaceful hour with Artemus Ward; that his true pleasure is serving in the local *crêche*, teaching the creed that is called, "How to get on and yet be good." I like to think of the millionaire talking freely in the street to some one who owns rather less, and with a green watering-can assisting into beauty a little bed of marigolds.

I think that impulse, which is purely American, arises from a desire to humanize the apparently inhuman. American business, shrewd as it is, seems to have a heart; it wants to do for individual men the fair and the generous thing. The whole trend of American civilization is toward stressing the human factor; indeed, the word "human" (in the sense of "friendly") is used in no other part of the English-speaking countries. Also, a certain reverence attaches to power; reverence is always apparent in the American character, curiously combined with irreverence. For instance, the magazine and novel continually present allusions to "the great surgeon" and "the great lawyer." The cynical European suspects that the great surgeon is a scrubby reactionary who does not read the medical journals; he views the great lawyer either as a foxy fee snatcher or as a toothless dodderer on the bench. But the American seems to invest these people with mental robes of ermine and scarlet. He is more easily impressed; his vision is more direct and less often leads him to doubt; where a European would doubt, an American often hates.

You find this seriousness extending even to the most ignoble of occupations, the arts. In civilized countries the arts are, as a rule, merely the resounding kettles tied to the tails of the hounds that are hunting the great quarry of profit. But in an American newspaper you will see headlines such as this, "Playwright Finds His Inspiration in Lonely Sand Dunes." No European would be interested in the playwright's inspiration, except as an object for jeers. The American takes the arts seriously, just as he takes seriously the funds for the restoration of churches. He is altogether more literal; he uses the words "right" and "wrong," as to the meaning of which many Europeans have become rather shaky. He takes his tradition more seriously. For instance, in Chicago I observed a headline in the newspaper, "Cotton Exchange Fifty Years Old To-day." That has an irresistible charm. One need not, from the false vantage of the Oxford turf, smile at a record of fifty years; one envies, rather, the contentment so aroused. Then, once more, American complexity appears—I contrast this headline with the fact that in nearly every American city I have visited hotels and office buildings, erected round about 1900, are being pulled down to give place to buildings that shall be up-to-date. America delights in tradition, and destroys it as she goes. She hates the thing she respects, burns the god that she worships. Once more, here is a sign of the immense vitality of the land; you discover it best in the headlines of the newspapers. . . .

Lyricism takes all forms. In the United States, one of the strangest from the European point of view is the adulation of business. As if America were reacting against the traditional adoration by England of the professions, she seems to set a peculiar value upon making, buying, and selling things. *The Dignity of Business* was written by an American, *The Romance of Commerce* was invented by another. To an extent this is a defense as well as an evangel, but it is certain that America has enshrined within business a portion of her romantic impulses. She respects the business man; while

ready to give his due to the professional man, and more than
his due to the artist, she intimately feels that business is the
finest, as well as the most valuable, function of man; she perceives in the business man the qualities of a hero; in her view,
he is doing the best that can be done by man. An evidence of
this is the prevalence in the magazines, not only of business
short stories (almost invariably concerned with smart selling), but of actual articles on business. In the *Saturday Evening Post* I found an article on the role of the purchasing
agent; in a single issue of the *American Magazine* I found
two business stories, and seven articles on business or inter-
views of big business men, total well over a third of the contributions. And these are not commercial journals, but popular magazines. It seems to me that in this America performs
a service; she is dragging down the wooden old traditions of
cultured leisure and setting up instead an ideal which some
may dislike, but which is a new ideal for new times.

One of the first things that impressed me in America is expressed in a large board that stands on every road outside
West Chester, Pennsylvania. On one side of the board we
read as follows:

THIS IS
WEST CHESTER.
COME RIGHT IN.
GLAD TO SEE YOU.

And on the other side:

GOOD-BY.
COME AGAIN.
COME OFTEN.
WEST CHESTER.

This board enraged my American companion, who happened to be an American artist of the highest order. He
mouthed a furious denunciation of this "fradulent cordiality." At last I told him that he knew nothing about it, being

merely an American, and that I could assure him that this sort of thing did mean something. It might not mean exactly what it said, for few human expressions do, but it did mean something. It represents a dominant streak in the American character. It means what I have everywhere experienced— that America is really hospitable, really sociable. Can anyone imagine an English village telling you to "Come right in"? An English village is not communicative enough even to tell you to get out, which at bottom is its only emotion. In America the stranger is not welcomed in a purely mercantile spirit. The American wants trade, but he also wants to know things, to secure new impressions, and, if you will let him, he wants to like you. This combines with the old pioneer spirit into true hospitality. It may be thought that I am stressing the pioneer spirit, which seems to elucidate the Middle West, but I do believe that America still carries the pioneer habit of giving hospitality to all. I am not deceived by the reasons for this; the pioneer had not a warmer heart than anybody else; he gave hospitality because in pioneer days he had to give hospitality so as to enjoy it himself when in need. For many years in America you had to take hospitality or die on the prairie; that taught all men hospitality, and much of the tradition stays in the American spirit. That is why the stranger finds America so delightful. He is readily admitted into the American home, while he may spend a lifetime in France and be admitted only to a restaurant.

I am perfectly sure that, on an average, the American is warmer hearted than the European. . . . An American will take immense trouble over you, waste his time over you, drive you about, get you introductions, secure you privileges. Sometimes this is ostentation, sometimes it is local pride; but human sentiments are always complex, and there runs through it an honest desire to oblige.

You find this particularly in the American of the middle-sized towns. New York is too large for anybody to be proud of; you cannot be town conscious in a city of that size, as

you can be, for instance, in Cincinnati. The American is almost invariably proud and fond of his home town. He is
always anxious that you should visit it; he will accompany
you and show you round; you will offend him if you refuse
to go and see the statue of Colonel Judson, who was killed
at Saratoga. I am afraid that I have offended many people
already by writing a book about America; nearly all those I
have met felt that the book ought to be about their city, or
at most about their state; I have been told everywhere that
"to stay only three days here" was akin to crime. . . .

Kindness is almost universal in America; in my first three
months I collected only three deliberate rudenesses, though,
doubtless, I deserved many more. I found everywhere assistance and, what the stranger needs so much, information.
Sometimes I found a little too much, for the American does
not always realize how lost is the stranger in this immense,
complicated system, and so burdens him with detail. The
American is often quiet, but he never refuses conversation,
and, on the whole, it is better that people should talk too
much than too little; this contributes to general sociability
and ease of intercourse. Also, conversation helps a man to
exhibit himself. Very few of us ever attempt to discover
what the other man thinks; we talk so as to assert to him what
we think; this helps us to discover what we really think. I
suspect that the American, more than any other kind of
man, his mind being filled with a vast number of physical
impressions, needs conversation to sort out these impressions.
Burdened by certain forms of national pride, local pride, and
personal pride, by old puritanic views and new efficiency
views, by sentiment and by ruthlessness, he needs conversation as a sort of clearing house. He has to formulate. . . .

I have met a few Americans who criticized America, but
they nearly all belonged to the intellectual class, which does
nothing but intellectualize. Those people take a queer pleasure in running down America. They vaunt the culture of
France and the courtesy of Spain; they read no American

books, but criticize them all the same. They are few, while the mass of Americans who openly boost their country is large. Many of them will criticize America in a temperate spirit, and, more and more, I suspect, the educated American is reacting against certain features of American civilization, such as haste and noise. One thing in him is noteworthy—he is always willing to discuss America. He will state her, explain her, defend her, and the subject never wearies him. That is a profound difference with the Englishman, who, confronted with a foreigner, is more likely to talk to him about the foreign land—that is, if he must. The Englishman would rather stick to safe topics, such as games, or London communications, but if he is dragged into national discussions he will avoid England. It is not that he lacks national pride, but that pride has become to him a habit of mind. He is really more arrogant than the American, for the American takes the trouble to speak for his country, and proclaims as an argument, "I am an American citizen." The Englishman is much worse. He does not trouble to proclaim, "I am a British subject." He expects you to know that, and at bottom does not care whether you know it or not, or what you say about it. The Englishman's complacency is immense: First, there is the Church-of-England God; then there is the Englishman; then there is the Englishman's bulldog; then there is nothing. So, realizing this, I am not with those who are offended by the occasionally loud American patriotism; I know only too well that its occasional loudness means that America doubts itself. . . .

I had not heard much about the soul until I came to America. In England the soul is an understood thing, to be taken out on Sunday for exercise; even then it has to behave, to be less evident than one's shadow. To expose one's soul is in England looked upon as a minor indecency. Even our magazine writers tend to let it alone, and cause heroes to love heroines from the bottom of their hearts; in the American magazine passion often goes a little deeper. . . .

Most Europeans look upon love as a comparatively simple and temporary reaction, which leaves behind it a certain sediment called affection. According to temperament, they look upon love as a regrettable physical excess, or as a natural desire for intimacy with a person of the other sex; or as a joke; or an act of business; but they very seldom look upon it as a sacrament. In America, I am not so sure of the men. The men do not talk much about love, and I have a suspicion that they do not place it on quite so lofty a plane as their women would desire. It is not in the nature of men to grow rhapsodic over anything; all great rhapsodies, it is true, have come from men, but always from unusual men; the ordinary man has a way of placing love and its consequences among the material facts of life; in Europe the women hold only slightly more refined views. But in America certain peculiarities appear in the conception of love which the American woman proclaims. (What actual conception she holds, as against the one she proclaims, may be a matter for further discussion.) The things that people proclaim are quite as important as the things they believe, because what people say to you is not always what they think, but what they would like to think, or what they would like you to think they think. The American woman's proclamation of the nature of love may be the proclamation of what she thinks love ought to be. Now from America came the phrase, "Divinity of Sex." . . . I suspect that the words, "Divinity of Sex," merely express the fact that the American woman sets upon herself a price higher than does the European. When giving herself in marriage to a man she appears to lay down that she is doing something significant, which honors him by preferment and her by self-sacrifice. Also, she conveys that she is the cradle of the race, forgetting that nature is so arranged as to demand that a masculine hand shall rock this cradle. It seems to be set up that "love" is wonderful; that "the child" is wonderful; that "the race" is wonderful; in other words, exaltation. Whether this is wholly sincere or wholly insincere does not matter very much; the American man hardly ever echoes the point of view, but he never controverts it; he maintains silence and seems to accept the feminine theory. I wonder. . . . Perhaps he does not care. . . .

The whole of the American civilization seems to me willfully, and often splendidly, excessive. The people seem to find a pleasure in the height of their buildings, in the size of their restaurants. The freak dinner, for instance, where a musical prodigy was concealed in a bush of roses and revealed only when coffee was served, where every guest was presented with a gift worth one thousand dollars, is not only an indication of reckless wealth, but also of a deliberate desire to do things largely, magnificently, excessively.

One discovers this in the lavish magnificence of American hospitality. It is delightful, but to a pallid European it sometimes proves exhausting. One rides to too many places in too many automobiles; one meets too many interesting people; visits to the opera, to the theater, to the country club, to the famous view over the valley—all this, so kindly, so generous, is part of the American tendency to do too much, too fast. They do not think that they themselves suffer from it, but I suspect that much of the sensitiveness of American public opinion to newspaper stunts is due to an over-stimulated condition of the nerves. Excess brings its penalty in the shape of reaction. The noise of America, the swift movement, the passion for automobiles, a passion so violent that people mortgage their house to buy one—all this is excess. . . .

The Englishman is not accustomed to the spaciousness of American hospitality. American hospitality will explain the difference between watermelon, honey dew, and casaba, while English hospitality consists in letting the lunch lie about for you to eat if you like. We are not accustomed to being shown a house in detail—the labor-saving appliances at work; told the story of the pieces of furniture, of the pictures. The Americans are never weary of this, because their

vitality is enormous. It is not only nerves which permit them
to do so many things in a single day; it is not only their magnificent climate, which is bright and bracing like champagne;
it is the rude strength of a race not yet sophisticated; it is the
hunger for impressions of a race just entering into possession
of its powers. Hunger and innocence, this defines a vast tract
of the American mind.

George, *Hail Columbia! Random Impressions of a Conservative English
Radical.*

28

AMERICANS ARE BOYS

SALVADOR DE MADARIAGA

ONE of the most distinguished Spaniards of our generation, Salvador de Madariaga has had a notable career in literature, scholarship, diplomacy and international affairs. Born in Spain in 1886 and educated at Madrid and Paris, Madariaga, like Santayana, was a cosmopolitan rather than a Spaniard. In 1916 he moved to London, contributing essays on Spanish literature to British journals; in 1922 he became director of the disarmament section of the League of Nations and in 1934 Secretary to the Temporary Mixed Commission on Disarmament. During the twenties he published a number of volumes on Spanish literature—*Shelley and Calderón, Spanish Folksongs* and *The Genius of Spain* are the best known—and in 1928 was appointed Professor of Spanish Studies at Oxford. Three years later he became Spanish Ambassador to the United States, and in 1934 Ambassador to France. During the thirties and forties he turned increasingly to public affairs and history: his later writings include volumes on *Disarmament* and *Theory and Practice of International Relations*, as well as biographies of Cortez and Columbus, and one novel, *Heart of Jade*. "Americans are Boys" is marked by the cynicism—and the superficiality—of the twenties: the animadversions on American intolerance seem to come strangely from the citizen of a country that has exhibited, during the last decade, a savage intolerance that Americans could not imitate if they would.

◇◇◇◇◇◇◇

Sooner or later the Spaniard feels the call of the blood and sallies forth in order to discover America. I have discovered America, which means, of course, that I know next to nothing about it. Yet, in all truth, America was not quite unknown to me. I had lived for six years in one of the most important American cities in Europe—Geneva—whose fertile soil brings forth every summer a plentiful harvest of distinguished Americans, all turning their faces to the League as sunflowers their corollas to the sun. I was then one of the rays in the League's Sun and grew to be quite conscious of the warmth and light which it was my privilege to convey from the Sun of Peace to the open, eager faces come from afar to behold it. I had grown to like those faces. They were clear, they were frank, they were earnest, with more fun than humor in their ever-youthful features. And by observing them year after year I had come to the conclusion that what I liked in them was that they reminded me of children.

Then I began to notice their English. I was impressed by the fact that they said "an elevator" instead of "a lift" and "an uplifting experience" instead of "an elevating experience." Now, Latin-English is the more refined, the nobler, and the more self-conscious of the two. This inversion in the use of Latin- and Saxon-English suggested, therefore, an inversion of the standard of values adopted in England. For the English, the more solemn of the two movements upwards is the moral; for the American, the physical. For the American, therefore, the world of tangible things is a noble and earnest world. The child believes in his toys and respects them.

America, then, appeared to me as an immense up-to-date nursery and boys' school fitted with the most wonderful toys and games you could imagine. Who was the gigantic Father Christmas who invented the skyscraper? That skyline which refused to reveal itself to us as the boat felt its way up New York haven in thick fog, was it not like a colossal Christmas shop window glittering with lights? And think of all that those beautiful towers and palaces conceal behind their embroidered cliffs! Think of the elevators (my hat off to their importance) coming and going behind their beautiful brass filigree cages, with all their neat little buttons and lights and arrows red and green, and the boy so spick and span you could hardly believe he was a real boy, least of all when he announces the floor in an unintelligible yell which seems to burst out of his stuffed body under mechanical compulsion. Think of the lovely marble floors, thick carpets, barber shops, all resplendent with mirrors and nickeled bars and, oh! the marvelous chairs pivoting in all meridians and parallels like telescopes for the barber to observe and operate on your beauty under every possible angle and light—and the mechanical appliances for brushing your hair and for drying it, all moving electrically, so fast and with so much wonderful noise. . . .

II

There is a boy in Detroit who had a capital idea. He made up his mind that every boy and girl in the house—I mean in America—was going to have a magnificent toy: a car on wheels and going by itself. None of those cars which had to be wound up, but a real automobile, which means that it goes on its own. A real thing, going for miles and miles without being wound at all—at least nowadays, for at first there was a bit of winding to do before the thing started and a not very pleasant job at that, particularly in winter. Now the fact is this boy has transformed the whole nursery and school with his idea, and everybody is so happy that no nursery was ever quieter in the world and the Nurse in Washington can knit the threads of her policy in blissful peace.

Boys are naturally given to boasting and exaggeration. The American language differs from English in that it seeks the top of expression while English seeks its lowly valleys. An Englishman would have found seemly and moderate, if vague, euphemisms for what America calls nowadays "wet" and "dry." But even these uncompromising expressions prove too weak for the American taste, and so we have come to read that Senator A is bone-dry while Governor B is drip-

ping wet. The *Times* (London) would have dropped an almost incomprehensible and labyrinthine hint in its City Columns to obtain the same effect which the Philadelphia *Ledger*
sought in saying on its first page: "The Department of State
came down to-day with both feet upon any and all proposals
to float loans in the United States for the benefit of Soviet
Russia." Some boy, that Department of State! And where an
English newspaper would have written, "Preparatory measures are being taken for an April primary by Senator D and
his friends," the Chicago *Tribune* announces that, "Senator
D and his associates jumped at full stride yesterday into the
race to get ready for an April primary." True the Chicago
Tribune has to live up to its claim: "The world's greatest
newspaper." Yet, the point is that it lives up to it by such
powerful "dramatizing" of facts, just as it dramatizes its own
building by making of it the tallest tower in Chicago, several
inches taller than (unless it is the reverse, which hardly matters) the tower built by a chewing-gum firm. But if a chewing-gum tower is not in its place in a nursery, what on earth
is your idea of a nursery, I ask? For my part, I find that
chewing-gum habit one of the most significant features of the
juvenile state of America. It is, moreover, subtly connected
with the boyish (and American) habit of exaggeration, for
all exaggerating phrases end in "the world" (the greatest paper in the world); and "the world" is pronounced by the
American Boy with a peculiar flourish of the tongue which
suggests an exceptional length of the said organ, as if it could
be, and was, twisted and turned and made into a knot—a fact
due no doubt to the gymnastical exercises which the American tongue goes through in gum-chewing.

Let us then make up our minds that the higher of the two
towers is the chewing-gum building. It must be. It should be.
It is. It stands for the innumerable sentences which represent
the refusal of every American Boy to accept any standard
below the topmost in the *worlrld*. Quantity is the first standard to appear in the scale of human values; and as the maxi-

mum is the quantity of quantity (all other levels of quantity
being but qualities of quantity), "the greatest in the world"
is the most frequent standard of comparison in the greatest
nursery in the world.

Pride? Perhaps. But how much simple humility under that
juvenile pride! Boys are proud with humble standards, and
it is the play of pride and humility which is attractive in
them.

They board one another like children, with no social reserve, no cold formality. "My name is John. Do you like to
play with me?"—so say children. And they, "My name is
Smith. I am much interested in your work. . . ." Or else, "I
came late to your lecture and did not hear the Chairman's
introduction. Who are you?" They are direct, frank, and
spontaneous, like children. They want to know because they
are curious, not because they seek some advantage from the
information they are asking. They just want to know. There
are so many things in the world and so thrilling, if only one
could know them. And the American Boy has kept intact
the juvenile capacity for being thrilled. So, being wealthy
children, they make their European uncles come over to tell
them stories. Every boat brings at least one of them, always,
of course, the most famous European uncle in the *worlrld*,
known the world over for his ability to spin yarns on a particular line—politics, philosophy, literature, or travel—and
the children go and listen to him and are thrilled and grateful
to the European uncle who has taught them so much and
kept them out of mischief for at least one hour.

They are hungry and thirsty for information—facts, stories. But they dislike thought, as all sound, healthy children
do. None of your highbrow stuff for fine lads who can enjoy
themselves making toys and playing with them. Knowledge,
yes. By all means. Some boys must know all about how toys
are made and moved to and fro, and distributed fairly in the
nursery, or there would be no fun. Knowledge, however, is
all right. It can be checked and put to some use, both made

something of and kept busy, so to say. It can be turned into a toy, so that by means of little machines with colored lamps and buttons and switches the springs of the soul-machine may be shown to the whole nursery. There is a mighty boy in Columbia University who is a master in that game. He's just discovered how blond girls are more sensitive than brunettes by showing them love films while they had all sorts of something-meters and what-d'you-call-them-graphs attached to their wrists and placed on their left breasts, their imagination meanwhile wandering God knows where. Great fun, I tell you, this knowledge game.

No wonder they like it. For knowledge is not only good fun but also useful and recognized as a commendable thing by all grown-ups. But principles and theories are quite another matter. They are dangerous things. God knows where they might lead. That is the way people turn radical, and once Boys began to be radicals, the whole nursery would be agog and the Boys divided for good, instead of just for a game of politics as they are divided now into Republicans and Democrats with not a pin to choose between them but, oh! such fierce quarrels and such agitation and shouting and organizing and playing at Committees and denouncing this and the other in dead earnest and choosing one particular lad and turning him into a hero, either because he speaks well or because he is always wonderfully silent, or because he is wet or maybe for being dry, or for descending from one of the masts of the *Mayflower*, or perhaps for being a self-made man—just someone to become a hero and a great man; and once chosen, they work for him and shout for him and fight for him and die for him and forget all about him when he is safely seated on his stately chair and the fun of the fight is over.

III

Splendid Boys! Their imagination is always at boiling point. With the little ones, it takes terrifying forms. They

dream of dreadful dangers and bogies—the Catholic Church
and the Rising Tide of Color, lurking in the night, ready to
devour the whole nursery with a snappy movement of their
powerful and sinister jaws. The little ones are terrified yet
brave. To give themselves a countenance, and in the hope of
frightening away the monsters, they grant one another
grand, high-sounding titles: "Imperial Wizard," they whis-
per; and then they rise from their cots, in their long white
nightgowns, and put masks on their faces and peaked caps
on their heads and weird paper ornaments on their chests,
and try to chase the dreaded fiends with yells and shouts and
dances and the magic power of the thrice-repeated letter K.

Happy in their spacious nursery, the Boys hardly ever
look through the window. Why should they? A wide street
of water separates them from the old house opposite whence
their parents came long ago, oh, so very, very, very long ago,
you know. . . . Longer, in fact, than any child's memory
can hold. They cannot see the old house, but they know it
only too well. Don't they know it? Some of them, the more
idle, venture over the water now and then. What for? I ask
you. Just to waste their money and to forget their good nursery manners over there. For it is a fact that the old place is
decrepit and dissolute and backward at that. They can't
make toys nearly as fast as we do, nor as cheap, and they cannot even agree among themselves. See. We are forty-eight
states living in perfect union. Why don't they follow our
example? The causes are exactly alike. We are all Americans.
They are all foreigners. Surely they might agree if they had
any decency. No wonder America remains aloof in her romantic dreams. Romantic and quixotic, she refuses to see
realities other than she imagines them, and she keeps loyal
to her sacred memories, regardless of her material interests.
She has made up her mind that every European statesman is
a super-intellectual machiavel, and it is no use showing her
photographs of European statesmen: she remains faithful to
her fond illusion. She has a vague notion that her beloved

Washington, long, oh, long ago, shook a tender yet stern finger at her, "Now, see you do not get entangled with Europeans!" and in vain her hard-boiled financiers point out to her that her European interests are worth several of her States: America half-closes her dreaming eyes and murmurs to herself, "HE told me I was to remain unentangled." Romantic America! . . .

Do you require further proofs? See the place which woman occupies in her life. The Boys have hoisted her on to a pedestal of admiration. Her power and privileges flow from the position she occupies as an idealized type of humanity. In her youth, the inspirer, in her maturer years, the leader of men. First, the sweetheart of the nation, then her aunt, woman governs America because America is a land of boys who refuse to grow up. She it is who rises to the activities reserved for grown-up people: general ideas, æsthetic enjoyment, culture, understanding of the world. The Boys around her live a life of fun and activity, caught in the "behaviorism" of club and school standards which they scrupulously respect, faithful to tradition and to a collective earth which their inexperienced minds are afraid to leave. She dares explore the Heaven and Hell of individualism, the wider responsibilities of thought, and the wider liberties of experience. The Boys look up to her—her beauty, first, then her intelligence, her culture, her wisdom. As the sweetheart of the nation, she keeps the Boys happy and healthy with her affection; as the nation's aunt, she made up her mind the Boys were not to drink, and the Boys are dry. Not that they like it overmuch, but, when asked, they sigh first, smile afterwards, cast a side glance at *Her* and concede, "We are better off as it is."

IV

Youth is also selfish, and the Boys are selfish enough. Toys or no toys, there is money in them, and everybody knows what is behind money—more toys, of course. Large colored boards yell their alluring promises to the "Successful" boy, tempting everyone to climb to the top with delicious vistas which no boy can resist—glossy cars, velvet-skinned beauties, travel, and cigarettes. Opportunities are large and numerous; skill and energy always sure of a reward. But every boy must look out for himself and "people don't go into business for their health." Boyish selfishness can be cruel.

But if boys are selfish, they can also be generous. These healthy and energetic Boys count the money they get but not the money they give.

For these children, so direct, so spontaneous, so ill-mannered at times, at times so ignorant and so secure in their self-satisfied limitations, these children so healthy and so strong even in their defects, are good. They are good children and they want to be good children. No nation, except perhaps that admirable England from whose old house they came (of that, there is no doubt) can show a higher sense of social duty and service than this Boy-Club which America is. Every boy and girl wants to serve. The lure of common service is so strong that many a woman fails to see in motherhood and the home a sufficient justification for her existence, and wants to be a citizen and a business woman rather than a mother or a wife. The common weal is the law; demagogues and political crooks can reach their ends only by pretending to be the champions of the community. The vices of American politics spring from ignorance and gullibility but not from lack of public spirit. It is with public spirit diverted to wrong ends that political mountebanks misgovern here and there in the wide country. Another juvenile feature comes here into play—an astounding credulity, an unbelievable faith in those who know. And Americans are justified in their credulity by the unbelievable things which they have witnessed in their lifetime. They believe in fairy tales partly because they are still in that age, partly because they live in the midst of them. They can spin fairy tales themselves with

that placid assurance of the child who begins by believing in
his inventions before inviting you to listen to them.

Children, for all their fuss about independence and individualism, are profoundly gregarious. American boys seek
one another's company for everything. Play and prayer,
feast and fast, lesson and leisure—all is arranged in common.
Even the most individualistic enterprises . . . America is
the land of "petting parties"! Kiwanis and Rotarians are but
symbolic institutions of a gregarious spirit which permeates
all American life. Let us meet. Let us meet for Heaven's sake.
Let us not remain alone. The mind is so queer. God knows
what it might be up to if we gave it a chance. Why! it might
even grow up and *think*. No. Let us clap one another's shoul-
der and be merry. We may even have a lecturer to spin a
yarn to us. It won't be long and we need not remember it
after he's gone. But let us meet.

That gregarious spirit is shaping the nation out of the heterogeneous elements which a century of immigration has
brought to it. A strong collective consciousness is the keynote.

v

These children are children of giants, and their toys are
huge. Their materialism is a mere phase in their development,
not an essential feature of their character. Let us remember
how it affects all their being, even their art, even their intellect, even the very movements of their soul.

They love "research" and recoil instinctively from speculative thought because research is the most material form of
intellectual exercise, and that in which mental initiative is
more closely guided and sustained by nature. Moreover, the
old house of Mother Nature is a wonderful place in which
to roam in search of odd corners and hidden rooms. In the
strong attachment towards research to be found in the
American I find, therefore, a sign of intellectual life in its

first phase: that of first acquaintance with the world outside, of still fresh appetite for adventure into the ocean of tangible things; and, further, the utilitarian sense of youth and the instinctive mistrust which young intellects feel of their own powers to fly into the thin air of speculation. But the strong tendency towards research is in itself a feature wholly dissimilar to the dislike of *all* intellectual effort which typifies the Englishman. Inherently, the American is not intellectually incurious. His curiosity is keen. And, therefore, though superficially some of his intellectual characteristics may recall those of the Englishman (and though historically and racially they are no doubt related to English traits), the American differs from the Englishman in that he is more energetically prone to intellectual work. Hence here is a distinctive promise of growth.

A similar conclusion suggests itself when American artistic life is considered. America excels in architecture. The fact deserves notice. Why should architecture be the American art par excellence? A mere glance at the arts will provide the answer. Art, I take it (I wish professors of æsthetics and critics would "take" it also) is the conveyance of spirit by means of matter. Now the arts may be classified in a kind of scale or hierarchy according to the weight and density of matter which they require. At the bottom end of the scale is architecture. Then come sculpture, painting, poetry, and finally music. Poetry needs ideas and concepts in which a shade of matter still lingers. In music, of the three elements which compose it, timbre still retains a shade of matter; rhythm and numbers are purely spiritual. Architecture, at the other end, is massive and utilitarian. Thus America's success in architecture appears to us as another manifestation of the material phase of her development.

Were America a land permanently poor in the arts, she might have shown herself relatively more proficient in some æsthetic form of life other than architecture. But the fact that, while but moderately successful in other arts, she should excel in architecture shows that we are in the presence of the *beginning* of a hopeful artistic career. Thus, after architecture, the best American art is sculpture, and then painting; while poetry and music come last.

For American sensibility is still profoundly material. Hence the tendency to material metaphors for describing the motions of the soul, generally represented in American language as movements of a body: *uplifted, thrilled,* are examples in point. But these examples in themselves (even when American exaggeration is discounted) as well as the obvious vitality of American architecture, show that American sensibility is naturally rich, just as we found that American intellect is naturally keen. The future of American life is, therefore, full of possibilities. The Boys will grow.

VI

Unless . . . A phase may be a mere phase and yet be dangerous for all that. Materialism begets its apostles and its pontiffs; it can (what can not?) be turned into a religion. The combination of materialism with the gregarious tendency is one of the most abominable enemies of true and healthy growth.

The visitor who wanders about among men and institutions soon realizes that the power of business over intellectual life is stronger in America than anywhere in Europe—leaving aside, of course, Russia, in which it is absolute. Here, it seems to me, must be found the cause of the relative uniformity of intellectual views which is one of the most striking facts for the visitor in contemporary America. When the Spanish State became a Church (a tendency alive to-day in the American State: see American flags on altars), the inquisition burned heretics. In America heretics are frozen out. The process requires a different temperature, yet is equally severe. But St. Augustine thought that it was good there should be heretics. And so do some of us.

Perhaps these are growth pains of the American boy. Perhaps he will outlive them. If not, the world will lose a great civilization. For the promise of America is great and its fulfilment should be desired by all those for whom life is to be loved for itself, out of all considerations of space, time, or race. Even now there are in America living witnesses of the spiritual power which she has in store. Her highest achievements are not her mighty factories—toys and toymaking, after all—nor her skyscrapers—toys, again—but the charm of some of her women. A charm which, indefinable as it is, independent of sex and age, is a definite spiritual wealth, a recognizable flower of life. It may be argued that of such women there are only a few. Of course. A woman of charm is as rare as a man of genius. But when a country gives forth a man of genius, she proves her worth for all time. And when a country is sprinkled with women of charm she proves that a life is in her which may yet make the world open its eyes and wonder.

Salvador de Madariaga, "Americans Are Boys."

29

THE MECHANIZATION AND
STANDARDIZATION OF
AMERICAN LIFE

RICHARD MÜLLER-FREIENFELS

LIKE his eminent compatriot Keyserling, Müller-Freienfels
was inclined to dive into mysticism when he wrote about
America—or almost anything else. Born in Bad Ems in 1882,
Müller-Freienfels studied at half a dozen European universities before he was appointed Professor of Aesthetics and
Psychology at the Berlin Academy of Music. His voluminous writings are largely in the field of aesthetics and
philosophy, and this selection is taken from his book on
The Mysteries of the Soul (1927), an interpretation of the
various expressions of the contemporary soul in Occidental
civilization. Müller-Freienfels' emphasis on the American
passion for quantity, on the mechanization and standardization of life, was no new thing, but his illustrations were more
relevant and his analysis more penetrating than most. His
other publications include *The Psychology of Art, Philosophy of Individualism*, and *The Evolution of Modern Psychology*.

❖❖❖❖❖❖❖

As THE first characteristic of the external image of America
I laid stress on its different dimensions, on the massive,
quantitative, gigantic nature of this world as compared with
Europe. What we learned in school, but never quite realized,
is here demonstrated by an object-lesson on the largest scale:
America is not a country, like Germany, France, or San Ma-

rino, but a continent. Even an inhabitant of Berlin feels a little provincial when he realizes, on studying the time-table, that in crossing this country one's watch must repeatedly be set back, since when it is noon or midnight in New York, it is eleven o'clock in Chicago, ten o'clock in Denver, and nine o'clock in San Francisco. In America they will ask you on your arrival in New York: "I suppose you will take in the Yellowstone Park and California?"—as though a man traveling from London to Berlin were asked whether he would not include in his journey an excursion to Leningrad and to Egypt. Spatially considered, the distance from New York to San Francisco is much greater than the distance from London to Leningrad, but psychically speaking the distance is trifling. No frontiers lie between them; the same language is spoken from the Atlantic to the Pacific; and there is no need to visit the money-changer. It is truly a continent that the traveler is crossing, but it is also a country, and *one* country of stupendous dimensions. Its provincial cities are larger than many European capitals; its lakes are small seas, wider in area than a European kingdom; its agricultural land is not divided up into small parcels, but the cornfields cover the plains like a shoreless ocean. Everything has other dimensions than with us: the coins are four or five times the size of European money, and compared with the newspapers, the great "dailies" of London, Paris, and Berlin seem small and insufficient. In short, we find that even in everyday things of secondary importance other quantitative notions prevail.

It may perhaps be objected that these great dimensions are something external. The American found his great country ready made! True, but he has not divided it; he has not made frontiers of mountains and rivers! That he has built up this vast country into a unity—that is his achievement. And though the many-storied sky-scrapers of New York may have been a sheer necessity, though the concentration of commercial life on the narrow island may have forced the houses upwards, since the mighty arms of the Hudson prevented them from spreading laterally, as elsewhere in the world, this necessity is absent in Chicago, in Detroit, and in all the other centres in which sky-scrapers are being built today. Here the Americans have imitated New York, not because they were compelled to do so, but because they delight in largeness, as a matter of taste—or the want of taste, as Europeans may possibly feel.

And here is the decisive point: *Quantity, in America, is not a fact, as with us; it is a value.* To say that something is large, massive, gigantic, is in America not a mere statement of fact, but the highest commendation. It is true that this may be so in Europe, but here the contrary valuation obtains as well; here small and graceful and modest things have a special value, while mere bulk may be felt as a defect, and colossal things are often regarded as crude, vulgar, and unqualitative. All this the American can hardly understand. The idyllic frame of mind which sees positive value in small and restrained and limited things is un-American, and occurs only as a reaction against Americanism, while in many European peoples it is a positive characteristic. In America everything big is blindly accepted. Magnitude, in the purely external sense of largeness, sets the standard of value. . . .

The second chief characteristic of Americanism is the technicalization or mechanization of life. Not that we Western Europeans are deficient in technique, but nowhere is it so obtrusive as in America. In Europe it is a servant—at least, in theory—but in America it is the almost undisputed despot of life. The decisive point is not the existence, but the different valuation of technical methods and knowledge. In Europe—at least, in intellectual circles—such terms as "mechanical" or "machine-made" are employed as terms of censure, which are opposed to "organic" or "artistic." In the same way the word "technique" seems often to savor of the superficial, unintellectual, and inartistic. The average American sets an absolute and positive value on technique. In the American cities it is not only the finished wares that are dis-

played in the stores; if possible they are actually manufac-
tured before the eyes of the passing crowd. You will see
the pressing-machine at work in the shop-windows, stretch-
ing, folding, and pressing a suit of clothes in the course of
a few minutes; cigar-makers will show anyone who cares
to linger before their windows how cigars are made by hand
and machine; or you may see—and this is quite an appetizing
sight—how sweets and pastry are made and cooked by neat
and pretty young women. Technique is not, as it should be
in theory, a means to an end, but is becoming an end in itself.
The clatter of machinery, which we find disturbing, is music
to the true American ear. Only by the fact that he does not
inwardly rebel against it can we explain the fact that the
American's nerves do not suffer from noise like those of the
European, who is distressed by these things because he inwardly protests against them.

In a purely external sense, the mechanization of life is
conditioned by the size of the country. To be sure, we Europeans too have need of our railways, telegraphs, and tele-
phones; but in America these are far more essential if the
different parts of the Continent are to be connected. A vast
network of railways covers the land; the telegraph and the
telephone, both largely American inventions, have reached
a high degree of development. The air-mail is a necessity,
not a kind of sport, as with us. Above all, the motor-car is
not a luxury, but an article of everyday utility, which is obvious from the shabby condition of most of the cars one sees.
The majority of the railways, whether above or below
ground, are single lines for one-way traffic, and there are separate tracks for the express trains. In the dwelling-houses
people ascend to their apartments not by the stairs, but by
elevators; in the larger buildings there are frequently a dozen
or more lifts at the inmates' disposal, and they may even be
divided into express and local elevators.

In the eyes of the American all these things have a positive
value. The average European takes his guest to the ancient

churches of his city; he shows you streets and localities that have a sentimental interest; it will seldom occur to him to invite you to visit the slaughter-house or a car factory. In Chicago the slaughter-houses are regarded as the thing best worth seeing, and after them the factories, docks, etc. It is not that we Europeans never inspect a dock or a factory, but we do so out of curiosity, or as a matter of unemotional interest, and not in a spirit of almost religious respect, as does the genuine American. In the country I was repeatedly taken to see wireless apparatus, which reproduced the great variety of messages with a considerable amount of noise. *What* was heard, whether Beethoven or jazz music, did not interest my hosts in the least; all that they considered was the technique of transmission and reception—technique as an end in itself.

This general mechanization of life is, of course, due to the co-operation of a number of factors. The lack of domestic servants, which I shall presently consider as a social factor, has of necessity resulted in the mechanization, even in the home, of many tasks which in Europe are performed by human labor. While visiting American acquaintances who lived in the country I was repeatedly led into the kitchen by my hostess, where she showed me her laboratory. Mechanical contrivances did the work of washing and drying plates and dishes; electrical machines prepared the inevitable ice-cream; and there were cooking appliances and vacuum-cleaners with refinements quite unknown to us. All these things are devised for "comfort," but American comfort is not what we call comfort in Europe. To us the word conveys a sense of ease and cosiness. The American railway-cars, with their spaciousness and their convenient corridors, which enable one to pass through the whole train more readily than is possible on most European expresses, are entirely comfortable, but they are not "cosy." . . .

Everyone who has visited the United States will be able to recall similar characteristics, all of which go to prove the same thing, namely, that the whole of life has been mechanized in a far greater degree than with us. Psychologically speaking, all these traits may be referred to an intellectual attitude on the part of the American, which is not indeed unknown in Europe, but is found in a purer form in America, and this attitude may be described as the rationalization of the soul. By rationalization I mean the prevalence of practical thinking, of the concentration of the intellect on the practical, useful, and efficient, and the obverse of this attitude is the repression and suppression of all that is merely agreeable, emotional, and irrational in the personality. This rationality, as a form of thinking and willing, expresses itself in constructions and instruments and machines which impress the purposeful will of humanity, with the aid of the inorganic forces of Nature, on the outer world. The machine is above all the typical creation and manifestation of the utilitarian and practical reason. It is pure practicality, embodied rationality.

Even organic and intellectual life are mechanized in accordance with the ideal of the rationally operating machine. A cow or a pig, which the German peasant will regard as a personality, and for which he often feels affection, is in America a machine for producing meat and leather. How should any personal relation to the animal be possible when animals are "produced" by the thousand? Even man himself is becoming mechanized, is considered solely with regard to his performance. What are the holders of the great athletic titles but machines for boxing, playing baseball, or running? And the workers in the factories? They too are machines, which indefatigably exercise the same function, a function rationally acquired, without any personal relation to the thing which they are making. How should the individual worker have any personal relation to his work when he is only one of thousands, who are all co-operating in a task which he cannot survey as a whole? Strictly speaking, the factory worker is not even a complete machine, but only a portion of a machine, with no more independence than a cog-wheel or driving-belt. Taylorism and Fordism are the systematic accomplishment of this mechanization of the human being. . . .

The mathematization and technicalization of life is connected inextricably with a further trait of Americanism— with the *typicalization*, or, to use the American expression, the *standardization* of life. Nowadays one may also call this *Fordization*, since Mr. Ford is regarded as peculiarly representative of his country. Standardization is a consequence of mass-production, mathematization, and mechanization, for it implies the unlimited mass-production—for the most part by mechanical means—of a definite type of product. The most importunate result of this process is the Ford car that rattles along every street.

This standardization will be obvious even to anyone crossing the continent. There are, of course, great differences in different parts of the States, yet they are trifling as compared with the uniformity which exists by their side. As compared with the special characteristics of German or Italian landscapes, in which every village almost, and at all events every town of any size, has an individuality of its own, the differences between American cities are trifling. At all events, an observant eye will note the conspicuous appearance of the same features everywhere, in spite of obvious differences. This typification will be seen in the most prominent features as well as in the least conspicuous. If you go shopping you will everywhere find the same standard wares in the window. All the men seem to be clothed by the same tailor, and all the women seem to have bought their hats at the same shop. As a matter of fact, they buy the same things in different shops. Everything reaches a most respectable standard, but everywhere this standard has the effect of a leveling, a standardization.

The most remarkable thing is that even the people impress one as having been standardized. All these clean-shaven men, all these girls, with their doll-like faces, which are generally painted, seem to have been produced somewhere in a Ford factory, not by the dozen but by the thousand. In no other country are the individuals reduced to such a dead-level as in the United States, and this appears all the more remarkable when we reflect that nowhere is there such a disorderly mixture of races and peoples as in this Eldorado of the needy and adventurous of all countries. And yet, surprisingly enough, after a few years as a rule, and certainly after a few generations, the immigrant, whether he was English, German, Russian, Syrian, or Greek, has become "an American." And this transformation affects even his features! We can understand that as regards his clothing and other externals he will do his best not to look a "greenhorn"; but it is not so easy to understand that even the member of such a race as the Jewish, which has preserved its type for thousands of years, will after a little while impress one as being not a Jew but an American. And if this transformation affects the features, which would seem to be independent of the will, it is naturally far more perceptible in the bearing and behavior, in speech and accent, and in social manners.

As in the case of "quantification" and mechanization, so in that of typification we are confronted by a different valuation. In Europe, time out of mind, people have preferred to maintain a distance, and therefore a difference, between races and classes and other social groups, and even between individuals. Distance, uniqueness, and originality are European values, which are foreign to the American. His values are the very reverse of these: adherence to type, agreement, similarity. In the Middle Ages the classes were divided by dress, custom, and many other characteristics; there was no intercourse between them. Even in Europe time has brought many changes; even in Europe the bourgeois is victorious, and noblemen and peasants alike wear bourgeois clothes. Nevertheless, these differences persist, even though they may not be visible; the spirit of caste still survives; classes and professional groups still regard one another with disfavor; the educated man looks down on the man of the people, and the man of the people is resentful of education; the officer has a special standing, and so forth. In America these differences do not exist. There the only difference that counts is a man's quantitative achievement and success, which in the last resort is expressed in dollars. Here is a marshal's baton which everyone carries in his knapsack. It does not matter how he makes his way; whether he succeeds as a professor, or a merchant, or an artisan, there is only the one method of valuation. There are no insuperable barriers, such as that of noble birth. If a man fails in one calling, he adopts another. No one looks down on a man who fails as a professor and then becomes a hotel-keeper, provided he is successful. This lack of social discrimination impresses the newcomer. People treat one another with a peculiarly equalitarian politeness, which to us often seems an obtrusive cordiality, but which is an attribute of the type, not of the individual. The American sees in his neighbor not a certain Mr. M—— or Mrs. N——, but simply an impersonal being, with whom he can exchange opinions, or rather the usual phrases, concerning the weather or the last glove-fight. This reduction of all to a dead-level has of course its advantages, but it deprives life of much that is desirable, and, above all, of a perception of personal quality.

Just as the American does not discriminate between the professions, so he has no perception of all those factors that in Europe separate, differentiate, and discriminate. What of the political parties, for example? In Europe they are divided by their social and political ideals. There are, of course, political differences in America, but in the first place they are very few, and in the second they are very slight. The European is surprised to find how little difference there is between the tendencies of the two principal parties, the Republicans and the Democrats. Men change their party without conscientious scruples, and they are not therefore accused of moral weakness. Even religion does not create such radical divisions as in Europe, although the number of sects and confusions is far greater than with us. But there is no "Center" party, as in Germany; no anti-Semitism as we understand it, no instinctive feeling of enmity against other ethnological species. Even such associations as the Ku-Klux-Klan do not attack any particular group of opponents, but simply wage war on all that is un-American—that is, on all that is not typical. If a thing is untypical it is worthless. Further, the difference between the sexes is not so great as it is—or used to be—with us. Women do not constitute a down-trodden caste; they are so dominant that some Europeans have spoken of gynocracy. Even the young girl behaves with an independence which is startling to the European, and seems to him "unfeminine"; and conversely, he often detects feminine traits in the American man. In both cases he is mistaken; the sexes have not interchanged their roles; it is only that the differences are not so extreme. Even age does not constitute a social difference in the States. While with us the relation of adults to children (like that of the husband to the wife) is from the sociological point of view very like that of master and servant, in America youth enjoys much more extensive rights. The result may often be regarded by the European as a lack of respect, disobedience, and libertinism, but it is not so regarded in America, since the adult does not ask for respect and subordination. Human typification finds an aesthetic expression in an "ideal beauty," which is propagated daily in a thousand magazines, cinemas, and theatres, and in which all the characteristic differences of race, sex, age, and class have completely disappeared.

Müller-Freienfels, *Mysteries of the Soul.*

30

LOVE IN AMERICA

RAOUL DE ROUSSY DE SALES

BORN in Paris in 1896, Roussy de Sales had a long association with America and Americans. During the First World
War he served as liasion officer with the American Red
Cross, then became an assistant director of the Rockefeller
Foundation in France. He came to the United States in 1932
as correspondent for various French newspapers, lectured
widely in this country, contributed to numerous American
and French periodicals, and translated *Mein Kampf* for
American publication. Returning to France at the outbreak
of the Second World War, Roussy de Sales lost his life on
December 3, 1942. This essay on "Love in America," which
appeared first in the *Atlantic Monthly* in 1938, illustrates
admirably the wit, the penetration, and the affection with
which he looked at the American scene.

AMERICA appears to be the only country in the world where
love is a national problem.

Nowhere else can one find a people devoting so much time
and so much study to the question of the relationship between men and women. Nowhere else is there such concern
about the fact that this relationship does not always make
for perfect happiness. The great majority of the Americans
of both sexes seem to be in a state of chronic bewilderment
in the face of a problem which they are certainly not the
first to confront, but which—unlike other people—they still
refuse to accept as one of those gifts of the gods which one

might just as well take as it is: a mixed blessing at times, and at other times a curse or merely a nuisance.

The prevailing conception of love, in America, is similar to the idea of democracy. It is fine in theory. It is the grandest system ever evolved by man to differentiate him from his ancestors, the poor brutes who lived in caverns, or from the apes. Love is perfect, in fact, and there is nothing better. But, like democracy, it does not work, and the Americans feel that something should be done about it. Their statesmen are intent on making democracy work. Everybody is trying to make love work, too.

In either case the result is not very satisfactory. The probable reason is that democracy and love are products of a long and complicated series of compromises between the desires of the heart and the exactions of reason. They have a peculiar way of crumbling into ashes as soon as one tries too hard to organize them too well.

The secret of making a success out of democracy and love in their practical applications is to allow for a fairly wide margin of errors, and not to forget that human beings are absolutely unable to submit to a uniform rule for any length of time. But this does not satisfy a nation that, in spite of its devotion to pragmatism, also believes in perfection.

For a foreigner to speak of the difficulties that the Americans encounter in such an intimate aspect of their mutual relationship may appear as an impertinence. But the truth is that no foreigner would ever think of bringing up such a subject of his own accord. In fact, foreigners who come to these shores are quite unsuspecting of the existence of such a national problem. It is their initial observation that the percentage of good-looking women and handsome men is high on this continent, that they are youthful and healthy in mind and body, and that their outlook on life is rather optimistic.

If the newcomers have seen enough American moving pictures before landing here—and they usually have—they must have gathered the impression that love in America is normally triumphant, and that, in spite of many unfortunate accidents, a love story cannot but end very well indeed. They will have noticed that these love stories which are acted in Hollywood may portray quite regrettable situations at times and that blissful unions get wrecked by all sorts of misfortunes. But they never remain wrecked: even when the happy couple is compelled to divorce, this is not the end of everything. In most cases it is only the beginning. Very soon they will remarry, sometimes with one another, and always— without ever an exception—for love.

The observant foreigner knows, of course, that he cannot trust the movies to give him a really reliable picture of the American attitude towards love, marriage, divorce, and re-marriage. But they nevertheless indicate that in such matters the popular mind likes to be entertained by the idea (1) that love is the only reason why a man and a woman should get married; (2) that love is always wholesome, genuine, up-lifting, and fresh, like a glass of Grade A milk; (3) that when, for some reason or other, it fails to keep you uplifted, wholesome, and fresh, the only thing to do is to begin all over again with another partner.

Thus forewarned, the foreigner who lands on these shores would be very tactless indeed if he started questioning the validity of these premises. Besides, it is much more likely that he himself will feel thoroughly transformed the moment he takes his first stroll in the streets of New York. His European skepticism will evaporate a little more at each step, and if he considers himself not very young any more he will be immensely gratified to find that maturity and even old age are merely European habits of thought, and that he might just as well adopt the American method, which is to be young and act young for the rest of his life—or at least until the expiration of his visa.

If his hotel room is equipped with a radio, his impression that he has at last reached the land of eternal youth and perfect love will be confirmed at any hour of the day and on any point of the dial. No country in the world consumes such a fabulous amount of love songs. Whether the song is gay or nostalgic, the tune catchy or banal, the verses clever or silly, the theme is always love and nothing but love.

Whenever I have gone back to France and listened to the radio, I have always been surprised to find that so many songs can be written on other subjects. I have no statistics on hand, but I think that a good 75 per cent of the songs one hears on the French radio programs deal with politics. There are love songs, of course, but most of them are far from romantic, and this is quite in keeping with the French point of view that love is very often an exceedingly comical affair.

In America the idea seems to be that love, like so much else, should be sold to the public, because it is a good thing. The very word, when heard indefinitely, becomes an obsession. It penetrates one's subconsciousness like the name of some unguent to cure heartaches or athlete's foot. It fits in with the other advertisements, and one feels tempted to write to the broadcasting station for a free sample of this thing called Love.

Thus the visitor from Europe is rapidly permeated with a delightful atmosphere of romanticism and sweetness. He wonders why Italy and Spain ever acquired their reputation of being the lands of romance. This, he says to himself, is the home of poetry and passion. The Americans are the real heirs of the troubadours, and station WXZQ is their love court.

To discover that all this ballyhoo about love (which is not confined to the radio or the movies) is nothing but an aspect of the national optimistic outlook on life does not take very long. It usually becomes evident when the foreign visitor receives the confidences of one or more of the charming American women he will chance to meet. This normally happens after the first or second cocktail party to which he has been invited.

II

I wish at this point to enter a plea in defense of the foreign visitor, against whom a great many accusations are often made either in print or in conversation. These accusations fall under two heads. If the foreigner seems to have no definite objective in visiting America, he is strongly suspected of trying to marry an heiress. If for any reason he cannot be suspected of this intention, then his alleged motives are considerably more sinister. Many American men, and quite a few women, believe that the art of wrecking a happy home is not indigenous to this continent, and that in Europe it has been perfected to such a point that to practice it has become a reflex with the visitors from abroad.

It is very true that some foreign visitors come over here to marry for money in exchange for a title or for some sort of glamour. But there are many more foreigners who marry American women for other reasons besides money, and I know quite a few who have become so Americanized that they actually have married for love and for nothing else.

As for the charge that the Europeans are more expert than the Americans in spoiling someone else's marital happiness, it seems to me an unfair accusation. In most cases the initiative of spoiling whatever it is that remains to be spoiled in a shaky marriage is normally taken by one of the married pair, and the wrecker of happiness does not need any special talent to finish the job.

What is quite true, however, is that the American woman entertains the delightful illusion that there *must* be some man on this earth who can understand her. It seems incredible to her that love, within legal bonds or outside of them, should not work out as advertised. From her earliest years she has been told that success is the ultimate aim of life. Her father and mother made an obvious success of their lives by creating her. Her husband is, or wants to be, a successful business man. Every day 130,000,000 people are panting and sweating to make a success of something or other. Success—the constant effort to make things work perfectly and the conviction that they can be made to—is the great national preoccupation.

And what does one do to make a success?

Well, the answer is very simple: one learns how, or one consults an expert.

That is what her husband does when he wants to invest his money or improve the efficiency of his business. That is what she did herself when she decided to "decorate" her house. In the American way of life there are no insoluble problems. You may not know the answer yourself, but nobody doubts that the answer exists—that there is some method or perhaps some trick by which all riddles can be solved and success achieved.

And so the European visitor is put to the task on the presumption that the accumulation of experience which he brings with him may qualify him as an expert in questions of sentiment.

The American woman does not want to be understood for the mere fun of it. What she actually wishes is to be helped to solve certain difficulties which, in her judgment, impede the successful development of her inner self. She seldom accepts the idea that maladjustments and misunderstandings are not only normal but bearable once you have made up your mind that, whatever may be the ultimate aim of our earthly existence, perfect happiness through love or any other form of expression is not part of the program.

III

One of the greatest moral revolutions that ever happened in America was the popularization of Freud's works.

Up to the time that occurred, as far as I am able to judge, America lived in a blissful state of puritanical repression. Love, as a sentiment, was glorified and sanctified by marriage.

There was a general impression that some sort of connection existed between the sexual impulses and the vagaries of the heart, but this connection was not emphasized, and the consensus of opinion was that the less said about it the better. The way certain nations, and particularly the French, correlated the physical manifestations of love and its more spiritual aspects was considered particularly objectionable. Love, in other words,—and that was not very long ago,—had not changed since the contrary efforts of the puritanically-minded and the romantic had finally stabilized it midway between the sublime and the parlor game.

The important point is that up to then (and ever since the first Pilgrims set foot on this continent) love had been set aside in the general scheme of American life as the one thing which could not be made to work better than it did. Each one had to cope with his own difficulties in his own way and solve them as privately as he could. It was not a national problem.

Whether or not people were happier under that system is beside the point. It probably does not matter very much whether we live and die with or without a full set of childish complexes and repressions. My own view is that most people are neither complex nor repressed enough as a rule; I wish sometimes for the coming of the Anti-Freud who will complicate and obscure everything again.

But the fact is that the revelations of psychoanalysis were greeted in America as the one missing link in the general program of universal improvement.

Here was a system, at last, that explained fully why love remained so imperfect. It reduced the whole dilemma of happiness to sexual maladjustments, which in turn were only the result of the mistakes made by one's father, mother, or nurse, at an age when one could certainly not be expected to foresee the consequences. Psychoanalysis integrated human emotions into a set of mechanistic formulas. One learned with great relief that the failure to find happiness was not irreparable. Love, as a sublime communion of souls and bodies, was not a legend, nor the mere fancy of the poets. It was real, and—more important still—practically attainable. Anybody could have it, merely by removing a few obstructions which had been growing within himself since childhood like mushrooms in a dark cellar. Love could be made to work like anything else.

It is true that not many people are interested in psychoanalysis any more. As a fad or a parlor game, it is dead. Modern débutantes will not know what you are talking about if you mention the Œdipus complex or refer to the symbolic meaning of umbrellas and top hats in dreams. Traditions die young these days. But the profound effect of the Freudian revelation has lasted. From its materialistic interpretation of sexual impulses, coupled with the American longing for moral perfection, a new science has been born: the dialectics of love; and also a new urge for the American people—they want to turn out, eventually, a perfect product. They want to get out of love as much enjoyment, comfort, safety, and general sense of satisfaction, as one gets out of a well-balanced diet or a good plumbing installation.

IV

Curiously enough, this fairly new point of view which implies that human relationships are governed by scientific laws has not destroyed the romantic ideal of love. Quite the contrary. Maladjustments, now that they are supposed to be scientifically determined, have become much more unbearable than in the horse-and-buggy age of love. Husbands and wives and lovers have no patience with their troubles. They want to be cured, and when they think they are incurable they become very intolerant. Reformers always are.

Usually, however, various attempts at readjustment are made with devastating candor. Married couples seem to spend many precious hours of the day and night discussing what is wrong with their relationship. The general idea is that—according to the teachings of most modern psychologists and pedagogues—one should face the truth fearlessly. Husbands and wives should be absolutely frank with one another, on the assumption that if love between them is real it will be made stronger and more real still if submitted, at frequent intervals, to the test of complete sincerity on both sides.

This is a fine theory, but it has seldom been practiced without disastrous results. There are several reasons why this should be so. First of all, truth is an explosive, and it should be handled with care, especially in marital life. It is not necessary to lie, but there is little profit in juggling with hand grenades just to show how brave one is. Secondly, the theory of absolute sincerity presupposes that, if love cannot withstand continuous blasting, then it is not worth saving anyway. Some people want their love life to be a permanent battle of Verdun. When the system of defense is destroyed beyond repair, then the clause of hopeless maladjustment is invoked by one side, or by both. The next thing to do is to divorce and find someone else to be recklessly frank with for a season.

Another reason why the method of adjustment through truthtelling is not always wise is that it develops fiendish traits of character which might otherwise remain dormant.

I know a woman whose eyes glitter with virtuous self-satisfaction every time she has had a "real heart-to-heart talk" with her husband, which means that she has spent several hours torturing him, or at best boring him to distraction, with a ruthless exposure of the deplorable status of their mutual relationship to date. She is usually so pleased with herself after these periodical inquests that she tells most of her friends, and also her coiffeur, about it. "Dick and I had such a wonderful time last evening. We made a real effort to find out the real truth about each other—or, at least, I certainly did. I honestly believe we have found a new basis of adjustment for ourselves. What a marvelous feeling that is—don't you think so?"

Dick, of course, if he happens to be present, looks rather nervous or glum, but that is not the point. The point is that Dick's wife feels all aglow because she has done her bit in the general campaign for the improvement of marital happiness through truth. She has been a good girl scout. . . .

V

The difference between an American cookbook and a French one is that the former is very accurate and the second exceedingly vague. A French recipe seldom tells you how many ounces of butter to use to make *crêpes Suzette,* or how many spoonfuls of oil should go into a salad dressing. French cookbooks are full of esoteric measurements such as a *pinch* of pepper, a *suspicion* of garlic, or a *generous sprinkling* of brandy. There are constant references to seasoning *to taste,* as if the recipe were merely intended to give a general direction, relying on the experience and innate art of the cook to make the dish turn out right.

American recipes look like doctors' prescriptions. Perfect cooking seems to depend on perfect dosage. Some of these books give you a table of calories and vitamins—as if that had anything to do with the problem of eating well!

In the same way, there is now flourishing in America a great crop of books which offer precise recipes for the things you should do, or avoid doing, in order to achieve happiness and keep the fires of love at a constant temperature. In an issue of *Time* magazine, four such books were reviewed together. Their titles are descriptive enough of the purpose of the authors as well as the state of mind of the readers: *Love and Happiness, So You're Going to Get Married, Marriages Are Made at Home, Getting Along Together.*

I have not read all these books, but, according to the reviewer, they all tend to give practical answers to the same

mysterious problem of living with someone of the opposite
sex. They try to establish sets of little rules and little tricks
which will guarantee marital bliss if carefully followed, in
the same way that cookbooks guarantee that you will obtain
pumpkin pie if you use the proper ingredients properly measured.

As the publisher of one of these books says on the jacket:
"There is nothing in this book about the complicated psychological problems that send men and women to psycho-
analysts, but there is a lot in it about the little incidents of
daily married life—the things that happen in the parlor,
bedroom and bath—that handled one way enable people to
live together happily forever after, and handled another way
lead to Reno."

Time's review of these books is very gloomy in its conclusion: "Despite their optimistic tone," it says, "the four volumes give a troubled picture of United States domestic life
—a world in which husbands are amorous when wives are
not, and vice versa; where conflicts spring up over reading
in bed or rumpling the evening paper . . . the whole grim
panorama giving the impression that Americans are irritable,
aggravated, dissatisfied people for whom marriage is an ordeal
that only heroes and heroines can bear."

But I believe that the editors of *Time* would be just as
dejected if they were reviewing four volumes about American cooking, and for the same reasons. You cannot possibly
feel cheerful when you see the art of love or the art of eating
thus reduced to such automatic formulas, even if the experts
in these matters are themselves cheerful and optimistic. Good
food, the pleasures of love, and those of marriage depend on
imponderables, individual taste, and no small amount of luck.

VI

Thus the problem of love in America seems to be the re-
sultant of conflicting and rather unrealistic ways of ap-

proaching it. Too many songs, too many stories, too many pictures, and too much romance on the one hand, and too much practical advice on the other. It is as if the experience of being in love could only be one of two things: a superhuman ecstasy, the way of reaching heaven on earth and in pairs; or a psychopathic condition to be treated by specialists.

Between these two extremes there is little room for compromise. That the relationship between men and women offers a wide scale of variations seldom occurs to the experts. It is not necessarily true that there is but one form of love worth bothering about, and that if you cannot get the de luxe model, with a life guarantee of perfect functioning, nothing else is worth-while. It is not true either that you can indefinitely pursue the same quest for perfection, or that if a man and a woman have not found ideal happiness together they will certainly find it with somebody else. Life unfortunately does not begin at forty, and when you reach that age, in America or anywhere else, to go on complaining about your sentimental or physiological maladjustments becomes slightly farcical.

It is not easy, nor perhaps of any use, to draw any conclusion from all this, especially for a European who has lost the fresh point of view of the visitor because he lives here, and who is not quite sure of what it means to be a European any more. I sometimes wonder if there is any real difference between the way men and women get along—or do not get along—together on this side of the Atlantic and on the other. There are probably no more real troubles here than anywhere else. Human nature being quite remarkably stable, why should there be? But there is no doubt that the revolt against this type of human inadequacy is very strong indeed here, especially among the women who imagine that the Europeans have found better ways of managing their hearts and their senses than the Americans.

If this is at all true, I believe the reason is to be found in a more philosophical attitude on the part of the Europeans towards such matters. There are no theories about marital bliss, no recipes to teach you how to solve difficulties which, in the Old World, are accepted as part of the common inheritance.

Men and women naturally want to be happy over there, and, if possible, with the help of one another; but they learn very young that compromise is not synonymous with defeat. Even in school (I am speaking more particularly of France now) they are taught, through the literature of centuries, that love is a phenomenon susceptible of innumerable variations, but that—even under the best circumstances—it is so intertwined with the other experiences of each individual life that to be over romantic or too dogmatic about it is of little practical use. *"La vérité est dans les nuances,"* wrote Benjamin Constant, who knew a good deal about such matters.

And, speaking of the truly practical and realistic nature of love, it is a very strange thing that American literature contains no work of any note, not even essays, on love as a psychological phenomenon. I know of no good study of the process of falling in and out of love, no analytical description of jealousy, coquettishness, or the development of tediousness. No classification of the various brands of love such as La Rochefoucauld, Pascal, Stendhal, Proust, and many others have elaborated has been attempted from the American angle. The interesting combinations of such passions as ambition, jealousy, religious fervor, and so forth, with love are only dimly perceived by most people and even by the novelists, who, with very few exceptions, seem to ignore or scorn these complicated patterns. These fine studies have been left to the psychiatrists, the charlatans, or the manufacturers of naïve recipes.

The reason for this neglect on the part of real thinkers and essayists may be that for a long time the standards imposed by the puritanical point of view made the whole study more or less taboo with respectable authors. And then the Freudian wave came along and carried the whole problem out of reach of the amateur observer and the artist. In other words, conditions have been such that there has been no occasion to fill this curious gap in American literature.

Of course, nothing is lost. The field remains open, and there is no reason to suppose that love in America will not cease to be a national problem, a hunting ground for the reformer, and that it will not become, as everywhere else, a personal affair very much worth the effort it takes to examine it as such. All that is necessary is for someone to forget for a while love as Hollywood—or the professor—sees it, and sit down and think about it as an eternally fascinating subject for purely human observation.

Roussy de Sales, "Love in America."

A CHINESE VIEW OF THE AMERICAN CHARACTER

NO YONG·PARK

CURIOUSLY enough, though many Orientals have come to the United States, few have written about it, and few of those who have written have done so with any understanding. No Yong-Park is an exception, and that, perhaps, because he became so largely Americanized. Born in Manchuria at the turn of the century, and educated in a Buddhist monastery, Park came to the United States in 1921 and at once immersed himself in American society. He studied first at Evansville College, in Indiana, and later at Northwestern, Minnesota, and Harvard Universities, taking a Ph.D. degree at the latter institution with a thesis on China and the League. In between he managed to tour with Chautauqua, teach at Western Reserve University, and lecture on the Orient to women's clubs and similar organizations. His most important book is an attack on Western imperialism called *Retreat of the West;* his *Oriental View of American Civilization*, from which this extract is taken, was written in 1933 in the midst of the great depression, and the observations on business, while general in character, are colored by that catastrophe.

❖❖❖❖❖❖

THE typical American is young and energetic, progressive and optimistic, and is a great "booster," a hardworking man, a good sport, and a genius as an organizer.

Of all the peoples of the world, Americans, to my mind,

are the most progressive. They are the ones who live in the future tense. Their mind and soul are always bent for the future. They never move backward and always march forward, even if they have to go all the way around the circle. They do not care to know from where they came. All that matters to them is where they are going. They do not care to know who their ancestors were. You ask them who their ancestors were. They will reply bluntly, "Who in hell wants to know?" Maybe they are right in this respect. What is the use of dwelling so long in the past? Let the archaeologists excavate all the tombs and examine all the bones of our long-dead ancestors. Let the historians search all the dust-covered books in all the libraries on earth. They will never be able to find a model civilization that will fit into the present situation. Destiny points to the future, not to the past. Rightly, the Americans waste little time on history. They study history only to find the faults of their ancestors, so that they may not repeat the same mistakes. They do not think that their ancestors who lived in the trees and in the caves knew or did any better, and they refuse to follow their fathers' trails.

This forward-looking frame of mind, as I see it, is one of the essential differences between the Occidental and the Oriental, particularly between the American and the old Chinese. The former always looks forward while the latter looks backward; the former is always progressive while the latter is conservative. The old-fashioned Chinese revered their ancestors so much as to worship them, and feared to do anything which their ancestors did not do. Hence, Chinese civilization, comparatively speaking, has been static and stagnant. I do not mean to give, however, the wrong notion that China has never progressed. Most often the superficially informed foreigners maintain that China, smitten by the cult of ancestor worship, made no progress during the past several thousand years. But that is not so. The Chinese historians glorified their ancestors so highly that no one would seem to equal them in virtue and achievement, but they were not so great as they were recorded in history. Whenever the Chinese wanted to be greater, they first made their ancestors appear still greater, and no matter how far the Chinese would have moved forward, they always seemed to lag far behind their ancestors. The Chinese notion of progress has been to struggle to catch up with their fathers, whereas the American idea is to do something which no one has yet done. Hence the Americans always look forward into the future and the Chinese always look backward into the past. In substance, both ideas are about the same, so far as progress is concerned. But the one gives rather a dull, pessimistic outlook on life whereas the other gives "pep," optimism and pride.

With such a pride and optimism and ever-progressive frame of mind, the American cannot help being a "booster." No doubt, he is the biggest booster in the world. He boosts himself, of course; he boosts his work; he boosts his family, his town, his state, his country and his race. He will tell you that his people are the most civilized and his country the best in the world. He will also tell you that his State is the best in the Union and that his town is the best in the state. You will hear the same statement in every state and in every town, hence all the states and all the towns in America are the best. In a small town in North Dakota, I was talking to an undertaker. Even that undertaker was boosting his town before me. He said that his town was the best in the state, business was better than in other towns, and more people died there than in any other town in the state! The booster looks at times very childish, and often foolish. But after all, I think it is better to boost everything than to pull it down.

The American does not stop with boosting. He works, works and works. I have never seen anyone who likes to work better than he. To him work is his religion, his recreation and life. You take work away from him, and you will kill him. He is born to work, he lives to work, and he dies for his work. He works when he has something to do; he works when he has nothing to do. He builds up when he can and he tears down when he has nothing to build. He has no time to be graceful, polite and stylish. He is always on the go. He runs, jumps and hops back and forth like a rabbit. Speed! Speed! Speed! It gets on one's nerves. But that is better than being lazy, idle and mischievous.

It is not only the poor that work in America. The rich work as well. In fact, the richer he is the harder a man works. Look at Ford. Look at Rockefeller, his son, and especially his grandson, who worked his way through Yale by waiting on table. What a contrast to China, where only the poor work with the sweat of their brow and the toil of their hands and the idle rich lie around like the lazzaroni of Naples, as Henry George says, and do nothing, make nothing and are good for nothing. To be sure there are, in America, a number of idle rich, wicked and corrupt. But the typical American is a hard-working, God-fearing man, who deserves a decent living on earth and a comfortable place in heaven.

Another thing which impresses me most about the American is his spirit of sportsmanship. Of course there are a lot of unfair people in every country, but the representative Babbitt is a good sport. In play or in work, he follows the rules of the game. He is willing to let his opponent have a fair chance. If he is defeated, he is a good loser; he does not cherish any animosities. He congratulates the victor cheerfully and consoles himself with being a good sport. Watch them in every political election. The opposing candidates fight each other like cats and dogs. They shout, yell, and assail their opponents in the strongest language that can be found. But after the election, the loser congratulates the winner, and he seals his mouth and lets his opponent have the floor. Sportsmanship, as I see it, is one of the great virtues of the Americans. To them sportsmanship is as important as honesty is to the Chinese. To be sure, that spirit is not absent in other countries but it is more outspoken in America than elsewhere.

Undoubtedly, the greatest of all American virtues is the ability to organize. Look into any city. There you will find literally hundreds and thousands of clubs and associations. Everything is organized from the bottom to the top. Look at the huge business organizations, the billion-dollar corporations, if you please. Look at all the men's clubs, Rotary, Kiwanis, and the like. Look at the women's clubs and see how well they are organized. Even the boys and girls are all organized into Boy Scouts and Camp Fire Girls, and the like. The Americans surely know how to organize. A humorist once remarked that even in Inferno there may be found some American associations.

There are curious similarities between the Chinese political chaos and the American industrial anarchy. The former may be described as political feudalism and the latter as economic feudalism. The political feudalism in China is the creation of armed bandits, and the economic feudalism in America has been the creation of gamblers and speculators. The collapse of Chinese political machinery is largely due to failure in controlling the armed bandits, and the collapse of the American industrial system has been largely due to failure in controlling the profit-makers and exploiters. In the one country a handful of arrogant and unscrupulous militarists wages political wars, endless and interminable, and in the other a small group of selfish and irresponsible capitalists has staged industrial wars which have been no less deadly in their effects. In the one country, the armed militarists are kings and dictators, and in the other the selfish capitalists are armed with industrial machinery. But in both countries, the sufferers have been the innocent people.

The capitalists in America have been as free as the militarists in China, and the people in the one country as much subjected to them as in the other. There is no other country in the world where the militarists are so free to exploit the masses as in China. Nor is there any other country where the capitalists have been so free and uncontrolled as in America. China is a country of free militarists and America has been a land of free capitalists, free to exploit, free to gamble, free to wage wars, free from all responsibilities. Nothing can explain the situation better than the gambling in stocks and other securities. Probably the most diabolical thing in the world is this gambling in securities. Hanging may be too good a reward for most of these speculators, but they have been left practically uncontrolled to cheat, rob the people of millions and to put the entire nation into jeopardy. A movement toward control is now under way. This control must not be so rigid as to smother individual initiative, but the extent of the freedom which the capitalists have hitherto enjoyed in America is beyond the imagination of any reasonable man. There can be no economic security in America until the irresponsible blood-suckers have been brought under control, as there can be no political order in China unless the armed militarists are brought under rule.

The American capitalists have been as irresponsible as the Chinese militarists in dealing with their fellow men. The Chinese militarist drags the poor fellows into his service. He pays them while they risk their lives in the battlefield, but when the crisis is over, he is not responsible for the well-being of his men. They are scattered throughout the country and become the burden of the people. Precisely the same situation has prevailed in America. A few years ago when business conditions were good the worker was paid well. The thrifty and hard-working saved a few dollars every week for the rainy day that might overtake them. Some bought stocks, some deposited their money in banks, others bought bonds. It seemed for some time that the wage earners would all be financially independent, sooner or later. But when prosperity vanished, millions of men were thrown out into the streets. . . .

No doubt some of them were the victims of their own sins, but most of them have been the victims of gamblers and speculators, who deserve nothing but an electric chair and a stone overcoat. No civilized state should allow its soldiers to use the instruments of war against the innocent population, nor should it allow its speculators and the reckless producers to use the machinery of industry to enslave and slaughter mankind. Both must be drastically controlled, or else civilization itself may be ruined and destroyed.

There is another striking similarity between the American industrial condition and the Chinese political situation. The Americans have gone as far with their business as the Chinese have with their politics. From time immemorial the Chinese have lived democracy, but their democracy has never extended beyond the walls of the little villages. Since the revolution in 1912 they have tried to extend the principle to the entire state, but so far they have failed. Therefore, there is turmoil and unrest in China. Similarly, the Americans demonstrated their business genius but their success has been confined only within the walls of the individual plants, and so far they have failed to extend the system, the plan and the mechanism operating within the factory to the entire state. Therefore chaos came in American industry.

No-Yong Park (Pao), *An Oriental View of American Civilization.*

CAPITALISM NURTURES AMERICA IN SPIRITUAL LASSITUDE

ILYA ILF AND EUGENE PETROV

IN 1932 Americans had read, with delight, a book called *Little Golden Calf,* one of the few humorous books on the Soviet Union which had been permitted to appear. Three years later the authors, Ilya Ilf and Eugene Petrov, came to the United States to look at life under capitalism and report their findings. It was a period of acute depression, and what they saw confirmed them in their belief that capitalism was headed for disaster. Yet, like Ilya Ehrenburg who came over in 1946, their view of America was a confused one. They were committed to disapproval, yet found much in American economy and society that excited their admiration. Something of that grudging admiration crept into their *Little Golden America,* from the concluding chapter of which this selection is taken.

O UR journey came to an end. Within two months we had been in twenty-five states and several hundred towns, we had breathed the dry air of deserts and prairies, had crossed the Rocky Mountains, had seen Indians, had talked with the young unemployed, with the old capitalists, with radical intellectuals, with revolutionary workers, with poets, with writers, with engineers. We had examined factories and parks, had admired roads and bridges, had climbed up the

Sierra Nevadas and descended into the Carlsbad Caves. We had traveled ten thousand miles.

And throughout that entire journey we never once stopped thinking of the Soviet Union.

We had traveled over American highways, but in our thoughts were Soviet highways. We spent nights in American hotels, but we thought about Soviet hotels. We examined Ford's factories, but in our thoughts we saw ourselves in our own automobile factories, and while conversing with Indians we thought of Kazakstan.

Through the tremendous distance that separated us from Soviet soil we envisioned it with special incisiveness. It is necessary to see the capitalist world to appreciate in a new way the world of socialism. All the attributes of the socialist arrangement of our life, which man ceases to notice because of daily contact with them, seem especially significant at a distance. We understood the mood of Maxim Gorky when upon his return to the Union after many years of life abroad, tirelessly, day in and day out, he repeated one and the same thing: "It's a remarkable thing you are doing, comrades! A great thing!"

We talked constantly about the Soviet Union, drew parallels, made comparisons. We noticed that the Soviet people whom we frequently met in America were of the same emotions. There was not a single conversation which in the end would not bring a reference to the Soviet Union: "But at home it is like this," "but at home it is like that," "it would be well to introduce it at home," "we don't know how to do that yet," "that we have already adopted." Soviet people abroad were not mere travelers, not merely engineers or diplomats on a mission. All of them were lovers who had been torn away from the object of their affection and who remembered it every minute. It is a unique patriotism that cannot be understood, let us say, by an American. In all probability the American is a good patriot. If he were asked he would sincerely say that he loves his country; but at the same time it will be found out that he does not love Morgan, that he does not know and does not care to know the names of the people who planned the suspension bridges in San Francisco, that he is not interested to know why in America drought increases every year, who built the Boulder Dam and why, why Negroes are lynched in the Southern states, or why he must eat frozen meat. He will say that he loves his country—yet he is profoundly indifferent to questions of agriculture, since he is not an agriculturist; to questions of industry, since he is not an industrialist; to finances, since he is not a financier; to art, since he is not an artist; and to military problems, since he is not a military man. He is a hard-working man who receives his hundred and thirty dollars a month, so he sneers at Washington with all its laws, at Chicago with its bandits, and at New York with its Wall Street. He asks only one thing of his country—to let him alone, and not to interfere with his listening to his radio or going to the movies. Of course, when he becomes unemployed, that's a different matter. Then he will begin to think about everything. No, he will not understand the patriotism of a Soviet man, who loves not his juridical native land which gives him merely the rights of citizenship, but a native land which is tangible, where to him belong the soil, the factories, the stores, the banks, the dreadnoughts, the airplanes, the theatres, and the books, where he himself is the politician and the master of all.

The average American cannot endure abstract conversations nor does he touch upon themes too far removed from him. He is interested only in what is directly connected with his house, his automobile, or his nearest neighbors. He shows an interest in the life of the country once in four years, at the time of the presidential election.

We do not at all insist that this absence of spirituality is an organic attribute of the American people. There was a time, after all, when the Northern armies marched off to liberate the Negroes from slavery! It is capitalism that has made these people thus, and in every way it nurtures in them this spiritual lassitude. Terrible are the crimes of American capitalism, which with amazing trickiness has palmed off on the people the most trivial of motion pictures, radio, and weekly journalistic tosh, while reserving for itself Tolstoy, Van Gogh, and Einstein, but remaining profoundly indifferent to them.

Essentially there is in the world only one noble striving of the human mind—to vanquish spiritual and material poverty, to make people happy. Yet those people in America who have made it their goal to attain that—the advanced workers, the radical intellectuals—are at best regarded as dangerous cranks, and in the worst case as the enemies of society. The result is that even indirect fighters for human happiness—men of learning, inventors, builders—are not popular in America. They and their works, inventions, and wonderful constructions, remain in the shadows, while all of fame goes to boxers, bandits, and the motion-picture stars. While among the people themselves—who see that with the increase in the number of machines, life becomes not better but worse—prevails even hatred of technical progress. There are people who are ready to break up machines, just like the drowning man who, in desperation to get out of the water, seizes his savior by the neck and drags him down to the bottom.

We have already said that the American, in spite of his business-like activity, has a passive nature. Some Hearst or some Hollywood shyster can manage to drag millions of good, honest, hard-working average Americans down to the spiritual level of a savage. But even these all-powerful men cannot divest the people of the notion that life must be improved. That notion is very widespread in America. But when it finally finds its expression in the form of political ideas, their level does not exceed the level of the average Hollywood picture. And such ideas have a colossal success. All the political ideas which tend to the improvement of the welfare of the American people are inevitably presented in the form of easy arithmetic problems for students of the third grade. In order to understand the idea, the voter need merely take a sheet of paper, a pencil, make a quick calculation, and it's done. As a matter of fact, all of them are not really ideas but tricks, suitable for advertising purposes only. They would hardly bear mentioning, if scores of millions of Americans were not carried away by them.

How to save America and improve its life?

Huey Long advises division of wealth. A sheet of paper and a pencil appear on the scene. The voter, puffing, adds, multiplies, subtracts, and divides. This is a terribly interesting occupation. What a smart fellow this Huey Long is! Everyone will get a large sum of money! People are so carried away by this impudent arithmetic that it does not even occur to them to think about where these millions will come from.

How to improve life? How to save America?

There arises a new titan of thought, another Socrates or Confucius, the physician Townsend. The thought which has entered the thinking head of this respectable practicing physician could have been born in any small European country only in a psychiatric hospital in a ward for the tranquil, quiet, polite, and utterly hopeless madmen. But in America it has a dizzying success. Here it isn't even necessary to bother with subtraction and multiplication. Here everything is quite simple. Every old man and every old woman in the United States upon attaining the age of sixty will receive two hundred dollars a month under obligation to spend these dollars. Then trade will increase automatically and automatically unemployment will disappear. Everything takes place automatically.

When we were leaving America the number of Townsend's followers was increasing at a frightful rate. Not a single politician dared to speak against this doctor of genius on the eve of elections.

But American capitalists understand that motion pictures,

ILYA ILF AND EUGENE PETROV

a radio broadcast, stories in weeklies, billboards about revolution "which can never happen in America," churches, and arithmetical plans may not prove sufficient, so there are already growing "American Legions" and "Liberty Leagues," and little by little fascist forces are trained, so that at the necessary moment they may be turned into the most genuine kind of storm troops, which will be ordered to stifle the revolutionary movement by force.

America is rich. But it is not merely rich. It is phenomenally rich. It has everything—oil, grain, coal, gold, cotton—everything that can only lie beneath the earth or grow upon the earth. It has people—the best workers in the world—capable, neat, efficient, honest, hard-working. America marched toward its enrichment at a quick rate of speed. The country reminds one of a man who has made a rapid career, who at first sells suspenders from a pushcart on the East Side, then opens his own store of ready-made clothes and moves to Brooklyn. Then he opens a department store, begins to play the stock market and moves to the Bronx. And finally he buys a railroad, hundreds of steamships, two motion picture factories, builds a skyscraper, opens a bank, joins a golf club, and moves to Park Avenue. He is a billionaire. He has striven for that goal all his life. He bought and sold everything in any old way. He dispossessed people, speculated, sat at the stock exchange from morning until night, he toiled sixteen hours a day, he awoke with the thought of money, he fell asleep with the same thought, and now he is monstrously wealthy. Now he may rest. He has villas by the ocean, he has yachts and castles, but he becomes ill with an incurable disease. He is dying, and no billions can save him.

The stimulus of American life has been and is money. Contemporary American technique grew up and developed so that money might be made faster. Everything that brings in money develops, and everything that does not bring money degenerates and wilts away. Gas, electricity, construction, and automobile companies, in their chase for money, have created a high standard of living. America has raised itself to a high degree of welfare, having left Europe far behind. But precisely at this point it becomes clear that America is seriously and dangerously ill. The country is now facing its own *reductio ad absurdum*. It is capable now, today, of feeding a billion people, and yet it cannot feed its own hundred and twenty millions. It has everything needed to create a peaceful life for its people, yet it has come to such a pass that the entire population is in a state of unrest; the unemployed fears that he will never again find a job; the employed fears that he will lose his job; the farmer fears a crop failure, because then prices will increase and it will cost him more to buy bread, but he also fears a good crop, because then prices will fall and he will have to sell his produce for a pittance. The rich fear that bandits will kidnap their children, bandits fear that they will be placed in the electric chair. Immigrants fear that they will be deported from America; Negroes fear that they will be lynched; politicians fear elections; the average man fears illness, because then doctors will take everything he owns; the merchant fears that racketeers will come and riddle his store counters with a machine-gun fusillade.

At the foundation of life of the Soviet Union lies the communist idea. We have a definite goal, toward which the country advances. The slogan that technique decides everything was given by Stalin after that idea triumphed. That is why we, the people, by comparison with Americans of the average kind are now already much calmer and happier than they, in the land of Morgan and Ford, of twenty-five million automobiles, of a million miles of ideal roads, the land of cold and hot water, of bathrooms, and of service. That is why technique does not seem to us an evil spirit sprung from a bottle. On the contrary, we want to catch up with technical America and to outstrip it.

America does not know what will happen with it tomorrow. We know, and we can tell with definite accuracy, what will happen with us fifty years from now.

Nevertheless, we can still learn much from America. We are doing that. But the lessons which we learn from America are episodic and too specialized.

To catch up with America! That task which Stalin set before our people is immense, but in order to carry out this task we must first of all study America, study not only its automobiles, its turbine generators and radio apparatuses (we are doing that), but likewise the very character of the work of American workers, engineers, business people, especially the business people, because if our Stakhanovists sometimes outstrip the norms of American workers, while the engineers are no worse at times than the American engineers (about that we heard frequently from Americans themselves), still, our business people or economists are considerably behind American business people and cannot compete with them in any way.

We will not discuss now the attributes of our economists, their loyalty to ideas, their devotion, their efficiency. These are the attributes of the Communist Party, which brought them up. Nor will we touch upon the deficiencies of American business people, their lack of loyalty to ideas, their lack of principle, their chase after the dollar. These are the defects of the capitalism which brought them up. It is important right now for us to study their attributes and our defects, because it is necessary for us to learn from them. Not only engineers but also economists, our business people, must learn from them.

The American businessman always finds time for a business conversation. The American sits in his office with his coat off and works. He works quietly, unobtrusively, without making any fuss. He is never late anywhere. He never hurries anywhere. He has only one telephone. No one waits for him in his reception room, because an appointment is usually made with absolute accuracy, and not a single extra minute is wasted during the interview. He is occupied only with his business, exclusively with his business. When he holds conferences nobody knows. In all likelihood, he holds conferences rarely.

Should an American say in the course of a conversation, even incidentally, "I'll do that," it is not necessary to remind him of anything at all in the future. Everything will be done. The ability to keep his word, to keep it firmly, accurately, to burst, but keep his word—that is the most important thing which our Soviet business people must learn from American business people.

We wrote about American democracy, which in fact does not give man freedom and only masks the exploitation of man by man. But in American life there is a phenomenon which should interest us no less than a new machine model. That phenomenon is democracy in intercourse between people, albeit that democracy, too, covers social inequality and is a purely outward form. The outward forms of such a democratism are splendid. They help a lot in work, deliver a blow to bureaucratism, and enhance human dignity.

We drove out of Washington to New York. In a few hours our journey over the American land would come to an end. We thought about America during those final hours. We think that in our book we have told everything that we have thought.

Americans are very angry with Europeans who come to America, enjoy its hospitality, and later scold it. Americans often told us about this with annoyance. But we do not understand such posing of the question; to scold or to praise. America is not the first night of a new play, and we are not theatre critics. We transmit to paper our impressions about that country and our thoughts about it.

What can be said about America, which simultaneously

horrifies, delights, calls forth pity, and sets examples worthy
of emulation, about a land which is rich, poor, talented, and
ungifted?

We can say honestly, with hand on heart, that we would
not like to live in America. It is interesting to observe this
country, but one does not care to live in it.

Ilya Ilf and Eugene Petrov, *Little Golden America.*

✦✦✦ 33 ✦✦✦

THE HOMELINESS AND FRIEND-
LINESS OF THE AMERICANS

JOHN BUCHAN

FEW contemporary novelists have been more widely read
than John Buchan, author of *Greenmantle, Thirty-nine
Steps, The Three Hostages, The Man from Norlands,* and
numerous other high-class thrillers. Buchan was far more
than a successful novelist, however. A soldier, he served on
General Haig's staff in the First World War and, later, as
Director of Information for the British Government, and
the material for many of his novels was quarried from the
files of the secret service. A distinguished historian, he wrote
one of the best histories of the First World War, and numerous biographies, of which those of Montrose, Walter
Scott, and Oliver Cromwell are the best. A lawyer and civil
servant, he served His Majesty's Government in many ca-
pacities and as Lord Tweedsmuir was appointed, in 1935,
Governor-General of Canada. He confessed three ambitions
—to write a biography of Robert E. Lee, to make the best
literature of all languages available to the poorest purse, and
"to help bring about the full understanding of America and
the British Empire." Certainly he did much to fulfill this last
ambition. These gracious pages on America—which he knew
well and for which he had a deep and abiding affection—are
taken from his charming autobiography, *Pilgrim's Way*
(1940).

✦✦✦✦✦✦✦

"AH, MY cabbages!" Henry Adams wrote, "when will you
ever fathom the American? Never in your sweet lives."
He proceeds in his genial way to make epigrams about his
own New Englanders: "Improvised Europeans we were and

—Lord God!—how thin!" "Thank God I never was cheerful. I come from the happy stock of the Mathers, who, as you remember, passed sweet mornings reflecting on the goodness of God and the damnation of infants." Where an Adams scrupled to tread it is not for a stranger to rush in. But I would humbly suggest a correction to one reading which, I think, has the authority of Robert Louis Stevenson. America is, no doubt, a vast country, though it can be comfortably put inside Canada. But it is not in every part a country of wide horizons. Dwellers on the Blue Ridge, on the prairies, and on the Western ranges may indeed live habitually with huge spaces of land and sky, but most of America, and some of its most famous parts, is pockety, snug and cosy, a sanctuary rather than a watch-tower. To people so domiciled its vastness must be like the mathematician's space-time, a concept apprehended by the mind and not a precept of the eye. "The largeness of Nature and of this nation were monstrous without a corresponding largeness and generosity of the spirit of the citizen." That is one of Walt Whitman's best-known sayings, but let us remember that the bigness of their country is for most Americans something to be learned and imaginatively understood, and not a natural deduction from cohabiting with physical immensities.

Racially they are the most variegated people on earth. The preponderance of the Anglo-Saxon stock disappeared in the Civil War. Look today at any list of names in a society or a profession and you will find that, except in the Navy, the bulk are from the continent of Europe. In his day Matthew Arnold thought that the chief source of the strength of the American people lay in their homogeneity and the absence of sharply defined classes, which made revolution unthinkable. Other observers, like Henry James, have deplored the lack of such homogeneity and wished for their country the "close and complete consciousness of the Scots." (I pause to note that I cannot imagine a more nightmare conception. What would happen to the world if a hundred and thirty million Scotsmen, with their tight, compact nationalism, were living in the same country?) I am inclined to query the alleged absence of classes, for I have never been in any part of the United States where class distinctions did not hold. There is an easy friendliness of manner which conceals a strong class pride, and the basis of that pride is not always, or oftenest, plutocratic. Apart from the social snobbery of the big cities, there seems to be everywhere an innocent love of grades and distinctions which is enough to make a communist weep. I have known places in the South where there was a magnificent aristocratic egalitarianism. Inside a charmed circle all were equal. The village postmistress, having had the right kind of great-great-grandmother, was an honored member of society, while the immigrant millionaire, who had built himself a palace, might as well have been dead. And this is true not only of the New England F.F.M.'s and the Virginian F.F.V.'s, the districts with long traditions, but of the raw little townships in the Middle West. They, too, have their "best" people who had ancestors, though the family tree may only have sprouted for two generations.

No country can show such a wide range of type and character, and I am so constituted that in nearly all I find something to interest and attract me. This is more than a temperamental bias, for I am very ready to give reasons for my liking. I am as much alive as anyone to the weak and ugly things in American life: areas, both urban and rural, where the human economy has gone rotten; the melting-pot which does not always melt; the eternal colored problem; a constitutional machine which I cannot think adequately represents the efficient good sense of the American people; a brand of journalism which fatigues with its ruthless snappiness and uses a speech so disintegrated that it is incapable of expressing any serious thought or emotion; the imbecile patter of high-pressure salesmanship; an academic jargon, used chiefly by psychologists and sociologists, which is hideous and almost meaningless. Honest Americans do not deny these blemishes; indeed they are apt to exaggerate them, for they are by far the sternest critics of their own country. For myself, I would make a double plea in extenuation. These are defects from which today no nation is exempt, for they are the fruits of a mechanical civilization, which perhaps are more patent in America, since everything there is on a large scale. Again, you can set an achievement very much the same in kind against nearly every failure. If her historic apparatus of government is cranky, she is capable of meeting the "instant need of things" with brilliant improvisations. Against economic plague-spots she can set great experiments in charity; against journalistic baby-talk a standard of popular writing in her best papers which is a model of idiom and perspicuity; against catch-penny trade methods many solidly founded, perfectly organized commercial enterprises; against the jargon of the half-educated professor much noble English prose in the great tradition. That is why it is so foolish to generalize about America. You no sooner construct a rule than it is shattered by the exceptions. . . .

I am less concerned with special types than with the American people as a whole. Let me try to set down certain qualities which seem to me to flourish more lustily in the United States than elsewhere. Again, let me repeat, I speak of America only as I know it; an observer with a different experience might not agree with my conclusions.

First, I would select what, for want of a better word, I should call homeliness. It is significant that the ordinary dwelling, though it be only a shack in the woods, is called not a house, but a home. This means that the family, the ultimate social unit, is given its proper status as the foundation of society. Even among the richer classes I seem to find a certain pleasing domesticity. English people of the same rank are separated by layers of servants from the basic work of the household, and know very little about it. In America the kitchen is not too far away from the drawing-room, and it is recognized, as Heraclitus said, that the gods may dwell there. But I am thinking chiefly of the ordinary folk, especially those of narrow means. It is often said that Americans are a nomad race, and it is true that they are very ready to shift their camp; but the camp, however bare, is always a home. The cohesion of the family is close, even when its members are scattered. This is due partly to the tradition of the first settlers, a handful in an unknown land; partly to the history of the frontier, where the hearthfire burnt brighter when all around was cold and darkness. The later immigrants from Europe, feeling at last secure, were able for the first time to establish a family base, and they cherished it zealously. This ardent domesticity has had its bad effects on American literature, inducing a sentimentality which makes a too crude frontal attack on the emotions, and which has produced as a reaction a not less sentimental "toughness." But as a social cement it is beyond price. There have been many to laugh at the dullness and pettiness of the "small town." From what I know of small-town life elsewhere, I suspect obtuseness in the satirists.

Second, I would choose the sincere and widespread friendliness of the people. Americans are interested in the human race, and in each other. Deriving doubtless from the old frontier days, there is a general helpfulness which I have not found in the same degree elsewhere. A homesteader in Dakota will accompany a traveler for miles to set him on the right road. The neighbors will rally round one of their number in distress with the loyalty of a Highland clan. This friendliness is not a self-conscious duty so much as an instinct. A squatter in a cabin will share his scanty provender and never dream that he is doing anything unusual.

American hospitality, long as I have enjoyed it, still leaves me breathless. The lavishness with which a busy man will give up precious time to entertain a stranger to whom he is in no way bound remains for me one of the wonders of the world. No doubt this friendliness, since it is an established

custom, has its fake side. The endless brotherhoods and
sodalities into which people brigade themselves encourage
a geniality which is more a mannerism than an index of character, a tiresome, noisy, back-slapping heartiness. But that is
the exception, not the rule. Americans like company, but
though they are gregarious they do not lose themselves in
the crowd. Waves of mass emotion may sweep the country,
but they are transient things and do not submerge for long
the stubborn rock of individualism. That is to say, people
can be led, but they will not be driven. Their love of human
companionship is based not on self-distrust, but on a genuine
liking for their kind. With them the sense of a common
humanity is a warm and constant instinct and not a doctrine
of the schools or a slogan of the hustings.

Lastly—and this may seem a paradox—I maintain that
they are fundamentally modest. Their interest in others is a
proof of it; the Aristotelian Magnificent Man was interested
in nobody but himself. As a nation they are said to be sensitive to criticism; that surely is modesty, for the truly arrogant care nothing for the opinion of other people. Above
all, they can laugh at themselves, which is not possible for
the immodest. They are their own shrewdest and most ribald
critics. It is charged against them that they are inclined to
boast unduly about those achievements and about the greatness of their country, but a smug glorying in them is found
only in the American of the caricaturist. They rejoice in
showing their marvels to a visitor with the gusto of children
exhibiting their toys to a stranger, an innocent desire, without any unfriendly gloating, to make others partakers in
their satisfaction. If now and then they are guilty of bombast,
it is surely a venial fault. The excited American talks of his
land very much, I suspect, as the Elizabethans in their cups
talked of England. The foreigner who strayed into the
Mermaid Tavern must often have listened to heroics which
upset his temper.

John Buchan (Lord Tweedsmuir), *Pilgrim's Way*.

❖❖❖ 34 ❖❖❖

A CAMBRIDGE PROFESSOR CELEBRATES THE AMERICAN PUBLIC SCHOOL

DENIS W. BROGAN

THE mantle of Tocqueville and Bryce has fallen, in our generation, upon the Professor of Political Science at Cambridge University, Denis Brogan. Born in Glasgow in 1900, Brogan was educated at the University of Glasgow and at Balliol College, Oxford, and studied, for a short time, at Harvard University. At the age of thirty-three he published a remarkable study of *The American Political System* which was widely hailed as the best thing of its kind since Bryce's *American Commonwealth*. Thereafter came, in rapid succession, a brief biography of Lincoln, an outline study of *Politics and Law in the United States,* and a wonderfully perspicacious and brilliant analysis of *The American Character* (1944). Brogan not only studied in this country, but almost every year he has managed to visit here, and during the war he was in charge of the American division of the British Broadcasting Company. No other Britisher of our time has brought to an understanding of the American character and institutions a more intimate familiarity with or a warmer affection for this country. That understanding is revealed at its best in this view of the American educational system—a subject which has usually excited nothing but disparagement among foreign critics. Besides his studies of American history and institutions, Professor Brogan has written learned and penetrating studies of French and British politics.

❖❖❖❖❖❖❖

THE word "school" in America covers every type of educational institution. Being "at school" may mean being at a kindergarten or at Harvard. School, too, has kept much of its Greek meaning. It is a system of organization and training for leisure as well as work. And it has become more and more adjusted to its environment, undertaking to do more than it can (which is very American) and doing much more than it seems to do (which is also very American).

The social and political role of American education cannot be understood if it is thought of as being primarily a means of formal instruction. If it is so thought of, it will be overrated and underrated. It will be overrated because the figures of two million college students, of seven million high school students, will dazzle the visitor used to seeing opportunities for higher education doled out (except in Soviet Russia) on a combined class-and-intellectual basis. It will be underrated if, at any stage below the highest (that is, below the great universities), the academic standards are compared with those of a good English, French, or pre-Hitler German school. If these millions of boys and girls are to be judged by their academic accomplishments, they will be judged harshly. But they are not to be so judged, for their schools are doing far more than instruct them: they are letting them instruct each other in how to live in America.

Of those millions, a large section will be the children of immigrants to whom English is still largely a foreign tongue. Of these millions, a very large proportion will be the children of migrants from different parts of the United States. Others will be the children of rural-bred parents, forced to adjust themselves to the new urban world. They have to learn a common language, common habits, common tolerances, a common political and national faith. And they do. It is this aim and this success that justifies the lavish buildings of the local high school; not merely the classrooms and the laboratories, but the gymnasium, the field-house where basketball can be played in comfort in the depth of the bitter winter, the swimming pools in which the summer heat can be endured.

It is true that the teachers are relatively badly paid and have an inferior social as well as economic standing, insecure tenure and politics making their condition worse. More money spent on men might get better results than more money spent on buildings. But it is easier to get the materials for buildings than the materials for teachers. As long as American society remains individualistic, competitive, confident that the answers to the present are in the future, not in the past, it is going to take more than money to seduce the right men and women in adequate numbers away from the life of action. And, a point too seldom remembered, the necessity for providing teachers for the two million college students hampers recruiting for high schools. In many cases, the colleges are doing what is really high school work and it matters comparatively little where the good teachers are, as long as they are teaching.

The political function of the schools is to teach Americanism, meaning not merely political and patriotic dogma, but the habits necessary to American life. This justifies the most extravagant items in the curriculum. Since the ability to play bridge is one of the marks of Americanism in a suburb, it is reasonable that there should be bridge clubs in schools. The main political achievement of the high schools and grammar schools is to bring together the young of all classes and all origins, to provide, artificially, the common background that in an old, rural society is provided by tradition, by the necessary collaboration of village life. The elementary schools —the "grade" schools—do this, too, but as far as an American town is broken up into racial blocs, the Ethan Allen Public School may have mainly Polish pupils, the Zachary Chandler mainly Welsh. Only in the Warren G. Harding High School is a big enough common pool formed in which Americans can be made.

Some of that Americanization is, of course, done deliber-

ately and formally. Mr. Carlton Hayes pointed out long ago
that the ritual of flag worship and oath-taking in an American school is a religious observance. Little boys and girls, in
a school from which religion in the old sense is barred, solemnly rising each morning and reciting together the "American's Creed" are performing a religious exercise as truly as
if they began the day with "I believe in God the Father Almighty" or asserted that "There is no God but God."

And that these daily rituals are religious has been at last
affirmed by the Supreme Court in a series of cases in which
the children of a fanatical sect, Jehovah's Witnesses, had
been excluded from schools for refusing to give to the flag
honors that, so their parents had taught them, were due to
God alone. In 1940, all the Court except Chief Justice Stone
held that flag worship was among the things that were Caesar's. Since that year, however, they have decided by a majority that the religious rights of the children were being in-
fringed. What is significant in the cases is not the Court's
reversal of itself but the reality of the issue presented to it.
For to the Court, and to the overwhelming majority of the
American people, the objections of the Witnesses were as
unintelligible as the objections of the Christians to making a
formal sacrifice to the Divine Emperor were to Trajan and
Pliny. The school board of Minersville, Pennsylvania, was
faced with a real problem when it was asked to admit that
children refusing to take part in the most sacred rite of the
day should be allowed to associate with the believing children of the formally unestablished national church of the
United States. So, too, was the state of Oregon when it found
Catholic and Lutheran children refusing to go to the schools
it provided. But in both cases the Supreme Court held, finally, that compulsory Americanism was not Americanism at
all, that coerced belief was not what the American people
needed to stay united. This was not Germany or Russia but
the country of Jefferson and Justice Holmes.

The flag worship of the American school and the American nation was brought home to the British public in an episode that, if funny, was also very revealing. For the London makers of ladies' underwear who adorned their garments with American flags were innocent of any insulting or even frivolous intention. At the same time, a revue chorus in London was attired in Union Jack handkerchiefs and nothing else—to the public indifference. But the flag, in America, is more than a mere symbol among many others. It is the regimental color of a regiment in which all Americans are enrolled. Its thirteen stripes and forty-eight stars are symbols far better understood than the complicated heraldry of crosses of Saint George, Saint Andrew, and Saint Patrick imposed on each other in a way that only experts understand. It was Lincoln's task to see that the number of stars in the flag was not diminished by eleven during his term of office. It was the discovery that the flag still flew over Fort McHenry, despite the British fleet, that moved Francis Scott Key to write:

Oh, say, can you see by the dawn's early light,
*   What so proudly we hailed at the twilight's last gleaming;*
Whose broad stripes and bright stars, thro' the perilous fight,
*   O'er the ramparts we watched were so gallantly streaming?*

What he wrote in 1814, tens of millions of Americans have since sung or tried to sing. And when Barbara Frietchie in Whittier's poem told-off Stonewall Jackson with:

"Shoot if you must this old gray head,
*   But spare your country's flag," she said,*

she was speaking for all Americans for whom the Stars and Stripes was still their country's flag as it had been, till recently, that of General Jackson.

Thus Americanization by ritual is an important and necessary part of the function of the American school. And because it is best carried out in schools, it matters little that the high school curriculum has been so widened that it no longer means a great deal that this boy or that girl has graduated from it—if we are looking for proof of academic achievement. But graduation from high school is reasonable proof that a great deal has been learned about American ways of life, that lessons in practical politics, in organization, in social ease have been learned that could not have been learned in factory or office.

And if the high school seems to devote too much time and money to social life, penalizing the poor boy or girl more than a theoretically less democratic educational system might do, it is thus early impressing an awkward truth on the boy or girl who is both mediocre and poor. It also penalizes the really able boy or girl who is not kept in good enough intellectual training. And if the main business of the school is, in fact, the Americanization of the children of newcomers, the parents of "old American stock" have a good reason (to add to less good ones) for not sending their children to learn what they know already, at the cost of diminishing their chance of learning what they do not know. If English is native to your children and to their home, it is not merely undemocratic to object to having their progress held up and their accent debased by the tone of a high school largely immigrant in composition.

For the task of an American school in many regions is to teach the American language, to enable it to compete with Spanish, with French, with Yiddish, with Polish, with German, with Swedish. Another task is to give, through the language and the literature of the language, a common vocabulary and a common fund of allusion, fable, and sentiment. With a fluid population this has not been easy. And the countless teachers who have labored, pedantically, formally, with complete and erroneous conviction that there were correct standards, have been heroes as important in the mass as was William McGuffey whose *Eclectic Readers* sold over one hundred and twenty million copies and helped to make the Union. The teachers were heroes because, although English won against all its rivals, it was itself going through important changes, in vocabulary, in grammar, in sound, becoming the new tongue we are beginning to call American. The teachers who stuck by the rules, who worshipped at the New England shrines in Concord, were bound to lose, but their struggle was not pure waste. For the common tongue, hammered out by millions of immigrants, by millions of migrants, would have been poor in vocabulary and structure but for the people Mr. Mencken calls the dominies and who call themselves schoolmen. The creation of general literacy and a common written and spoken tongue, intelligible everywhere except possibly in the deep South, is an achievement as remarkable as the creation of Mandarin Chinese or Low Latin or Hellenistic Greek, and this tongue is certain to be the new *lingua franca* of the world.

The making of American has been mixed-up in English minds with the making of American slang. Slang, as we should know, is one of the great sources of language. French is improved Latin slang. And slang has contributed a good deal to American. It is a generation since Mr. Dooley said that when his countrymen had finished with the English language it would look as if it had been run over by a musical comedy. Since then it has been run over by *Hellzapoppin*. But it is possible, indeed very easy, to overestimate the role of slang. It is more and more the creation of professional artists, "makers." The Hollywood prose masters provide a current and often short-lived jargon; the boys and girls, men and women, who wish to be on the beam or in the groove, may murmur with admiration, "I wish I had said that." And Whistler's classical answer to Wilde is certainly appropriate: "You will, Oscar—you will!" But not for long. Some slang will enter the language; some words will lose their meanings or acquire new ones; syntax will be loosened up. But formal speech as taught in schools will still be very important. The high school English teacher, for all her pedantry, is as much a maker of the American language as Messrs. Runyon and

O'Hara. Two streams of language may run roughly parallel, but in time they will merge; they will provide America with many interesting variations, do for American what its dual Germanic and Latin character does for English. That time has not yet come, but it is on the way. And the future character of this truly national tongue is foreshadowed in the drawing by Mr. Peter Arno in which an indignant citizen tells another: "I consider your conduct unethical and lousy."

Most American parents do not want, or are not able, to send their children to anything but public high schools, and the life in such a school is a training in life for America. It may be and often is a training in life *against* Europe. For Europe is the background from which many of the children are reacting and from which they must be delivered if they are to be Americanized. For nearly all immigrants, America is promotion, and this promotion is more clearly felt by their children. The old people may hanker after the old country, but the children—whatever sentimental feelings for their ancestral homes they may have, especially when provoked—are, above all else, anxious to be Americans.

Necessarily something is lost here. The least-common-denominator Americanism of the schools is not a complete substitute for a native culture. What the first-generation American children learn to despise may include elements in their moral diet that are not replaced. A new American whose pride in that promotion involves mere contempt for the habits, what Americans call the "folkways" or "mores," of his parents is not necessarily a good American. So attempts are made to instill pride in the ancestral cultures of the European lands from which the immigrants come. The University of Pittsburgh, located in one of the main melting pots of America, has a set of rooms illustrating the culture of various European countries. In the case of the Greeks, the room may instill adequate pride; in the case of the Scots (if any such need is felt) a shrine of Robert Burns may serve. But, for many of the peasant immigrants, the old country is backward though beloved, while for their children it is merely backward.

Americanization comes not from preservation of Slovak or Italian peasant culture, but from speedy assimilation to "American" culture. And that assimilation may take the form of distinction in anything that the American world obviously values. In the narrow sense of culture, there may even be a temptation to go for those courses that have no immigrant stigma on them. Thus I have been told by an eminent Scandinavian-American that it is difficult to get good students of Scandinavian literature and language at the University of Minnesota, although most of the students have fairly recent Scandinavian connections. They will study French but not Swedish, for "French is not a servant's language." Latin, emblem of functionless "culture," plays something of the same role; it is a symbol of liberation.

Study is not the only way up to Americanization, to acceptation. Sport is another—and one that does the job more dramatically for the newcomers gifted with what it takes to excel in competitive contests, with what is needed to win personal and community and institutional glory.

When Fanny Ellsler, the ballet dancer, came to Boston, her performance was solemnly inspected from the highest motives by Emerson and Margaret Fuller. "The dance began; both sat serenely silent; at last Emerson spoke. 'Margaret,' he said, 'this is poetry.' 'No, Waldo,' replied Margaret; 'it is not poetry, it is religion.' " And the great football games of today are religious ceremonies in this sense. It is significant that the graduating classes in Muncie High School a generation ago took such mottoes as "Deo duce" and today take mottoes stressing the "Bearcat Spirit," the "Bearcats" being the school basketball team. But a Greek would know where he was at a basketball game uniting boys and girls, parents and civic leaders, in a common passion for competitive achievement. It may be hard on the academic work of the school. It may even slightly annoy a schoolboy, who like

Mr. Burton Rascoe combines excellence in gymnastic and music (as the Greeks put it), to find that his views on literature are less interesting to the other sex than his prowess at football. But sport, school sport, college sport, does unite the parents, the children, and the community. And sport is rigorously democratic. The sons of Czechs and Poles can score there, can break through the barriers that stand in the way of the children of "Bohunks" and "Polacks." And although Harvard may secretly rejoice when it can put a winning team on to Soldiers' Field whose names suggest the *Mayflower*, it would rather put on a team that can beat Yale, even though it is not a "Yankee" team, than go down to defeat with the descendants of generations of Brahmins. And in the Middle West, sport is a real means of promotion. The Ohio high school that produced the great Negro runner, Jesse Owens, was prouder of him than if he had made Phi Beta Kappa at Ohio State; and Hitler would have made a less serious mistake if he had snubbed a great American scholar whose race he didn't like than he did by sulking at the Olympic Games when the Herrenvolk were beaten by a Negro. It is a frontier tradition; Lincoln's great strength gave him a prestige that helped him as a lawyer and politician. The great athlete performing for the glory of the school, college, state, or nation, is a less egoistic figure than the great scholar pursuing his own studies with an undemocratic concentration. And the Negroes, whose greatest hero is Joe Louis, not Paul Robeson, are not substantially wrong so far. In American society as it is, a Negro heavy-weight champion, like a Negro tap-dancer, is a better adjusted figure than a great Negro artist—or America is a less maladjusted society for them. Of course, this will not and should not last. The Irish were rising when their great hero became Governor Al Smith, rather than a successor of John L. Sullivan, the "Boston strong boy." But to get assent to a Negro's *right* to be heavy-weight champion is something—as those will agree who remember the frenzied search round 1910 for a "white hope" to save the heavy-weight championship from the indignity of being held by Jack Johnson. Great Indian athletes like Jim Thorpe, great Negro football heroes like Paul Robeson in his earlier days, the polyglot teams put on the field by the great Swedish coach Knut Rockne for the "Irish" of Notre Dame—these become "All American" figures in a wider and deeper sense than that in which the Yale of Walter Camp understood the term.

The cheer leaders, the new "jongleurs de Notre Dame," the "majorettes," shapely young women more or less involved with musical instruments, the massed cheering sections of the students, the massed yelling sections of the alumni—these are the equivalent of the crowds at the great Hellenic festivals in which barbarians were not allowed to compete. The Rose Bowl, the Cotton Bowl, the other intersectional games—these are instruments of national unity, and the provision of such instruments is no mean duty of colleges and universities. It is a religious exercise of a kind a Greek would have understood, however remote it may be from the university as understood by Abelard or Saint Thomas Aquinas or John Harvard.

The university, as these men understood it, exists all the same and exists to play a great national part, for the level of academic learning in America is perhaps the only branch of American life where the promise of rapid progress upward has been consistently kept. It is not as easy to define the nature of that progress as it is to affirm its existence.

Things have changed a great deal since the ideal of American college education was "Mark Hopkins at one end of a log and a student at the other." Then the college existed to provide a common background for lawyers and doctors and divines; it was small and select, not select in a social or financial sense, but select in that only those who accepted the old intellectual order of things were catered for. It was a decisive moment when President Eliot of Harvard (which had long ceased to concentrate on providing for a "learned ministry")

introduced the elective system. The college abandoned any
idea of imposing a hierarchy of subjects. The student could
select what he wanted from the menu provided; *à la carte*
had succeeded *table d'hôte*. But in newer, less secure, less
rich institutions than Harvard, the change went farther than
that, for not only was the student free to choose from what
was offered—he was entitled to complain if the college did
not offer what he wanted to learn, or even what he wanted
to learn in the sense that it was all he could hope to learn. As
more and more students came to college with varying school
preparation, as life grew more complex and the techniques of
life and business more impressive in their results, the unity of
college life disappeared. Boys and girls were no longer taken
in hand by a successor of Mark Hopkins and given a few
general ethical and philosophical ideas suitable to a world
still pretty much agreed on fundamentals. They were visitors
to an institution that seemed to have more in common with
the Mark Hopkins Hotel in San Francisco than with the Wil-
liams College of a century ago; and from the glass-walled
bar, "The Top of the Mark," they could see the modern
world, the bridges and skyscrapers of San Francisco, and
across the Bay the lights of Berkeley where the University of
California provides for all tastes from addicts of the Greek
theater to the most modern biological and physical techniques.

In this necessary adaptation of the old university ideal to
the modern American world, much was lost, or not provided; there was not as yet a common standard of reference
for educated men; a mass of information was stored and techniques were imparted in institutes physically associated for
historical reasons. But of course, the universities and colleges
like the high schools, served other than merely academic
ends. *Our Town* illustrates high school mating which would
have taken place anyway. *The Miracle of Morgan's Creek*
shows a suitor taking cookery so as to be close to his beloved

during her high school career, but he was bound to be close to her anyway. But the college movie, play (*The Poor Nut*) and novel rightly illustrates the more important phenomenon of exogamous marriage, of the bringing together boys and girls who otherwise would not meet at all.

And the very success of the school system in Americanizing the American young may result in the killing of natural curiosity. For example, the cult of the Constitution leads to the exclusive identification of a political concept like "liberty" with the American constitutional system. This being so, a Latin-American "republic" with a paper constitution like the American is regarded as "free" while Canada is not. For Canada is part of an "empire" with a monarch at the head of it. Some two-thirds of the American people, accordingly, think that Canada pays taxes to Britain; even in the states bordering on the Dominion, about half the Americans think this! In the same way, the word "republic" has an almost magical significance for the Americans. Plutarch, as Mr. Wells once suggested, had a good deal to do with this; but, whatever the origins of the belief, it is now part of the American credo that only citizens of a republic can be free. And no matter what romantic interest Americans may display in the human side of monarchy, it should never be forgotten that, politically, they regard it as a childish institution. Mark Twain, a very pro-English American, refused for that very reason to write one of his amusing, critical travel books about England. But he did write two books about England, all the same: *The Prince and the Pauper* and *A Connecticut Yankee at the Court of King Arthur*. How deeply anti-monarchical, anti-clerical, anti-traditional, those books are!

And in *Huckleberry Finn*, the traditional American view of royalty as expensive foolishness is admirably set forth in Huck's remark to Nigger Jim: "Sometimes I wish we could hear of a country that's out of kings."

A great many Americans still think like Huck Finn. And

it must be remembered that for Americans the great event of their own and of world history was the destruction of the royal power of George III and the establishment of a Constitution guaranteeing to each State "a republican form of government." It is in that light that the modern world is seen by nearly all Americans.

Brogan, *The American Character*.

THE AMERICAN BELIEVES
IN TOMORROW

VICTOR VINDE

WE bring our selection of interpretations of America to a close, appropriately enough, with this sanguine view of the American character under the strain and stress of war. Victor Vinde, a prominent Swedish journalist, came to the United States early in 1942 on the invitation of the United Press Club, and for six months traveled through the whole of the country, visiting farms and factories, mines and shipyards, seeing at first-hand how America organized herself for war. His enthusiastic reports to the Swedish press, coming at a time when the prospect of Allied victory seemed distant and dim, did much to strengthen Swedish faith in ultimate Allied victory. Vinde concluded his interpretation of America with a quotation from the most famous of Swedish commentators on the United States, Frederika Bremer: "If you ask me what the people of the New World have got that the Old World lacks, then I would answer, warmer hearts, and a more energetic and youthful way of life."

THERE is scarcely any country with a white population which has given rise to so many deeply rooted prejudices in Europe as the U. S. A. Perhaps it is principally the fault of the Americans themselves, because they have seldom or never paid any attention to outside criticism. They have not bothered about the misconceptions which have prevailed in Europe during the course of years. But some responsibility certainly also lies upon the Europeans, who, with few exceptions, have looked upon the Americans superficially and airily.

These prejudices have often been shared by cultured Europeans and statesmen. One need only remember the perverted portrait which was made of President Wilson after the failure of Versailles. As a rule one has judged the Americans harshly. When they withdrew after 1919, or when some years later they demanded payment for their war supplies, there was a bitter storm of reproaches in France and Britain. The U. S. A. had gone into the war in order to make money, it was said. People forgot the enthusiasm with which a large part of the American people had entered the war and that anyhow some hundreds of thousands of American dead and wounded had fallen on French battlefields. And was it not, after all, the sudden appearance of the U. S. A. on the world stage in 1917 which gave the Western Powers new courage? There is no doubt, too, that it was with American capital that defeated Germany paid reparations to France and Belgium. Some of the serious mistakes of which Americans were subsequently guilty during the fateful years after the First World War might have been avoided if the leaders of Europe had looked differently upon the U. S. A.

The misunderstanding has, however, not been confined to questions of high policy. It is true that it is long since we regarded the American as an upstart with gold-filled teeth and a big cigar in his mouth, but it is not so very long since leading European newspapers had a standing caption "Latest folly from the U. S. A."

The more one travels and the more one comes in contact with other countries and other peoples the more one understands the ignorance which governs the relations between countries and peoples. This is doubly true as regards continents such as the U. S. A. and Europe.

After the last war, especially during prohibition and the boom, and afterwards during the depression, there appeared a whole literature on the U. S. A. and its problems. It was frequently based on fleeting observations and referred in reality only to a crisis period in American history; it did not want to understand, only to condemn. It reacted against lawlessness, gangsterism, the domination of business in American society, the dissolution of American home life, the decay of morals—the mechanization of life. Mechanization and stultification were translated by "Americanization." When it was said of a European country that it was Americanized, then the suggestion was of demoralization, ruin and looseness of morals. . . .

Nothing seems to irritate a European more, be he a French cultural pessimist like Georges Duhamel or a propagandist for dictatorship and racial doctrine like Colin Ross, than the fact that the U. S. A. in one century has absorbed foreign races and to a large extent even assimilated them. That fact refutes the author's race feelings, though Duhamel translates the conception of "race" by "culture."

One cannot escape the fact that the Americans were originally immigrants. But if one goes back in time to the great migration in Europe it would appear that the European countries were also cultivated and inhabited by immigrants. The difference is that thanks to modern technique the process has been much swifter and more brutal.

It was in fact only in the 'eighties that the volume of immigration into the U. S. A. assumed such vast proportions—only to be increased still further in the early 20th century. It would have continued to grow after the last war, when millions of people wished to flee from economic misery or changed political conditions, if strong nationalistic demands in the U. S. A. had not literally put a full stop to immigration. The great period of immigration was consequently between 1880 and 1921, i.e. during forty years.

The last available American census is thirteen or fourteen years old and does not reveal the present position. But it may be mentioned that at that time there were 38,000,000 persons in the U. S. A. who were either born abroad or whose parents immigrated from a foreign country. One may assume therefore that thirteen or fourteen years ago there were between 15 and 20 million persons born outside the U. S. A. Bearing in mind that the population was then over 125,000,-000, this figure of immigrants is not overwhelming.

In the year 1942 there were published for the first time statistics of foreign languages spoken in the U. S. A., from which it appeared that 80 per cent of the population had English as their native language, that is to say, their parents' language was English. Whereas the immigrant population and their children born in the U. S. A. in 1928–29 constituted about 30 per cent of the whole population, yet thirteen years later they represented only 20 per cent, or even less. America has therefore entered into a new period of its history. Immigration ceased in 1921. In two decades the foreign elements have been assimilated, whilst new arrivals from abroad have not disturbed the assimilation process. It is very clear that now and in the future this fact will influence the U. S. A. in many respects.

It is nevertheless true that there still exist typical immigration centres. In New York, which is a modern Babel, or in some of the great industrial centres of the Eastern States, the foreign element is striking. English names certainly predominate in telephone directories, but foreign names are conspicuous. In Rochester or Buffalo one finds types and languages which shout of Eastern Europe. Thus, Buffalo, for example, has among its 600,000 inhabitants, 225,000 Poles, 50,000 Germans, 50,000 Italians and 100,000 Hungarians. These national groups live in different parts of the town, have their own business streets, their own restaurants, their own newspapers and their own churches—in other words their own community life, separate from that of the others.

Here it is a question of people who immigrated immediately before or after the last war. They arrived destitute, often unable to read or write. For that reason they have been obliged to live in national groups. The sense of alienage in a foreign country has naturally driven them together. The Southern and Eastern European immigrants have been usually taken in hand by the Catholic Church, which has successfully isolated them from the outer world. It has meant much for a Hungarian, Polish or Italian Catholic community that the new arrivals did not learn English, but were dependent on their native language and the Church. By becoming Americanized they would understand the new language and perhaps become indifferent to the Church, or in any case to the Church which obstinately stuck to the mother tongue.

Approximately the same may be said of the Protestant and free churches. They have had enormous significance for the millions of people who immigrated after being torn up from their native soil, but they have nevertheless been a restraint. They have resisted assimilation and have induced many hundreds of thousands immigrants to form provincial national islands in modern America.

If one disregards the Eastern American immigration centers of recent origin, one has a feeling that the process of absorption is on the whole being completed. Foreign newspapers disappear more and more or have a languishing existence. The new World War will probably deal a death blow to the German Press which before the war was still considerable. Unique, for example, is the French-speaking population of Louisiana, which for the most part came over 125 years ago and has both French and Spanish blood. Where this population is isolated in country districts and is in charge of a French-speaking Catholic church the language may perhaps survive for generations among the lower classes. But even in Louisiana the majority of the descendants of the French nevertheless speak English. There is no longer a daily newspaper printed in French, and the French-speaking population which still exists is not a French minority, but a surviving fragment of the Franco-American colonist system of the beginning of the 19th century.

In the U. S. A. one still talks of a Swede, a German, a Pole or a Scotsman, but it means much the same as a Provencal, a Breton or a Norman in France or a Prussian, Rhinelander or Bavarian in Germany. By it they do not mean a Swede, a German, a Pole or a Scotsman, but an American whose parents, father or grandfather or great grandfather's parents, emigrated from this or that country to America. Whoever obstinately continues to speak and think of the U. S. A. as a country populated by Germans, Italians, Swedes or Poles will find it difficult to understand future American developments.

The great American collapse in the beginning of the 'thirties led many European observers to draw the conclusion that this was a material civilization which was going under. What joy had the American from his car, his wireless, his refrigerator when he no longer had any income or anything to eat? It was said that the U. S. A. had defied natural laws. Material civilization, soulless mechanization had led to a *cul-de-sac*. "I see men enough in America," said Georges Duhamel, "but where are their souls?"

Here we shall not even attempt to analyse the deeper causes of American social crises, but we may nevertheless affirm that contrary to what is generally supposed, it was not mechanization which in the great crisis led to the collapse, but the individualism of the capitalistic system of production. Up to a certain point it was American individualism which received its death blow. It was a reaction against a lack of social conscience and a large-scale swindle which caused the mighty revulsion of 1932 and brought Franklin Roosevelt to power in 1933. Mechanization, Americanization appear, therefore, not to have suffered any check— Americans in 1943 have more wireless apparatus and refrigerators, to say nothing of mechanical improvements, than they had in 1929.

It is easy to overlook the fact that mechanization, of which the fantastic development of communications is only one

part, has imparted to American daily life a uniform character, and is the cause, more important than any other, of universal habits and customs throughout the immense continent.
It may be that a Frenchman dreaming of a little inn in a provincial French village may be indignant that an American
lunch bar, a so-called drug-store, lacks all individuality. But
it is this drug-store which has carried not only hygiene, but
also rational diet far out into the prairie. Certainly the film
has its bad sides and equally certainly it is no substitute for
Shakespeare, but it signifies that millions of human beings
who used to live completely isolated in the wilds now not
only have a most desirable entertainment but have also come
into contact with the unknown world around them. Any
attempt to feed the American millions on classical literature
would certainly have been labour in vain. The same may be
said of the wireless, which provides from hundreds of miles
away great and good music for the enjoyment of everybody
—to what extent is it worse than a concert given at any European court during the 19th century? It may sound quite
silly, but it is perhaps of importance to point out that mechanization—the popularization of music, literature or films—
has given to the American masses something which they
would never have had if they had sat quietly waiting for
Greek tragedies or the great men of the second Parnassus.
Neither has it ever been affirmed by the Americans that the
cinema or the refrigerator are any substitute for culture.

The U. S. A. has its culture in its vivid modern literature
and *belles-lettres*. A further testimony to this culture is also
to be found in the humanistic research conducted in the great
American universities, of which Europe unfortunately
knows too little. No European country has such scientific
laboratories as the U. S. A. and no country has received with
such warmth the great men of science expelled from Europe,
men whom the free countries of Europe frequently would
not receive, from contemptible motives. The U. S. A. has
culture and research centers which it has never so noisily ad-

vertised as it has so much else that is American. Nevertheless it will in the future of the world be of great importance.

Naturally, mass production of consumption goods has contributed enormously to the improvement of the conditions of life—indeed it has been the preliminary to a higher standard of living. It by no means indicates that the individual task has been completely levelled out or that taste has deteriorated. The wholesale ready-made clothing industry for women, for example, has made triumphant progress throughout the world and has made it possible for those of smaller means to be well dressed. Nowhere, however, has the industry brought about such a revolution as in the U. S. A. It has bestowed on the woman of the U. S. A. gifts which the European woman has every reason to envy. That up to a point it brings monotony is true of all countries: it is only the rich and a few exceptional members of society who can afford to indulge their own habits and customs. American mass production has never directed itself to the rich or to the few.

Nowadays one can travel hundreds and hundreds of miles on the American continent and everywhere encounter the same features, that is to say the same drug-store, the same standard clothing for men and women, the same store, the same cinema, the same big hotel. Naturally one notices, if one is observant, certain variations due to climate or other local causes. But what is most conspicuous is the uniformity. It is this uniformity of daily life which in the course of time puts its stamp on human beings. They all acquire the same habits: they become Americans. It is a fact that week after week in the whole of the continent one meets people whom one can identify as Americans as a generalization, without being able to say exactly from where they come. One must travel to the Southern States or up into the mountain regions of the northwest to find a social type whose development has been arrested or which adapts itself more slowly, i.e. which does not exactly fit in with the formula "American."

It would not seem that this mechanical process of unification has killed or uprooted anything of value of what we are used to call the good old times! One cannot say, as in many cases one can in Europe, that ancient and venerable historical relics and traditions have been sacrificed. Where they existed they really survive, as in Louisiana and Virginia. On the other hand the process has been one of the contributory causes of the creation of uniform conditions of life throughout the continent.

It would be superficial, however, not to emphasize the enormous role which school and education have played in the development of the American. Even for the descendants of millions of immigrants America's historical past is a living reality—because it has been absorbed in school life and has been fortified by constant reminders out of school. An American certainly need not have had his ancestors in the U. S. A. in Abraham Lincoln's day in order to be full of reverence and affection for that historical figure. That comes from education and surroundings. In the third or fourth generation George Washington is just as great a national hero to the man of German descent in Wisconsin as to the descendant of an English family which came over in the *Mayflower* in 1620.

The greatest asset of the American, so often ridiculed by Europeans, is his belief in progress and his profession of democracy—a profession which is not always made with the lips, but which has often stood, and still stands, in glaring contrast to everyday reality. What a belief in progress meant to the American appeared quite clearly during the depression, when for a time it was lost. The depression has left traces in most people in the U. S. A., perhaps not so much because of the troubles which accompanied it as because of the despair and hopelessness for the morrow which characterized it. It was the first time in his history that the American doubted himself or the future of his country. Belief in progress, however, is stronger in America today than it has ever been.

It is true that the Americans' sense of democratic values

more often finds expression in unmeasured criticism of prevailing conditions than in organized action to promote reforms, but this is surely due in a large degree to the development of political life—politically the U. S. A. is only now
beginning to grow out of the old regional or local straight-
jacket. An expression of opinion does in fact more easily influence a chief of state than do the political parties, which in
many respects are still living in the 19th century. One may
say that the ready-made clothes industry has conquered provincialism in dress, but that the parties have not freed themselves from provincialism in politics. Nothing has been a
greater obstacle to democratization than just this. Nevertheless, American democracy during the last ten years made gigantic progress: in nearly every field a beginning has been
made and there has been a breach with the past. It remains
to be seen whether the leading classes of the country with the
help of the wireless will succeed in creating that vigorous and
widespread social sense without which the great structure of
society cannot be fulfilled.

The American is almost always smiling and amiable. That
is one of the banal assertions which conceal a good deal of
truth. One can call it amiability or willingness to be of service. Service is a typical American conception. It has spread
from business life to private and administrative life. For example, you may order a cup of coffee in a restaurant and
have the feeling that the waiter takes a special pleasure in
serving just you. The American is willing to be of service
because he knows that his willingness creates an atmosphere
of well-being around him. Nothing is more necessary in a
community than a sense of well-being. It is often said that the
American's smile is not genuine, that it is a mask. It may be
that he does not put his whole heart into his smile, but it inspires a confidence and a candour in human intercourse
which have their value.

He thrives in company; he has no distrust of strangers. The
U. S. A. is probably the only country in the world in which

you can travel for months without ever being something so despicable as a "foreigner." Cafés and restaurants are wide open to life: you never feel yourself shut out in the U. S. A. It is commonly said that people who live in the wildernesses with great distances and sparse population become hermits, self-centred and folk-shy. The American is the exact opposite.

What surprises and attracts the European greatly is the American's social adaptability. In the European democracies there has been much talk of class fluidity. French democracy used to be proud of it. Swedish and Swiss democracies point out with pride how simple men of no standing could rise to leading positions in the community. And yet in these countries this has been the exception rather than the rule. In the U. S. A. it is almost a natural law. Manual labour is in no way degrading. Many leaders of industry send their sons as workmen into the factories. In the high schools and universities there are hundreds of thousands of young boys and girls doing ordinary manual labour in order to earn money for their upkeep and study. Often they change over from one vocation to another. There are no insurmountable walls between university education and business. Academically trained people are no mandarins. If a person fails in one place the country is so great that he can quite anonymously start his life all over again in another place. This creates a mobility which is unknown to Europe. One can be poor one day and rich the next or one may have been rich and become ruined suddenly without being quite thrown out of the saddle and declassed. The wild carousal ride which American enterprise and unrestained capitalism have offered to the American people during the first quarter of this century have loosened the joints of the social structure and have perhaps laid the foundations of a future social levelling.

There is much to irritate the European in the U. S. A. and much he would like to smile at. The power of advertisement is wonderful. For example, thanks to simply murderous advertisement such a wretched soft drink as coca-cola has become the property of the whole American people, as indispensable as air or light. The American does not share the European's hereditary distrust of everything new; he cannot defend himself against advertisement and lets himself be caught.

The power of standardization over the senses may also assume strange forms. Every American drinks iced water at lunch or dinner. The custom probably arose from the painful thirst of the hot season on the East Coast. But standardization has had the consequence that iced water is now drunk where there are no hot seasons, and it is drunk all the year round, even when there is ice on the window-panes. Again, there are only certain groups of the population in Louisiana and some other Southern States who retain their old-world customs.

One can also travel from east to west at a time when the trees are loaded with the most wonderful fruits and yet find it impossible to obtain fresh fruit for dessert even in the best restaurants. One always gets—both in restaurants and homes —preserved fruit. If one makes a protest about it the waiter or the headwaiter will come with a hidden winter apple, which, however, is entirely out of season. There are perhaps various reasons for this curious phenomenon. Is it a survival from the times when, owing to the immense distances and the absence of refrigerators, the fruit could not be transported or kept and was therefore preserved? Or is it the canning trusts which by their advertisements have succeeded in convincing the consumer that preserved fruit is healthier than fresh fruit? Anyhow, it is certainly true that behind many American customs and peculiarities which at first sight seem incomprehensible there are quite natural reasons based on historical developments or on the corruption of taste by advertisement.

In the midst of this external uniformity one suddenly encounters something which resists their general homogeneity—and such resistance is not necessarily good. It is simply different. This is true, for example, of the various laws relating to the sale of spirituous liquors, by which in one State one can obtain spirit both in the bars and in restaurants, in another only in State spirit-centres and in yet another not at all. It is true of the thousand-and-one old, but still valid, laws relating to public and private morals, so that at least theoretically it is laid down by law that one must read the Bible in elementary schools in certain States or one may be sentenced to imprisonment for maintaining that man is descended from the ape. Here is an inexhaustible field for the collector of curios.

The American goes to church just as much as other people, but whereas in most European countries the Church, so to speak, stands outside life, in the U. S. A. it stands right inside it. This observation is probably more true of the Middle West than, for example, of the Southern States, more true of the Protestant Free Church than of the Catholic Church. The importance of the contribution of the Church in the stormy periods of the growing U. S. A. can scarcely be exaggerated. This influence still remains in its high schools, clubs and societies; the churches were once the focus of all social life in the U. S. A., as in Europe.

The American is certainly not more religious than other people. But he is seldom an atheist. The President, the political leaders, the trade-union leaders all belong to some religious community. The religion of the Americans is, like so much else in the U. S. A., fresh and go-ahead, but it has naturally not entirely escaped the suspicion of the prevalent advertisement virus.

There is some humbug in American religious life, but one wonders whether it is fundamentally more widespread than in Europe. Perhaps it is more visible. Sinclair Lewis's *Elmer Gantry* is not a common American type. Southern California, to which rich people retire with their millions,

has a sort of monopoly of religious charlatanry. Aimee Mc-
Pherson is only one of many. Suddenly there pops up a
new maker of religion, does splendid business for a year
or two, then vanishes and makes way for another. There
are very few Americans who take this sort of religion
seriously. There is some humbug also about Father Divine,
the negro priest who represents himself as God the Father
Almighty descended to earth, though one never really knows
where the limit is to be found. He has some hundred thousand
followers and believers. He cures cramps and makes busi-
nesses flourish. In his paper one can read the advertisement,
for example, of a butcher or a grocer thanking Father Divine
because his business has multiplied its turnover since it was
blessed by God the Father Almighty. Everyone becomes
blessed or rich in his own way. There have been workers of
miracles and religious charlatans everywhere since the world
was populated by man. It is nothing especially American.
Only—Father Divine advertises, and that is perhaps more
American.

"I see the people, but where are their souls?" said Georges
Duhamel. It was on an August night on the Rio Grande
Railway between Denver and Salt Lake City. The long train
wound up the mountain-sides into the Rocky Mountains,
whilst the moon illuminated the ghost-like landscape and
good American citizens slept the sleep of the just behind
the drawn curtains of the Pullman car. In the drawing-
room sat the conductor—a fine old man of sixty-five years
of age. A loud snore occasionally penetrated to us whilst
the old man unravelled the tangled skein which is called
world politics. He did it with finesse, with knowledge and
with a sure judgment, but at the same time with an humble-
ness before great things which carried his listener to higher
spheres. He saw the man behind the big name, he realized
Roosevelt and Stalin and Churchill as men of flesh and blood.
He gave continents and countries and events their proper

proportions. He knew Adler, Spengler, Freud and Jung. He did not lecture; he answered no questions—he *put* them. Then he broke off in the middle of a sentence—"I shall be back soon," he said—and vanished into the corridor to attend to his sleeping fellow creatures, as if he had never concerned himself with the riddles of the world in all his life. The sun already began to creep up behind the high plateaux of Utah, and still he sat, this wise old Socrates of the Rio Grande Railway, passionately engaged in questioning events and mankind.

He was perhaps the sort of soul for Georges Duhamel. But he was a man of the rarer sort.

It is possibly only romance. Or it may be a reflection of one's own imaginary world. But away over on the West Coast of America one sometimes thought one could sense something new in process of being. Was it the joy in life, or was it some sort of new sense of living. One could not define it, but one felt it. It seemed to be in the air. It might be in one of the simple San Francisco bars where some hundreds of young men and women, mostly factory workers, or men in uniform, sat crowded together on worn plush sofas, whilst a small negro orchestra hour after hour improvized its rhythmic disharmony, and everybody listened intently, beating out the rhythm with hand, foot, or the whole body—and in spite of the late hour everything was as orderly and decent as at a family party. There was an atmosphere of collective and intense and yet quiet happiness which one does not find in New York—nor any longer in London or Paris.

It might perhaps equally well have been up in Vallejo, outside San Francisco, where the young architects stand bent over their plans for a new community which will grow up in a few months. They stand there with one foot in the present —the other already in a future of whose greatness they dream. Due west is the Pacific, from the window one sees the curling of the waves. Enthusiasm, unselfishness, love of work. And there is in the air something of the atmosphere of the little bar in San Francisco—something of the same intense, common joy.

Consciously or unconsciously it is for this conception of life, this indefinable joy of life, slowly emerging from the undisciplined capitalism of the 'twenties and the depression and social experiments of the 'thirties that the American is fighting.

He knows: there will be a tomorrow. And he believes in tomorrow.

Vinde: *America at War.*

BIBLIOGRAPHY

1. Michel-Guillaume Jean de Crèvecoeur, *Letters from an American Farmer; Describing Certain Provincial Situations, Manners, and Customs, Not Generally Known . . . Written for the Information of a Friend in England,* by J. Hector St. John, A Farmer in Pennsylvania. Letter III. London, 1782 and many subsequent editions.

2. Jacques Pierre Brissot de Warville, *New Travels in the United States of America.* Preface. Performed in 1788. London, 1792.

3. William Cobbett, *A Year's Residence in America.* pp. 204–214. London, 1828.

4. Francis Lieber, *Letters to a Gentleman in Germany,* edited by Francis Lieber. Philadelphia, 1834.

5. Alexis de Tocqueville, *Democracy in America.* 1835 and 1840 and many subsequent editions. This selection is taken from the edition ed. by H. S. Commager, New York, 1947. Vol. 2, Chapters XXIII and XXXIII.

6. Harriet Martineau, *Retrospect of Western Travel,* 3 vols. Vol. II. London, 1838.

7. Frederick Marryat, *A Diary in America.* 3 vols. Vol. II. London, 1839.

8. Francis Joseph Grund, *The Americans in their Moral, Social, and Political Relations.* 2 vols. in one. Boston, 1837.

9. Charles Dickens, *American Notes.* Chap. XVIII. London, 1842 and many subsequent editions.

10. Alexander Mackay, *The Western World, or Travels in the United States in 1846 and 1847*. Vol. III. Philadelphia, 1849.

11. Ole Munch Raeder, *America in the Forties. The Letters of Ole Munch Raeder*, trans. and ed. by Gunnar J. Malmin. Published for the Norwegian-American Historical Association by the University of Minnesota Press. Minneapolis, 1929.

12. Thomas Colley Grattan, *Civilized America*, 2 vols. Vol. I. London, 1859.

13. Francis and Theresa Pulszky, *White, Red, Black; Sketches of American Society in the United States During the Visit of Their Guests*. 2 vols. Vol. II. New York, 1853.

14. Philip Schaff, *A Sketch of the Political, Social, and Religious Character of the United States*, in two lectures. Trans. from the German. New York, 1855.

15. Adam G. de Gurowski, *America and Europe*. New York, 1857.

16. "Lord Macaulay on American Institutions," *Harper's New Monthly Magazine*, Vol. LIV (Dec. 1876 to May 1877).

17. Edward Dicey, *Six Months in the Federal States*, 2 vols. Vol. I. New York, 1863.

18. James D. Burn, *Three Years among the Working Classes in the United States during the War*, by the Author of *The Autobiography of a Beggar-Boy*, London, 1865.

19. Matthew Arnold, *Civilization in the United States, First and Last Impressions of America*. Boston, 1888.

20. James Bryce, *The American Commonwealth*, 2 vols. Vol. II. New York, 1888.

21. Paul Bourget, *Outre-Mer. Impressions of America*. New York, 1895.

22. George Warrington Steevens, *The Land of the Dollar*. New York, 1898.

23. Hugo Munsterberg, *The Americans*. New York, 1914.

24. Gilbert Keith Chesterton, *Heretics*. New York, 1905.

25. Monsignor Count Vay de Vaya and Luskod, *The Inner Life of the United States*. E. P. Dutton & Co., New York, 1908.

26. George Birmingham (Canon James Hannay), *From Connaught to Chicago*, New York, 1914.

27. Walter Lionel George, *Hail Columbia! Random Impressions of a Conservative English Radical*. New York, 1921.

28. Salvador de Madariaga, "Americans Are Boys," *Harper's Monthly Magazine*, July, 1928.

29. Richard Müller-Freienfels, *Mysteries of the Soul*, trans. by Bernard Miall. New York, 1929.

30. Raoul de Roussy de Sales, "Love in America," *The Atlantic Monthly*, May, 1938.

31. No Yong-Park (Pao), *An Oriental View of American Civilization*. Boston and New York, 1934.

32. Ilya Ilf and Eugene Petrov, *Little Golden America*. Rinehart & Company, New York, 1937.

33. John Buchan, *Pilgrim's Way*. Cambridge, 1940.

34. Denis W. Brogan, *The American Character*. Alfred A. Knopf, Inc., New York, 1944.

35. Victor Vinde, *America at War*, trans. by E. Classen, London, 1945.